More Exceptional

The C++ In-Depth Series

Bjarne Stroustrup, Editor

"I have made this letter longer than usual, because I lack the time to make it short."
   —BLAISE PASCAL

The advent of the ISO/ANSI C++ standard marked the beginning of a new era for C++ programmers. The standard offers many new facilities and opportunities, but how can a real-world programmer find the time to discover the key nuggets of wisdom within this mass of information? **The C++ In-Depth Series** minimizes learning time and confusion by giving programmers concise, focused guides to specific topics.

Each book in this series presents a single topic, at a technical level appropriate to that topic. The Series' practical approach is designed to lift professionals to their next level of programming skills. Written by experts in the field, these short, in-depth monographs can be read and referenced without the distraction of unrelated material. The books are cross-referenced within the Series, and also reference *The C++ Programming Language* by Bjarne Stroustrup.

As you develop your skills in C++, it becomes increasingly important to separate essential information from hype and glitz, and to find the in-depth content you need in order to grow. The C++ In-Depth Series provides the tools, concepts, techniques, and new approaches to C++ that will give you a critical edge.

Titles in the Series

Accelerated C++: Practical Programming by Example, Andrew Koenig and Barbara E. Moo

Applied C++: Practical Techniques for Building Better Software, Philip Romanik and Amy Muntz

The Boost Graph Library: User Guide and Reference Manual, Jeremy G. Siek, Lie-Quan Lee, and Andrew Lumsdaine

C++ In-Depth Box Set, Bjarne Stroustrup, Andrei Alexandrescu, Andrew Koenig, Barbara E. Moo, Stanley B. Lippman, and Herb Sutter

C++ Network Programming, Volume 1: Mastering Complexity Using ACE and Patterns, Douglas C. Schmidt and Stephen D. Huston

C++ Network Programming, Volume 2: Systematic Reuse with ACE and Frameworks, Douglas C. Schmidt and Stephen D. Huston

Essential C++, Stanley B. Lippman

Exceptional C++: 47 Engineering Puzzles, Programming Problems, and Solutions, Herb Sutter

Modern C++ Design: Generic Programming and Design Patterns Applied, Andrei Alexandrescu

More Exceptional C++: 40 New Engineering Puzzles, Programming Problems, and Solutions, Herb Sutter

For more information, check out the series web site at www.awprofessional.com/series/indepth/

More Exceptional C++

40 New Engineering Puzzles, Programming Problems, and Solutions

Herb Sutter

♦♦ Addison-Wesley

**Boston • San Francisco • New York • Toronto • Montreal
London • Munich • Paris • Madrid
Capetown • Sydney • Tokyo • Singapore • Mexico City**

The publisher offers discounts on this book when ordered in quantity for special sales. For more information, please contact

U.S Corporate and Government Sales
(800) 382-3419
corpsales@pearsontechgroup.com

Visit Addison-Wesley on the Web: www.awprofessional.com

Library of Congress Cataloging-in-Publication Data

Sutter, Herb.
    More exceptional C++ : 40 new engineering puzzles, programming problems, and solutions / Herb Sutter.
        p. cm—(The C++ in-depth series)
    Includes bibliographical references and index.
    ISBN 0-201-70434-X
    1. C++ (Computer program language) I. Title. II. Series.

QA76.73.C153 S89 2002
005.13'3—dc21

2001046436

Text printed on recycled and acid-free paper.
ISBN   020170434X
4 5 6 7 8 9   CRS   06 05 04 03
4th Printing   January 2004

For Günter and Elisabeth

Contents

Foreword

How do you become an expert? The answer is the same in all the fields I've seen:

1. Learn the basics.
2. Study the same material again—but this time, concentrate on the details you didn't realize were important the first time around.

If you pick the right details and master them so thoroughly that you no longer have to think about them, you will be much closer to being an expert. However, until you've become an expert, how do you know which details to pick? You'll learn a lot faster, and enjoy it more, if someone who's already been there picks the right details for you.

For example, I once took a photo workshop given by a fine photographer named Fred Picker. He told us that the only two hard parts of photography were where to put the camera and when to press the button. He then spent most of the workshop teaching us technical details about exposure, processing, and printing—details we had to absorb completely before we could control our photographs well enough for it even to make sense for us to concentrate on the two "hard" parts.

A particularly entertaining way to learn about the details of C++ programming is to try to answer questions about C++ programs. For example:

- Do f(a++); and f(a); ++a; have the same effect?
- Can you use an iterator to change the contents of a set?
- Suppose you're using a vector named v that has grown to use an uncomfortable amount of memory. You'd like to clear the vector and return that memory to the system. Will calling v.clear() do the trick?

You have probably guessed that the answers to these seemingly obvious questions must be no—otherwise I wouldn't have asked them—but do you know why the answers are no? Are you sure?

This book answers these questions and many other thoughtfully chosen questions about seemingly ordinary programs. There aren't many other books like it—except, of course, its predecessor, *Exceptional C++*. Most C++ books that claim to be "advanced" are either about specialized topics—which is fine if you want to master those particular topics, but not if you are trying to look more deeply into everyday programs—or they use the word "advanced" merely to attract readers.

Once you understand these questions and answers thoroughly, you will no longer have to think so much about the details when you program; you will be free to concentrate on the problems you are really trying to solve.

Andrew Koenig
June 2001

Preface

The Greek philosopher Socrates taught by asking his students questions—questions designed to guide them and help them draw conclusions from what they already knew, and to show them how the things they were learning related to each other and to their existing knowledge. This method has become so famous that we now call it the "Socratic method." From our point of view as students, Socrates' approach involves us, makes us think, and helps us relate and apply what we already know to new information.

This book takes a page from Socrates, as did its predecessor, *Exceptional C++* [Sutter00]. It assumes you're involved in some aspect of writing production C++ software today, and uses a question-answer format to teach you how to make effective use of standard C++ and its standard library with a particular focus on sound software engineering in modern C++. Many of the problems are drawn directly from experiences I and others have encountered while working with production C++ code. The goal of the questions is to help you draw conclusions from things you already know as well as things you've just learned, and to show how they interrelate. The puzzles will show how to reason about C++ design and programming issues—some of them common issues, some not so common; some of them plain issues, some more esoteric; and a couple because, well, just because they're fun.

This book is about all aspects of C++. I don't mean to say that it touches on every detail of C++—that would require many more pages—but rather that it draws from the wide palette of the C++ language and library features to show how apparently unrelated items can be used together to synthesize novel solutions to common problems. It also shows how apparently unrelated parts of the palette interrelate on their own, even when you don't want them to, and what to do about it. You will find material here about templates and namespaces, exceptions and inheritance, solid class design and design patterns, generic programming and macro magic—and not just as randomized tidbits, but as cohesive Items showing the interrelationships among all of these parts of modern C++.

What's "More?"

More Exceptional C++ continues where *Exceptional C++* left off. This book follows in the tradition of the first: It delivers new material, organized in bite-sized Items and grouped into themed sections. Readers of the first book will find some familiar section themes, now including new material, such as exception safety, generic programming, and memory management techniques. The two books overlap in structure and theme, not in content.

Where else does *More Exceptional C++* differ? This book has a much stronger emphasis on generic programming and on using the C++ standard library effectively, including coverage of important techniques such as traits and predicates. Several Items provide in-depth looks at considerations to keep in mind when using the standard containers and algorithms; many of these considerations I've not seen covered elsewhere. There's a new section and two appendixes that focus on optimization in single- and multithreaded environments—issues that are now more than ever of practical consequence for development shops writing production code.

Versions of most Items originally appeared in Internet and magazine columns, particularly as *Guru of the Week* [GotW] issues #31 to 62, and as print columns and articles I've written for *C/C++ Users Journal, Dr. Dobb's Journal*, the former *C++ Report*, and other publications. The material in this book has been significantly revised, expanded, corrected, and updated since those initial versions, and this book (along with its *de rigueur* errata list available at *www.gotw.ca*) should be treated as the current and authoritative version of that original material.

What I Assume You Know

I expect that you already know the basics of C++. If you don't, start with a good C++ introduction and overview. Good choices are a classic tome like Bjarne Stroustrup's *The C++ Programming Language* [Stroustrup00], or Stan Lippman and Josée Lajoie's *C++ Primer, Third Edition* [Lippman98]. Next, be sure to pick up a style guide such as Scott Meyers' classic *Effective C++* books [Meyers96] [Meyers97]. I find the browser-based CD version [Meyers99] convenient and useful.

How to Read This Book

Each Item in this book is presented as a puzzle or problem, with an introductory header that resembles the following:

ITEM #: THE TOPIC OF THIS PUZZLE   DIFFICULTY: X

The topic tag and difficulty rating gives you a hint of what you're in for. Note that the difficulty rating is my subjective guess at how difficult I expect most people will find each problem, so you may well find that a "7" problem is easier for you than some "5" problem. Since writing *Exceptional C++*, I've regularly received e-mail saying that "Item #N is easier (or harder) than that!" It's common for different people to vote "easier!" and "harder!" for the same Item. Ratings are personal; any Item's actual difficulty for you really depends on your knowledge and experience and could be easier or harder for someone else. In most cases, though, you should find the rating to be a good rule-of-thumb guide to what to expect.

You might choose to read the whole book front to back; that's great, but you don't have to. You might decide to read all the Items in a section together because you're particularly interested in that section's topic; that's cool, too. Except where there are what I call a "miniseries" of related problems which you'll see designated as "Part 1," "Part 2," and so on, the Items are pretty independent, and you should feel free to jump around, following the many cross-references among the Items in the book, as well as some references to *Exceptional C++*. The only guidance I'll offer is that the miniseries are designed to be read consecutively as a group; other than that, the choice is yours.

Namespaces, Typename, References, and Other Conventions

I make quite a few recommendations in this book, and I won't give you guidelines that tell you to do something I don't already do myself. That includes what I do in my own example code throughout this book. I'll also bow to existing practice and modern style, even when it really makes no material difference.

On that note, a word about namespaces: In the code examples, if you see a using-directive at file scope in one example and at function scope in another example a few pages or Items later, there's no deeper reason than that's what felt right and aesthetically pleasing to me for that particular case; for the rationale, turn to Item 40. In the narrative text itself, I've chosen to qualify standard library names with `std::` when I want to emphasize that it's the standard facility I'm talking about. Once that's established, I'll generally switch back to using the unqualified name.

When it comes to declaring template parameters, I sometimes come across people who think that writing `class` instead of `typename` is old-fashioned, even though there's no functional difference between the two and the standard itself uses `class` most everywhere. Purely for style, and to emphasize that this book is about today's modern C++, I've switched to using `typename` instead of `class` to declare template parameters. The only exception is one place in Item 33, where I quote directly from the standard; the standard says `class`, so I left it in there.

Unless I call something a "complete program," it's probably not. Remember that the code examples are usually just snippets or partial programs and aren't expected to compile in isolation. You'll usually have to provide some obvious scaffolding to make a complete program out of the snippet shown.

Finally, a word about URLs: On the Web, stuff moves. In particular, stuff I have no control over moves. That makes it a real pain to publish random Web URLs in a print book lest they become out of date before the book makes it to the printer's, never mind after it's been sitting on your desk for five years. When I reference other people's articles or Web sites in this book, I do it via a URL on my own Web site, *www.gotw.ca*, which I can control and which contains just a straight redirect to the real Web page. If you find that a link printed in this book no longer works, send me e-mail and tell me; I'll update that redirector to point to the new page's location (if I can find the page again) or to say that the page no longer exists (if I can't). Either way, this book's URLs will stay up-to-date despite the rigors of print media in an Internet world. Whew.

Acknowledgments

Many thanks to series editor Bjarne Stroustrup, and to Debbie Lafferty, Tyrrell Albaugh, Chanda Leary-Coutu, Charles Leddy, Curt Johnson, and the rest of the Addison-Wesley team for their assistance and persistence during this project. It's hard to imagine a better bunch of people to work with, and their enthusiasm and cooperation has helped make this book everything I'd hoped it would become.

One other group of people deserves thanks and credit, namely the many expert reviewers who generously offered their insightful comments and savage criticisms exactly where they were needed. Their efforts have made the text you hold in your hands that much more complete, more readable, and more useful than it would otherwise have been. Special thanks to (in the approximate order that I received their review comments) Scott Meyers, Jan Christiaan van Winkel, Steve Dewhurst, Dennis Mancl, Jim Hyslop, Steve Clamage, Kevlin Henney, Andrew Koenig, Patrick McKillen, as well as several anonymous reviewers. The remaining errors, omissions, and shameless puns are mine, not theirs.

Finally, thanks most of all to my family and friends for always being there, during this project and otherwise.

Herb Sutter
Toronto, June 2001

Generic Programming and the C++ Standard Library

One of C++'s most powerful features is its support for generic programming. This power is reflected directly in the flexibility of the C++ standard library, especially in its containers, iterators, and algorithms portion, originally known as the standard template library (STL).

This opening section focuses on how to make the best use of the C++ standard library, particularly the STL. When and how can you make best use of `std::vector` and `std::deque`? What pitfalls might you encounter when using `std::map` and `std::set`, and how can you safely avoid them? Why doesn't `std::remove()` actually remove anything?

This section also highlights some useful techniques, as well as pitfalls, that occur when writing generic code of your own, including code that's meant to work with and extend the STL. What kinds of predicates are safe to use with the STL; what kinds aren't, and why? What techniques are available for writing powerful generic template code that can change its own behavior based on the capabilities of the types it's given to work with? How can you switch easily between different kinds of input and output streams? How does template specialization and overloading work? And what's with this funny `typename` keyword, anyway?

This and more, as we delve into topics related to generic programming and the C++ standard library.

ITEM 1: SWITCHING STREAMS   DIFFICULTY: 2

What's the best way to dynamically use different stream sources and targets, including the standard console streams and files?

1. What are the types of `std::cin` and `std::cout`?
2. Write an ECHO program that simply echoes its input and that can be invoked equivalently in the two following ways:

```
ECHO <infile >outfile

ECHO infile outfile
```

In most popular command-line environments, the first command assumes that the program takes input from `cin` and sends output to `cout`. The second command tells the program to take its input from the file named *infile* and to produce output in the file named *outfile*. The program should be able to support all of the above input/output options.

 SOLUTION

1. **What are the types of `std::cin` and `std::cout`?**

   The short answer is that `cin` boils down to:

   ```
   std::basic_istream<char, std::char_traits<char> >
   ```
   and cout boils down to:

   ```
   std::basic_ostream<char, std::char_traits<char> >
   ```

   The longer answer shows the connection by following some standard `typedefs` and templates. First, `cin` and `cout` have type `std::istream` and `std::ostream`, respectively. In turn, those are `typdef`'d as `std::basic_istream<char>` and `std::basic_ostream<char>`. Finally, after accounting for the default template arguments, we get the above.

   Note: If you are using a prestandard implementation of the iostreams subsystem, you might still see intermediate classes, such as `istream_with_assign`. Those classes do not appear in the standard.

2. **Write an ECHO program that simply echoes its input and that can be invoked equivalently in the two following ways:**

   ```
   ECHO <infile >outfile

   ECHO infile outfile
   ```

The Tersest Solution

For those who like terse code, the tersest solution is a program containing just a single statement:

```
// Example 1-1: A one-statement wonder
//
#include <fstream>
#include <iostream>

int main( int argc, char* argv[] )
{
  using namespace std;

  (argc > 2
    ? ofstream(argv[2], ios::out | ios::binary)
    : cout)
  <<
  (argc > 1
    ? ifstream(argv[1], ios::in | ios::binary)
    : cin)
  .rdbuf();
}
```

This works because of two cooperating facilities: First, basic_ios provides a convenient rdbuf() member function that returns the streambuf used inside a given stream object, in this case either cin or a temporary ifstream, both of which are derived from basic_ios. Second, basic_ostream provides an operator<<() that accepts just such a basic_streambuf object as its input, which it then happily reads to exhaustion. As the French would say, "*C'est ça*" ("and that's it").

Toward More-Flexible Solutions

The approach in Example 1-1 has two major drawbacks: First, the terseness is border-line, and extreme terseness is not suitable for production code.

> **↗ Guideline**
>
> *Prefer readability. Avoid writing terse code (brief, but difficult to understand and maintain). Eschew obfuscation.*

Second, although Example 1-1 answers the immediate question, it's only good when you want to copy the input verbatim. That may be enough today, but what if tomorrow you need to do other processing on the input, such as converting it to upper case or calculating a total or removing every third character? That may well be a reasonable thing to want to do in the future, so it would be better right now to encapsulate the processing work in a separate function that can use the right kind of input or output object polymorphically:

```
#include <fstream>
#include <iostream>

int main( int argc, char* argv[] )
{
  using namespace std;

  fstream in, out;
  if( argc > 1 ) in.open ( argv[1], ios::in  | ios::binary );
  if( argc > 2 ) out.open( argv[2], ios::out | ios::binary );

  Process( in.is_open()  ? in  : cin,
           out.is_open() ? out : cout );
}
```

But how do we implement Process()? In C++, there are four major ways to get polymorphic behavior: virtual functions, templates, overloading, and conversions. The first two methods are directly applicable here to express the kind of polymorphism we need.

Method A: Templates (Compile-Time Polymorphism)

The first way is to use compile-time polymorphism using templates, which merely requires the passed objects to have a suitable interface (such as a member function named rdbuf()):

```
// Example 1-2(a): A templatized Process()
//
template<typename In, typename Out>
void Process( In& in, Out& out )
{
  // ... do something more sophisticated,
  //     or just plain "out << in.rdbuf();"...
}
```

Method B: Virtual Functions (Run-Time Polymorphism)

The second way is to use run-time polymorphism, which makes use of the fact that there is a common base class with a suitable interface:

```
// Example 1-2(b): First attempt, sort of okay
//
void Process( basic_istream<char>& in,
              basic_ostream<char>& out )
{
  // ... do something more sophisticated,
  //     or just plain "out << in.rdbuf();"...
}
```

Note that in Example 1-2(b), the parameters to Process() are not of type basic_ios<char>& because that wouldn't permit the use of operator<<().

Of course, the approach in Example 1-2(b) depends on the input and output streams being derived from basic_istream<char> and basic_ostream<char>. That happens to be good enough for our example, but not all streams are based on plain chars or even on char_traits<char>. For example, wide character streams are based on wchar_t, and *Exceptional C++* [Sutter00] Items 2 and 3 showed the potential usefulness of user-defined traits with different behavior (in those cases, ci_char_traits provided case insensitivity).

So even Method B ought to use templates and let the compiler deduce the arguments appropriately:

```
// Example 1-2(c): Better solution
//
template<typename C, typename T>
void Process( basic_istream<C,T>& in,
              basic_ostream<C,T>& out )
{
  // ... do something more sophisticated,
  //     or just plain "out << in.rdbuf();"...
}
```

Sound Engineering Principles

All of these answers are "right" as far as they go, but in this situation I personally tend to prefer Method A. This is because of two valuable guidelines. The first is this:

 Guideline

Prefer extensibility.

Avoid writing code that solves only the immediate problem. Writing an extensible solution is almost always better—as long as we don't go overboard, of course.

Balanced judgment is one hallmark of the experienced programmer. In particular, experienced programmers understand how to strike the right balance between writing special-purpose code that solves only the immediate problem (shortsighted, hard to extend) and writing a grandiose general framework to solve what should be a simple problem (rabid overdesign).

Compared with the approach in Example 1-1, Method A has about the same overall complexity but it's easier to understand and more extensible, to boot. Compared with Method B, Method A is at once simpler and more flexible; it is more adaptable to new situations because it avoids being hardwired to work with the iostreams hierarchy only.

So if two options require about the same effort to design and implement and are about equally clear and maintainable, prefer extensibility. This advice is *not* intended as an open license to go overboard and overdesign what ought to be a simple system; we all do that too much already. This advice is, however, encouragement to do more than just solve the immediate problem, when a little thought lets you discover that the problem you're solving is a special case of a more general problem. This is especially true because designing for extensibility often implicitly means designing for encapsulation.

 Guideline

Prefer encapsulation. Separate concerns.

As far as possible, one piece of code—function or class—should know about and be responsible for one thing.

Arguably best of all, Method A exhibits good separation of concerns. The code that knows about the possible differences in input/output sources and sinks is separated from the code that knows how to actually do the work. This separation also makes the intent of the code clearer, easier for a human to read and digest. Good separation of concerns is a second hallmark of sound engineering, and one we'll see time and again in these Items.

ITEM 2: PREDICATES, PART 1: WHAT remove() REMOVES   DIFFICULTY: 4

This Item lets you test your standard algorithm skills. What does the standard library algorithm remove() actually do, and how would you go about writing a generic function to remove only the third element in a container?

1. What does the `std::remove()` algorithm do? Be specific.
2. Write code that eliminates all values equal to 3 from a `std::vector<int>`.
3. A programmer working on your team wrote the following alternative pieces of code to remove the *n*-th element of a container.

```
// Method 1: Write a special-purpose
// remove_nth algorithm.
//
template<typename FwdIter>
FwdIter remove_nth( FwdIter first, FwdIter last, size_t n )
{
  /* ... */
}
```

```
// Method 2: Write a function object which returns
// true the nth time it's applied, and use
// that as a predicate for remove_if.
//
class FlagNth
{
public:
  FlagNth( size_t n ) : current_(0), n_(n) { }

  template<typename T>
  bool operator()( const T& ) { return ++current_ == n_; }

private:
  size_t      current_;
  const size_t n_;
};

// Example invocation
... remove_if( v.begin(), v.end(), FlagNth(3) ) ...
```

a) Implement the missing part of Method 1.

b) Which method is better? Why? Discuss anything that might be problematic about either solution.

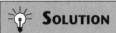 **SOLUTION**

What remove() Removes

1. What does the `std::remove()` algorithm do? Be specific.

The standard algorithm remove() does not physically remove objects from a container; the size of the container is unchanged after remove() has done its thing. Rather, remove() shuffles up the "unremoved" objects to fill in the gaps left by removed objects, leaving at the end one "dead" object for each removed object. Finally, remove() returns an iterator pointing at the first "dead" object, or, if no objects were removed, remove() returns the end() iterator.

For example, consider a vector<int> v that contains the following nine elements:

1 2 3 1 2 3 1 2 3

Say that you used the following code to try to remove all 3's from the container:

```
// Example 2-1
//
remove( v.begin(), v.end(), 3 );   // subtly wrong
```

What would happen? The answer is something like this:

```
1 2 1 2 1 2 ? ? ?
‿‿‿‿‿‿‿‿ ‿‿‿

unremoved   "dead"
            objects

            ↑
            iterator returned by
            remove() points to
            the third-last object
            (because three were
            removed)
```

Three objects had to be removed, and the rest were copied to fill in the gaps. The objects at the end of the container may have their original values (1 2 3), or they may not; don't rely on that. Again, note that the size of the container is left unchanged.

If you're wondering why remove() works that way, the most basic reason is that remove() doesn't operate on a container, but rather on a range of iterators, and there's no such iterator operation as "remove the element this iterator points to from whatever container it's in." To do that, we have to actually get at the container directly. For further information about remove(), see also Andrew Koenig's thorough treatment of this topic in [Koenig99].

2. Write code that removes all values equal to 3 from a std::vector<int>.

Here's a one-liner to do it, where v is a vector<int>:

```
// Example 2-2: Removing 3's from a vector<int> v
//
v.erase( remove( v.begin(), v.end(), 3 ), v.end() );
```

The call to remove(v.begin(), v.end(), 3) does the actual work, and returns an iterator pointing to the first "dead" element. The call to erase() from that point until v.end() gets rid of the dead elements so that the vector contains only the unremoved objects.

3. A programmer working on your team wrote the following alternative pieces of code to remove the n-th element of a container.

```cpp
// Example 2-3(a)
//
// Method 1: Write a special-purpose
// remove_nth algorithm.
//
template<typename FwdIter>
FwdIter remove_nth( FwdIter first, FwdIter last, size_t n )
{
  /* ... */
}

// Example 2-3(b)
//
// Method 2: Write a function object which returns
// true the nth time it's applied, and use
// that as a predicate for remove_if.
//
class FlagNth
{
public:
  FlagNth( size_t n ) : current_(0), n_(n) { }

  template<typename T>
  bool operator()( const T& ) { return ++current_ == n_; }

private:
  size_t      current_;
  const size_t n_;
};

// Example invocation
... remove_if( v.begin(), v.end(), FlagNth(3) ) ...
```

a) Implement the missing part of Method 1.

People often propose implementations that have the same bug as the following code. Did you?

```cpp
// Example 2-3(c): Can you see the problem(s)?
//
template<typename FwdIter>
FwdIter remove_nth( FwdIter first, FwdIter last, size_t n )
{
  for( ; n > 0; ++first, --n )
    ;
  if( first != last )
  {
    FwdIter dest = first;
    return copy( ++first, last, dest );
  }
  return last;
}
```

There is one problem in Example 2-3(c), and that one problem has two aspects:

1. Correct preconditions: We don't require that n <= distance(first, last), so the initial loop may move first past last, and then [first,last) is no longer a valid iterator range. If so, then in the remainder of the function, Bad Things will happen.

2. Efficiency: Let's say we decided to document (and test!) a precondition that n be valid for the given range, as a way of addressing problem #1. Then we should still dispense with the iterator-advancing loop entirely and simply write advance(first, n). The standard advance() algorithm for iterators is already aware of iterator categories, and is automatically optimized for random-access iterators. In particular, it will take constant time for random-access iterators, instead of the linear time required for other iterators.

Here is a reasonable implementation:

```
// Example 2-3(d): Solving the problems
//
// Precondition:
//  - n must not exceed the size of the range
//
template<typename FwdIter>
FwdIter remove_nth( FwdIter first, FwdIter last, size_t n )
{
  // Check precondition. Incurs overhead in debug mode only.
  assert( distance( first, last ) >= n );

  // The real work.
  advance( first, n );
  if( first != last )
  {
    FwdIter dest = first;
    return copy( ++first, last, dest );
  }
  return last;
}
```

b) Which method is better? Why? Discuss anything that might be problematic about either solution.

Method 1 has two main advantages:

1. It is correct.

2. It can take advantage of iterator traits, specifically the iterator category, and so can perform better for random-access iterators.

Method 2 has corresponding disadvantages, which we'll analyze in detail in the second part of this miniseries.

ITEM 3: PREDICATES, PART 2: MATTERS OF STATE   DIFFICULTY: 7

Following up from the introduction given in Item 2, we now examine "stateful" predicates. What are they? When are they useful? How compatible are they with standard containers and algorithms?

1. What are predicates, and how are they used in STL? Give an example.

2. When would a "stateful" predicate be useful? Give examples.

3. What requirements on algorithms are necessary in order to make stateful predicates work correctly?

 SOLUTION

Unary and Binary Predicates

1. What are predicates, and how are they used in STL?

A predicate is a pointer to a function, or a function object (an object that supplies the function call operator, operator()()), that gives a yes/no answer to a question about an object. Many algorithms use a predicate to make a decision about each element they operate on, so a predicate pred should work correctly when used as follows:

```
// Example 3-1(a): Using a unary predicate
//
if( pred( *first ) )
{
  /* ... */
}
```

As you can see from this example, pred should return a value that can be tested as true. Note that a predicate is allowed to use const functions only through the dereferenced iterator.

Some predicates are binary—that is, they take two objects (often dereferenced iterators) as arguments. This means that a binary predicate bpred should work correctly when used as follows:

```
// Example 3-1(b): Using a binary predicate
//
if( bpred( *first1, *first2 ) )
{
  /* ... */
}
```

Give an example.

Consider the following implementation of the standard algorithm find_if():

```
// Example 3-1(c): A sample find_if()
//
template<typename Iter, typename Pred> inline
Iter find_if( Iter first, Iter last, Pred pred )
{
  while( first != last && !pred(*first) )
  {
    ++first;
  }
  return first;
}
```

This implementation of the algorithm visits every element in the range [first, last) in order, applying the predicate function pointer, or object pred, to each element. If there is an element for which the predicate evaluates to true, find_if() returns an iterator pointing to the first such element. Otherwise, find_if() returns last to signal that an element satisfying the predicate was not found.

We can use find_if() with a function pointer predicate as follows:

```
// Example 3-1(d):
// Using find_if() with a function pointer.
//
bool GreaterThanFive( int i )
{
  return i > 5;
}

bool IsAnyElementGreaterThanFive( vector<int>& v )
{
  return find_if( v.begin(), v.end(), GreaterThanFive )
         != v.end();
}
```

Here's the same example, only using find_if() with a function object instead of a free function:

```
// Example 3-1(e):
// Using find_if() with a function object.
//
class GreaterThanFive
  : public std::unary_function<int, bool>
{
public:
  bool operator()( int i ) const
  {
    return i > 5;
  }
};
```

```
bool IsAnyElementGreaterThanFive( vector<int>& v )
{
  return find_if( v.begin(), v.end(), GreaterThanFive() )
         != v.end();
}
```

In this example, there's not much benefit to using a function object over a free function, is there? But this leads us nicely into our other questions, in which the function object shows much greater flexibility.

2. When would a "stateful" predicate be useful? Give examples.

Continuing on from Examples 3-1(d) and 3-1(e), here's something a free function can't do as easily without using something like a static variable:

```
// Example 3-2(a):
// Using find_if() with a more general function object.
//
class GreaterThan
  : public std::unary_function<int, bool>
{
public:
  GreaterThan( int value ) : value_( value ) { }
  bool operator()( int i ) const
  {
    return i > value_;
  }
private:
  const int value_;
};

bool IsAnyElementGreaterThanFive( vector<int>& v )
{
  return find_if( v.begin(), v.end(), GreaterThan(5) )
         != v.end();
}
```

This GreaterThan predicate has member data that remembers a value, in this case the value it should compare each element against. You can already see that this version is much more usable—and reusable—than the special-purpose code in Examples 3-1(d) and 3-1(e), and a lot of the power comes from the ability to store local information inside the object like this.

Taking it one step further, we end up with something even more generalized:

```
// Example 3-2(b):
// Using find_if() with a fully general function object.
//
```

```
template<typename T>
class GreaterThan
  : public std::unary_function<T, bool>
{
public:
  GreaterThan( T value ) : value_( value ) { }

  bool operator()( const T& t ) const
  {
    return t > value_;
  }

private:
  const T value_;
};

bool IsAnyElementGreaterThanFive( vector<int>& v )
{
  return find_if( v.begin(), v.end(), GreaterThan<int>(5) )
         != v.end();
}
```

So we can see some usability benefits from using predicates that store value.

The Next Step: Stateful Predicates

The predicates in both Examples 3-2(a) and 3-2(b) have an important property: Copies are equivalent. That is, if you make a copy of a GreaterThan<int> object, it behaves in all respects just like the original one and can be used interchangeably. This turns out to be important, as we shall see in Question #3.

Some people have tried to write *stateful* predicates that go further, by changing as they're used—that is, the result of applying a predicate depends on its history of previous applications. In Examples 3-2(a) and 3-2(b), the objects did carry some internal values, but these were fixed at construction time; they were not state that could change during the lifetime of the object. When we talk about stateful predicates, we mean primarily predicates having state *that can change* so that the predicate object is sensitive to what's happened to it over time, like a little state machine.[1]

Examples of such stateful predicates appear in books. In particular, people have tried to write predicates that keep track of various information about the elements they were applied to. For example, people have proposed predicates that remember the values of the objects they were applied to in order to perform calculations (for example, a predicate that returns true as long as the average of the values it was applied to so far

---

1. As John D. Hickin so elegantly describes it: "The input [first, last) is somewhat like the tape fed to a Turing machine and the stateful predicate is like a program."

is more than 50, or the total is less than 100, and so on). We just saw a specific example of this kind of stateful predicate in Item 2, Question #3:

```
// Example 3-2(c)
// (From Item 2, Example 2-3(b))
//
// Method 2: Write a function object which returns
// true the nth time it's applied, and use
// that as a predicate for remove_if.
//
class FlagNth
{
public:
  FlagNth( size_t n ) : current_(0), n_(n) { }

  template<typename T>
  bool operator()( const T& ) { return ++current_ == n_; }

private:
  size_t        current_;
  const size_t n_;
};
```

Stateful predicates like the above are sensitive to the way they are applied to elements in the range that is operated on. This one in particular depends on both the number of times it has been applied and on the order in which it is applied to the elements in the range (if used in conjunction with something like remove_if(), for example).

The major difference between predicates that are stateful and those that aren't is that, for stateful predicates, copies are *not* equivalent. Clearly an algorithm couldn't make a copy of a FlagNth object and apply one object to some elements and the other object to other elements. That wouldn't give the expected results at all, because the two predicate objects would update their counts independently and neither would be able to flag the correct *n*-th element; each could flag only the *n*-th element it itself happened to be applied to.

The problem is that, in Example 3-2(c), Method 2 possibly tried to use a FlagNth object in just such a way:

```
// Example invocation

... remove_if( v.begin(), v.end(), FlagNth(3) ) ...
```

"Looks reasonable, and I've used this technique," some may say. "I just read a C++ book that demonstrates this technique, so it must be fine," some may say. Well, the truth is that this technique may happen to work on your implementation (or on the implementation that the author of the book with the error in it was using), but it is *not* guaranteed to work portably on all implementations, or even on the next version of the implementation you are (or that author is) using now.

Let's see why, by examining `remove_if()` in a little more detail in Question #3:

3. What requirements on algorithms are necessary in order to make stateful predicates work correctly?

For stateful predicates to be really useful with an algorithm, the algorithm must generally guarantee two things about how it uses the predicate:

a) the algorithm must not make copies of the predicate (that is, it should consistently use the same object that it was given), and

b) the algorithm must apply the predicate to the elements in the range in some known order (usually, first to last).

Alas, the standard does not require that the standard algorithms meet these two guarantees. Even though stateful predicates have appeared in books, in a battle between the standard and a book, the standard wins. The standard does mandate other things for standard algorithms, such as the performance complexity and the number of times a predicate is applied, but in particular it never specifies requirement (a) for any algorithm.

For example, consider `std::remove_if()`:

a) It's common for standard library implementations to implement `remove_if()` in terms of `find_if()`, and pass the predicate along to `find_if()` by value. This will make the predicate behave unexpectedly, because the predicate object actually passed to `remove_if()` is not necessarily applied once to every element in the range. Rather, the predicate object *or a copy of the predicate object* is what is guaranteed to be applied once to every element. This is because a conforming `remove_if()` is allowed to assume that copies of the predicate are equivalent.

b) The standard requires that the predicate supplied to `remove_if()` be applied exactly `last - first` times, but it doesn't say in what order. It's possible, albeit a little obnoxious, to write a conforming implementation of `remove_if()` that doesn't apply the predicate to the elements in order. The point is that if it's not required by the standard, you can't portably depend on it.

"Well," you ask, "isn't there any way to make stateful predicates such as `FlagNth` work reliably with the standard algorithms?" Unfortunately, the answer is no.

All right, all right, I can already hear the howls of outrage from the folks who write predicates that use reference-counting techniques to solve the predicate-copying problem (a) above. Yes, you can share the predicate state so that a predicate can be safely copied without changing its semantics when it is applied to objects. The following code uses this technique (for a suitable `CountedPtr` template; follow-up question: provide a suitable implementation of `CountedPtr`):

```
// Example 3-3(a): A (partial) solution
// that shares state between copies.
//
class FlagNthImpl
```

```
{
public:
  FlagNthImpl( size_t nn ) : i(0), n(nn) { }
  size_t      i;
  const size_t n;
};

class FlagNth
{
public:
  FlagNth( size_t n )
    : pimpl_( new FlagNthImpl( n ) )
  {
  }

  template<typename T>
  bool operator()( const T& )
  {
    return ++(pimpl_->i) == pimpl_->n;
  }

private:
  CountedPtr<FlagNthImpl> pimpl_;
};
```

But this doesn't, and can't, solve the ordering problem (b) above. That is, you, the programmer, are entirely dependent on the order in which the predicate is applied by the algorithm. There's no way around this, not even with fancy pointer techniques, unless the algorithm itself guarantees a traversal order.

Follow-Up Question

The follow-up question, above, was to provide a suitable implementation of Counted Ptr, a smart pointer for which making a new copy just points at the same representation, and the last copy to be destroyed cleans up the allocated object. Here is one that works, although it could be beefed up further for production use:

```
template<typename T>
class CountedPtr
{
private:
  class Impl
  {
  public:
    Impl( T* pp ) : p( pp ), refs( 1 ) { }

    ~Impl() { delete p; }

    T*      p;
    size_t refs;
  };
  Impl* impl_;
```

```
public:
  explicit CountedPtr( T* p )
    : impl_( new Impl( p ) ) { }

  ~CountedPtr() { Decrement(); }

  CountedPtr( const CountedPtr& other )
    : impl_( other.impl_ )
  {
    Increment();
  }

  CountedPtr& operator=( const CountedPtr& other )
  {
    if( impl_ != other.impl_ )
    {
      Decrement();
      impl_ = other.impl_;
      Increment();
    }
    return *this;
  }

  T* operator->() const
  {
    return impl_->p;
  }

  T& operator*() const
  {
    return *(impl_->p);
  }

private:
  void Decrement()
  {
    if( --(impl_->refs) == 0 )
    {
      delete impl_;
    }
  }

  void Increment()
  {
    ++(impl_->refs);
  }
};
```

ITEM 4: EXTENSIBLE TEMPLATES: VIA INHERITANCE OR TRAITS?   DIFFICULTY: 7

This Item reviews traits templates and demonstrates some cool traits techniques. Even without traits, what can a template figure out about its type—and what can it do about it? The answers are nifty and illuminating, and not just for people who write C++ libraries.

1. What is a traits class?

2. Demonstrate how to detect and make use of template parameters' members, using the following motivating case: You want to write a class template C that can be instantiated only on types that have a const member function named Clone() that takes no parameters and returns a pointer to the same kind of object.

```
// T must provide T* T::Clone() const
template<typename T>
class C
{
  // ...
};
```

Note: It's obvious that if C writes code that just tries to invoke T::Clone() without parameters, then such code will fail to compile if there isn't a T::Clone() that can be called without parameters. But that's not enough to answer this question, because just trying to call T::Clone() without parameters would also succeed in calling a Clone() that has default parameters and/or does not return a T*. The goal here is to specifically enforce that T provide a function that looks exactly like this: T* T::Clone() const.

3. A programmer wants to write a template that can require (or just detect) whether the type on which it is instantiated has a Clone() member function. The programmer decides to do this by requiring that classes offering such a Clone() must derive from a predetermined Cloneable base class. Demonstrate how to write the following template:

```
template<typename T>
class X
{
  // ...
};
```

a) to require that T be derived from Cloneable; and

b) to provide an alternative implementation if T is derived from Cloneable, and work in some default mode otherwise.

4. Is the approach in #3 the best way to require/detect the availability of a Clone()? Describe alternatives.

5. How useful is it for a template to know that its parameter type T is derived from some other type? Does knowing about such derivation give any benefit that couldn't also be achieved without the inheritance relationship?

💡 SOLUTION

1. What is a traits class?

Quoting 17.1.18 in the C++ standard [C++98], a traits class is

> *a class that encapsulates a set of types and functions necessary for template classes and template functions to manipulate objects of types for which they are instantiated.*[2]

The idea is that traits classes are instances of templates, and are used to carry extra information—especially information that other templates can use—about the types on which the traits template is instantiated. The nice thing is that the traits class T<C> lets us record such extra information about a class C, without requiring any change at all to C.

For example, in the standard itself std::char_traits<T> gives information about the character-like type T, particularly how to compare and manipulate such T objects. This information is used in such templates as std::basic_string and std::basic_ostream to allow them to work with character types that are not necessarily char or wchar_t, including working with user-defined types for which you provide a suitable specialization of std::char_traits. Similarly, std::iterator_traits provides information about iterators that other templates, particularly algorithms and containers, can put to good use. Even std::numeric_limits gets into the traits act, providing information about the capabilities and behavior of various kinds of numeric types as they're implemented on your particular platform and compiler.

For more examples, see:

- Items 30 and 31 on smart pointer members
- *Exceptional C++* [Sutter00] Items 2 and 3, which show how to customize std::char_traits to customize the behavior of std::basic_string
- The April, May, and June 2000 issues of *C++ Report*, which contained several excellent columns about traits

---

2. Here *encapsulate*s is used in the sense of bringing together in one place, rather than hiding behind a shell. It's common for everything in traits classes to be public, and indeed they are typically implemented as struct templates.

Requiring Member Functions

2. Demonstrate how to detect and make use of template parameters' members, using the following motivating case: You want to write a class template C that can be instantiated only on types that have a member function named Clone() that takes no parameters and returns a pointer to the same kind of object.

```
// Example 4-2
//
// T must provide T* T::Clone() const
template<typename T>
class C
{
  // ...
};
```

Note: It's obvious that if C writes code that just tries to invoke T::Clone() without parameters, then such code will fail to compile if there isn't a T::Clone() that can be called without parameters.

For an example to illustrate that last note, consider the following:

```
// Example 4-2(a): Initial attempt,
// sort of requires Clone()
//
// T must provide /*...*/ T::Clone( /*...*/ )
template<typename T>
class C
{
public:
  void SomeFunc( const T* t )
  {
    // ...
    t->Clone();
    // ...
  }
};
```

The first problem with Example 4-2(a) is that it doesn't necessarily require anything at all. In a template, only the member functions that are actually used will be instantiated.[3] If SomeFunc() is never used, it will never be instantiated, so C can easily be instantiated with types T that don't have anything resembling Clone().

The solution is to put the code that enforces the requirement into a function that's sure to be instantiated. Many people put it in the constructor, because it's impossible to use C without invoking its constructor somewhere, right? (This approach is mentioned, for example, in [Stroustrup94].) True enough, but there could be multiple constructors. Then, to be safe, we'd have to put the requirement-enforcing code into every

---

3. Eventually, all compilers will get this rule right. Yours might still instantiate all functions, not just the ones that are used.

constructor. An easier solution is to put it in the destructor. After all, there's only one destructor, and it's unlikely that C will be used without invoking its destructor (by creating a C object dynamically and never deleting it). So, perhaps, the destructor is a somewhat simpler place for the requirement-enforcing code to live:

```
// Example 4-2(b): Revised attempt, requires Clone()
//
// T must provide /*...*/ T::Clone( /*...*/ )
template<typename T>
class C
{
public:
  ~C()
  {
    // ...
    const T t; // kind of wasteful, plus also requires
               // that T have a default constructor
    t.Clone();
    // ...
  }
};
```

That's still not entirely satisfactory. Let's set this aside for now, but we'll soon come back and improve this enforcement further, after we've done a bit more thinking about it.

This leaves us with the second problem: Both Examples 4-2(a) and 4-2(b) don't so much test the constraint as simply rely on it. (In the case of Example 4-2(b), it's even worse because 4(b) does it in a wasteful way that adds unnecessary runtime code just to try to enforce a constraint.)

But that's not enough to answer this question, because just trying to call `T::Clone()` **without parameters would also succeed in calling a** `Clone()` **that has defaulted parameters and/or does not return a** `T*`.

The code in Examples 4-2(a) and 4-2(b) will indeed work most swimmingly if there is a function that looks like `T* T::Clone()`. The problem is that it will also work most swimmingly if there is a function `void T::Clone()`, or `T* T::Clone( int = 42 )`, or with some other oddball variant signature, like `T* T::Clone( const char* = "xyzzy" )`, just as long as it can be called without parameters. (For that matter, it will work even if there isn't a `Clone()` member function at all, as long as there's a macro that changes the name `Clone` to something else, but there's little we can do about that.)

All that may be fine in some applications, but it's not what the question asked for. What we want to achieve is stronger:

The goal here is to specifically enforce that `T` **provide a function that looks exactly like this:** `T* T::Clone() const`.

So here's one way we can do it:

```
// Example 4-2(c): Better, requires
// exactly T* T::Clone() const
//
// T must provide T* T::Clone() const
template<typename T>
class C
{
public:
  // in C's destructor (easier than putting it
  // in every C constructor):
  ~C()
  {
    T* (T::*test)() const = &T::Clone;
    test; // suppress warnings about unused variables
    // this unused variable is likely to be optimized
    // away entirely

    // ...
  }

  // ...
};
```

Or, a little more cleanly and extensibly:

```
// Example 4-2(d): Alternative way of requiring
// exactly T* T::Clone() const
//
// T must provide T* T::Clone() const
template<typename T>
class C
{
  bool ValidateRequirements() const
  {
    T* (T::*test)() const = &T::Clone;
    test; // suppress warnings about unused variables
    // ...
    return true;
  }

public:
  // in C's destructor (easier than putting it
  // in every C constructor):
  ~C()
  {
    assert( ValidateRequirements() );
  }

  // ...
};
```

Having a `ValidateRequirements()` function is extensible, for it gives us a nice clean place to add any future requirements checks. Calling it within an `assert()` further ensures that all traces of the requirements machinery will disappear from release builds.

Constraints Classes

There's an even cleaner way to do it, though. The following technique is publicized by Bjarne Stroustrup in his *C++ Style and Technique FAQ* [StroustrupFAQ], crediting Alex Stepanov and Jeremy Siek for the use of pointer to function.[4]

Suppose we write the following `HasClone` constraints class:

```
// Example 4-2(e): Using constraint inheritance
// to require exactly T* T::Clone() const
//

// HasClone requires that T must provide
// T* T::Clone() const
template<typename T>
class HasClone
{
public:
  static void Constraints()
  {
    T* (T::*test)() const = &T::Clone;
    test; // suppress warnings about unused variables
  }
  HasClone() { void (*p)() = Constraints; }
};
```

Now we have an elegant—dare I say "cool"?—way to enforce the constraint at compile time:

```
template<typename T>
class C : HasClone<T>
{
  // ...
};
```

The idea is simple: Every C constructor must invoke the `HasClone<T>` default constructor, which does nothing but test the constraint. If the constraint test fails, most compilers will emit a fairly readable error message. The `HasClone<T>` derivation amounts to an assertion about a characteristic of T in a way that's easy to diagnose.

---

4. See *http://www.gotw.ca/publications/mxc++/bs_constraints.htm.*

Requiring Inheritance, Take 1:
IsDerivedFrom1 **Value Helper**

3. **A programmer wants to write a template that can require (or just detect) whether the type on which it is instantiated has a Clone() member function. The programmer decides to do this by requiring that classes offering such a Clone() must derive from a predetermined Cloneable base class. Demonstrate how to write the following template:**

```
template<typename T>
class X
{
  // ...
};
```

a) to require that T be derived from Cloneable

We'll take a look at two approaches. Both work. The first approach is a bit tricky and complex; the second is simple and elegant. It's valuable to consider both approaches because they both demonstrate interesting techniques that are good to know about, even though one technique happens to be more applicable here.

The first approach is based on Andrei Alexandrescu's ideas in "Mappings Between Types and Values" [Alexandrescu00a]. First, we define a helper template that tests whether a candidate type D is derived from B. It determines this by determining whether a pointer to D can be converted to a pointer to B. Here's one way to do it, similar to Alexandrescu's approach:

```
// Example 4-3(a): An IsDerivedFrom1 value helper
//
// Advantages: Can be used for compile-time value test
// Drawbacks:  Pretty complex
//
template<typename D, typename B>
class IsDerivedFrom1
{
  class No { };
  class Yes { No no[2]; };

  static Yes Test( B* ); // declared, but not defined
  static No Test( ... ); // declared, but not defined

public:
  enum { Is = sizeof(Test(static_cast<D*>(0))) == sizeof(Yes) };
};
```

Get it? Think about this code for a moment before reading on.

* * * * *

The above trick relies on three things:

1. Yes and No have different sizes. This is guaranteed by having a Yes contain an array of more than one No object. (And anyway, two negatives sometimes do make a positive. This time it's not really a No no.)

2. Overload resolution and determining the value of sizeof are both performed at compile time, not runtime.

3. Enum values are evaluated, and can be used, at compile time.

Let's analyze the enum definition in more detail. First, the innermost part is:

```
Test(static_cast<D*>(0))
```

All this does is mention a function named Test and pretend to pass it a D*—in this case, a suitably cast null pointer will do. Note that nothing is actually being done here, and no code is being generated, so the pointer is never dereferenced or, for that matter, even ever actually created. All we're doing is creating a typed expression. Now, the compiler knows what D is, and will apply overload resolution at compile time to decide which of the two overloads of Test() ought to be chosen: If a D* can be converted to a B*, then Test(B*), which returns a Yes, would get selected; otherwise, Test(...), which returns a No, would get selected.

The obvious next step, then, is to check which overload would get selected:

```
sizeof(Test(static_cast<D*>(0))) == sizeof(Yes)
```

This expression, still evaluated entirely at compile time, will yield 1 if a D* can be converted to a B*, and 0 otherwise. That's pretty much all we want to know, because a D* can be converted to a B* if and only if D is derived from B, or D is the same as B.[5]

So now that we've calculated what we need to know, we just need to store the result someplace. The said "someplace" has to be a place that can be set and the value used, all at compile time. Fortunately, an enum fits the bill nicely:

```
enum { Is = sizeof(Test(static_cast<D*>(0))) == sizeof(Yes) };
```

In this case, for our Cloneable purposes, we don't care if D and B are the same type. We just want to know whether a D can be used polymorphically as a B, and that's what's being tested in IsDerivedFrom1. It's trivially true that a B can be used as a B.

That's it. We can now use this facility to help build an answer to the question, to wit:

```
// Example 4-3(a), continued: Using IsDerivedFrom1
// helper to enforce derivation from Cloneable
//
template<typename T>
class X
```

---

5. Or B happens to be void.

```
{
  bool ValidateRequirements() const
  {
    // typedef needed because otherwise the , will be
    // interpreted as delimiting macro parameters to assert
    typedef IsDerivedFrom1<T, Cloneable> Y;

    // a runtime check, but one that can be turned
    // into a compile-time check without much work
    assert( Y::Is );

    return true;
  }

public:
  // in X's destructor (easier than putting it
  // in every X constructor):
  ~X()
  {
  assert( ValidateRequirements() );
  }

  // ...
};
```

Requiring Inheritance, Take 2: IsDerivedFrom2 Constraints Base Class

By now you've probably noticed that we could use Stroustrup's approach to create a functionally equivalent version, which is syntactically nicer:

```
// Example 4-3(b): An IsDerivedFrom2 constraints base class
//
// Advantages: Compile-time evaluation
//             Simpler to use directly
// Drawbacks:  Not directly usable for compile-time value test
//
template<typename D, typename B>
class IsDerivedFrom2
{
  static void Constraints(D* p)
  {
    B* pb = p;
    pb = p; // suppress warnings about unused variables
  }

protected:
  IsDerivedFrom2() { void(*p)(D*) = Constraints; }
};
```

```
// Force it to fail in the case where B is void
template<typename D>
class IsDerivedFrom2<D, void>
{
   IsDerivedFrom2() { char* p = (int*)0; /* error */ }
};
```

Now the check is much simpler:

```
// Example 4-3(b), continued: Using IsDerivedFrom2
// constraints base to enforce derivation from Cloneable
//
template<typename T>
class X : IsDerivedFrom2<T,Cloneable>
{
   // ...
};
```

Requiring Inheritance, Take 3: A Merged IsDerivedFrom

The main advantage of IsDerivedFrom1 over IsDerivedFrom2 is that IsDerived From1 provides an enum value that's generated, and can be tested, at compile time. This isn't important to the class X example shown here, but it will be important in the following section, when we want to switch on just such a value to select different traits implementations at compile time. On the other hand, IsDerivedFrom2 provides significant ease of use for the common case, when we just need to place a requirement on a template parameter to ensure some facility will exist, but without doing anything fancy, such as selecting from among alternative implementations. We could just provide both versions, but the duplicated and similar functionality is a problem, especially for naming. We can't do much better to distinguish them than we have done, namely by tacking on some wart to make the names different, so that users would always have to remember whether they wanted IsDerivedFrom1 or IsDerivedFrom2. That's ugly.

Why not have our cake and eat it, too? Let's just merge the two approaches:

```
// Example 4-3(c): An IsDerivedFrom constraints base
// with testable value
//
template<typename D, typename B>
class IsDerivedFrom
{
   class No { };
   class Yes { No no[2]; };

   static Yes Test( B* ); // not defined
   static No Test( ... ); // not defined
```

```
static void Constraints(D* p) { B* pb = p; pb = p; }

public:
  enum { Is = sizeof(Test(static_cast<D*>(0))) == sizeof(Yes) };

  IsDerivedFrom() { void(*p)(D*) = Constraints; }
};
```

Selecting Alternative Implementations

The solutions in 3(a) are nice and all, and they'll make sure T must be a Cloneable. But what if T isn't a Cloneable? What if there were some alternative action we could take? Perhaps we could make things even more flexible—which brings us to the second part of the question.

b) [...] provide an alternative implementation if T is derived from Cloneable, and work in some default mode otherwise.

To do this, we introduce the proverbial "extra level of indirection" that solves many computing problems. In this case, the extra level of indirection takes the form of a helper template: X will use IsDerivedFrom from Example 4-3(c), and use partial specialization of the helper to switch between "is-Cloneable" and "isn't-Cloneable" implementations. (Note that this requires the compile-time testable value from IsDerivedFrom1, also incorporated into IsDerivedFrom, so that we have something we can test in order to switch among different implementations.)

```
// Example 4-3(d): Using IsDerivedFrom to make use of
// derivation from Cloneable if available, and do
// something else otherwise.
//
template<typename T, int>
class XImpl
{
  // general case: T is not derived from Cloneable
};

template<typename T>
class XImpl<T, 1>
{
  // T is derived from Cloneable
};

template<typename T>
class X
{
  XImpl<T, IsDerivedFrom<T, Cloneable>::Is> impl_;
  // ... delegates to impl_ ...
};
```

Do you see how this works? Let's work through it with a quick example:

```
class MyCloneable : public Cloneable { /*...*/ };

X<MyCloneable> x1;
```

X<T>'s impl_ has type:

```
XImpl<T, IsDerivedFrom<T, Cloneable>::Is>
```

In this case, T is MyCloneable, and so X<MyCloneable>'s impl_ has type:

```
XImpl<MyCloneable, IsDerivedFrom<MyCloneable, Cloneable>::Is>
```

which evaluates to

```
XImpl<MyCloneable, 1>
```

which uses the specialization of XImpl that makes use of the fact that MyCloneable is derived from Cloneable. But what if we instantiate X with some other type? Consider:

```
X<int> x2;
```

Now T is int, and so X<int>'s impl_ has type

```
XImpl<int, IsDerivedFrom<int, Cloneable>::Is>
```

which evaluates to

```
XImpl<int, 0>
```

which uses the unspecialized XImpl. Nifty, isn't it? It's not even hard to use, once written. From the user's point of view, the complexity is hidden inside X. From the point of view of X's author, it's just a matter of directly reusing the machinery already encapsulated in IsDerivedFrom, without needing to understand how the magic works.

Note that we're not proliferating template instantiations. Exactly one XImpl <T,...> will ever be instantiated for any given T, either XImpl<T,0> or XImpl<T,1>. Although XImpl's second parameter could theoretically take any integer value, we've set things up here so that the integer can only ever be 0 or 1. (In that case, why not use a bool instead of an int? The answer is, for extensibility: It doesn't hurt to use an int, and doing so allows additional alternative implementations to be added easily in the future as needed—for example, if we later want to add support for another hierarchy that has a Cloneable-like base class with a different interface.)

Requirements versus Traits

4. Is the approach in #3 the best way to require/detect the availability of a Clone()? Describe alternatives.

The approach in Question #3 is nifty, but I tend to like traits better in many cases—they're about as simple (except when they have to be specialized for every class in a hierarchy), and they're more extensible as shown in Items 30 and 31.

The idea is to create a traits template whose sole purpose in life, in this case, is to implement a Clone() operation. The traits template looks a lot like XImpl, in that there'll be a general-purpose unspecialized version that does something general-purpose, as well as possibly multiple specialized versions that deal with classes that provide better or just different ways of cloning.

```
// Example 4-4: Using traits instead of IsDerivedFrom
// to make use of Cloneability if available, and do
// something else otherwise. Requires writing a
// specialization for each Cloneable class.
//
template<typename T>
class XTraits
{
public:
  // general case: use copy constructor
  static T* Clone( const T* p ) { return new T( *p ); }
};

template<>
class XTraits<MyCloneable>
{
public:
  // MyCloneable is derived from Cloneable, so use Clone()
  static MyCloneable* Clone( const MyCloneable* p )
  {
    return p->Clone();
  }
};

// ... etc. for every class derived from Cloneable
```

X<T> then simply calls XTraits<T>::Clone() where appropriate, and it will do the right thing.

The main difference between traits and the plain old XImpl shown in Example 4-3(b) is that, with traits, when the user defines some new type, the most work that has to be done to use it with X is external to X —just specialize the traits template to "do the right thing" for the new type. That's more extensible than the relatively hard-wired approach in #3 above, which does all the selection inside the implementation of XImpl instead of opening it up for extensibility. It also allows for other cloning methods, not just a function specifically named Clone() that is inherited from a specifically named base class, and this too provides extra flexibility.

For more details, including a longer sample implementation of traits for a very similar example, see Item 31, Examples 31-2(d) and 31-2(e).

Note: The main drawback of the traits approach above is that it requires individual specializations for every class in a hierarchy. There are ways to provide traits for a whole hierarchy of classes at a time, instead of tediously writing lots of specializations. See [Alexandrescu00b], which describes a nifty technique to do just this. His technique requires minor surgery on the base class of the outside class hierarchy—in this case, Cloneable.

Inheritance versus Traits

5. **How useful is it for a template to know that its parameter type T is derived from some other type? Does knowing about such derivation give any benefit that couldn't also be achieved without the inheritance relationship?**

There is little extra benefit a template can gain from knowing that one of its template parameters is derived from some given base class that it couldn't gain more extensibly via traits. The only real drawback to using traits is that traits can require writing lots of specializations to handle many classes in a big hierarchy, but there are techniques that mitigate or eliminate this drawback.

A principal motivator for this Item was to demonstrate that "using inheritance for categorization in templates" is perhaps not as necessary a reason to use inheritance as some have thought. Traits provide a more general mechanism that's more extensible when it comes time to instantiate an existing template on new types—such as types that come from a third-party library—that may not be easy to derive from a foreordained base class.

ITEM 5: TYPENAME   **DIFFICULTY: 7**

"What's in a (type) name?" Here's an exercise that demonstrates why and how to use typename, *using an idiom that's common in the standard library.*

---

1. What is typename, and what does it do?

2. What, if anything, is wrong with the code below?

```
template<typename T>
class X_base
{
public:
  typedef T instantiated_type;
};

template<typename A, typename B>
class X : public X_base<B>
{
public:
  bool operator()( const instantiated_type& i ) const
  {
    return i != instantiated_type();
  }

  // ... more stuff ...
};
```

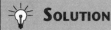 **SOLUTION**

1. What is `typename`, and what does it do?

This gets us back into the field of name lookup. A motivating example is dependent names in templates—that is, given the following code:

```
// Example 5-1
//
template<typename T>
void f()
{
  T::A* pa; // what does this line do?
}
```

the name `T::A` is a *dependent name* because it depends on the template parameter T. In this case, the programmer probably expects `T::A` to be a nested class or `typedef` within T, because the code will not compile correctly if it is something else, such as a static member variable or function. The problem is that the standard says:

> *A name used in a template declaration or definition and that is dependent on a template-parameter is assumed not to name a type unless the applicable name lookup finds a type name or the name is qualified by the keyword* typename.

This brings us to the main question:

2. What, if anything, is wrong with the code below?

This example illustrates the issue of why and how to use `typename` to refer to dependent names, and may shed some light on the question: "What's in a name?"

```
// Example 5-2
//
template<typename T>
class X_base
{
public:
  typedef T instantiated_type;
};

template<typename A, typename B>
class X : public X_base<B>
{
public:
  bool operator()( const instantiated_type& i ) const
  {
    return i != instantiated_type();
  }
```

```
    // ... more stuff ...
  };
```

1. Use `typename` for Dependent Names

The problem with X is that `instantiated_type` is meant to refer to the `typedef` supposedly inherited from the base class X_base<B>. Unfortunately, at the time the compiler parses the inlined definition of X<A,B>::operator()(), dependent names (again, names that depend on the template parameters, such as the inherited X_Base::instantiated_type) are not visible, and so the compiler will complain that it doesn't know what `instantiated_type` is supposed to mean. Dependent names become visible only later, at the point where the template is actually instantiated.

If you're wondering why the compiler couldn't just figure it out anyway, pretend that you're a compiler and ask yourself how you would figure out what `instantiated_type` means here. It's an illuminating exercise. Bottom line: You can't figure it out because you don't know what B is yet, and whether later on there might be a specialization for X_base<B> that makes X_base<B>::instantiated_type something unexpected—any type name, or even a member variable. In the unspecialized X_base template above, X_base<T>::instantiated_type will always be T, but there's nothing preventing someone from changing that when specializing. For example:

```
template<>
class X_base<int>
{
public:
  typedef Y instantiated_type;
};
```

Granted, the `typedef`'s name would be a little misleading if they did that, but it's legal. Or even:

```
template<>
class X_base<double>
{
public:
  double instantiated_type;
};
```

Now the name is less misleading, but template X cannot work with X_base <double> as a base class, because `instantiated_type` is a member variable, not a type name.

In summary, the compiler won't know how to parse the definition of X<A,B>::operator()() unless we tell it what `instantiated_type` is—at minimum, whether it's a type or something else. Here we want it to be a type.

The way to tell the compiler that something like this is a type name is to throw in the keyword `typename`. There are two ways to go about it here. The less elegant is to simply write `typename` wherever we refer to `instantiated_type`:

```
// Example 5-2(a): Somewhat horrid
//
template<typename A, typename B>
class X : public X_base<B>
{
public:
  bool operator()(
    const typename X_base<B>::instantiated_type& i
    ) const
  {
    return i != typename X_base<B>::instantiated_type();
  }

  // ... more stuff ...
};
```

I hope you winced when you read that. As usual, `typedef`s make this sort of thing much more readable, and by providing another `typedef`, the rest of the definition works as originally written:

```
// Example 5-2(b): Better
//
template<typename A, typename B>
class X : public X_base<B>
{
public:
  typedef typename X_base<B>::instantiated_type
          instantiated_type;

  bool operator()( const instantiated_type& i ) const
  {
    return i != instantiated_type();
  }

  // ... more stuff ...
};
```

Before reading on, does anything about adding this `typedef` seem unusual to you?

2. The Secondary (and Subtle) Point

I could have used simpler examples to illustrate this (several appear in the standard, in section 14.6/2), but that wouldn't have pointed out the unusual thing: The whole reason the empty base `X_base` appears to exist is to provide the `typedef`. However, derived classes usually end up just `typedef`ing it again anyway.

Doesn't that seem redundant? It is, but only a little. After all, it's still the specialization of X_base that's responsible for determining what the appropriate type should be, and that type can change for different specializations.

The standard library contains base classes like this, namely "bags-o-typedefs" which are intended to be used in just this way. Hopefully, this Item will help avert some of the questions about why derived classes re-typedef those typedefs, seemingly redundantly, and show that this effect is not really a language design glitch as much as it is just another facet of the age-old question:

"What's in a name?"

Postscript

As a bonus, here's a little typename-related code joke:

```cpp
#include <iostream>

class Rose {};

class A { public: typedef Rose rose; };

template<typename T>
class B : public T { public: typedef typename T::rose foo; };

template<typename T>
void smell( T ) { std::cout << "awful"; }

void smell( Rose ) { std::cout << "sweet"; }

int main()
{
  smell( A::rose() );
  smell( B<A>::foo() );   // :-)
}
```

ITEM 6: CONTAINERS, POINTERS, AND CONTAINERS THAT AREN'T   DIFFICULTY: 5

Oil and water just don't mix. Do pointers and standard containers mix any better?

1. Consider the following code:

```cpp
vector<char> v;
```

```
// ... populate v ...

char* p = &v[0];

// ... do something with *p ...
```

Is this code valid? Whether it's valid or not, how could it be improved?

2. Now consider the following code:

```
template<typename T>
void f( T& t )
{
  typename T::value_type* p1 = &t[0];
  typename T::value_type* p2 = &*t.begin();
  // ... do something with *p1 and *p2 ...
}
```

Is this code valid? Discuss.

 SOLUTION

Prelude

Little Stanislaus watched his mother as she rummaged busily in the refrigerator. "Be a dear, Stan," she said to him, without looking around, "and get me a container I can pour this juice into."

Stanislaus was a good boy, and he was pretty sure he knew what a container was. He looked about and saw just the thing—a bright and shiny plastic bowl with a mesh bottom. Well, little Stanislaus knew that a bowl was a container, so happily he fetched it and held it out for his mother. She, busy, started to pour the juice before she'd quite got a good look at what she was pouring it into, and as Stanislaus held the sieve with a helpful smile, the juice ran merrily into the sieve... and through it, onto the floor.

Stanislaus got a scolding that day. He didn't really think it was his fault, though. The bowl with the mesh bottom looked a lot like the other bowls. How was he to know it didn't meet his mother's container requirements?

In this Item, we'll take a look at some of the C++ standard's container requirements, some reasons to use the technique of taking pointers into a container, and—to your possible consternation and likely surprise—a standard container that isn't really a container at all.

Why Take Pointers or References into Containers?

1. Consider the following code:

```
// Example 6-1(a): Is this code valid? safe? good?
//
vector<char> v;

// ... populate v ...

char* p = &v[0];

// ... do something with *p ...
```

Is this code valid?

The standard guarantees that if a conforming sequence (such as `vector<char>`) provides `operator[]()`, that operator must return an lvalue of type `char`, which in turn can have its address taken.[6] So the answer to the question is: Yes, as long as v is not empty, the code in Example 6-1(a) is perfectly valid.

Is this code safe? Some C++ programmers are initially surprised at the idea of taking a pointer into a container, but the answer is: Yes, it's safe, as long as we remain aware of when the pointer might be invalidated, which is pretty much whenever an equivalent iterator would be invalidated. For example, clearly, if we decide to start inserting or erasing elements of the container, not only iterators but also any pointers into the container will be invalidated as the underlying memory moves.

But does this code make sense? Again, yes; it can make perfect sense to have pointers or references into a container. One common case is when you read a data structure into memory once, say on program startup, and thereafter you never modify it, but you do need to access it in different ways. In that case, it can make sense to have additional data structures that contain pointers into the main container to optimize different access methods. I'll give a simple example in the next section.

How Could the Code Be Improved?

Whether it's valid or not, how could it be improved?

Example 6-1(a) could be improved in the following way:

```
// Example 6-1(b): An improvement (when it's possible)
//
vector<char> v;
```

---

6. In this Item, I use different phrases for this term—for example, "pointer into a container," "pointer to an object inside a container," and "pointer to a contained object"—but they are all intended to mean the same thing.

```
// ... populate v ...

vector<char>::iterator i = v.begin();

// ... do something with *i ...
```

In general, it's not a bad guideline to prefer using iterators instead of pointers when you want to point at an object that's inside a container. After all, iterators are invalidated at mostly the same times and in the same ways as pointers, and one reason iterators exist is to provide a way to "point" at a contained object. If you have a choice, prefer to use iterators into containers.

Unfortunately, you can't always get the same effect with iterators that you get with pointers into a container. There are two main potential drawbacks to the iterator method, and when either applies we have to continue to use pointers:

1. You can't always conveniently use an iterator where you can use a pointer (see example below).
2. Using iterators might incur extra space and performance overhead when the iterator is an object and not just a bald pointer.

For example, say you have a map<Name,PhoneNumber> that is loaded once at program startup and thereafter is only queried. The idea is that, given a name, this makes it easy to look up the corresponding phone number in the fixed dictionary. But what if you need to do the reverse lookup too? A clean solution could be to build a second structure, perhaps a map<PhoneNumber*,Name*,Deref> that enables the reverse lookup but avoids doubling the storage overhead, because, using pointers, there's no need to store each name and phone number twice. The second structure simply has pointers into the first.

That's fine, and it will work well, but note that this effect would be more difficult to achieve using iterators instead of pointers. Why? Because the natural iterator candidate, map<Name,PhoneNumber>::iterator, points to a pair<Name,PhoneNumber>, and there's no handy way to get an iterator to just the name or phone number part individually. (We could store the entire iterator and always explicitly say ->first and ->second everywhere, but that's inconvenient to code, and it would mean that the reverse-lookup map would have to be redesigned or replaced by a different structure.)

This brings us to the next (and in my opinion, the most interesting) point of this Item's theme:

2. Now consider the following code:

```
// Example 6-2: Is this code valid?
//
template<typename T>
void f( T& t )
{
  typename T::value_type* p1 = &t[0];
  typename T::value_type* p2 = &*t.begin();
```

```
    // ... do something with *p1 and *p2 ...
  }
```

Before reading on, think about these questions: Is this code valid? If yes, under what conditions is it valid? Specifically, what kinds of things can we say about a T that makes this code valid? (Ignore runtime considerations, such as whether t happens to be in a suitable state to have t[0] called on it. We're interested in program legality here.)

When Is a Container Not a Container?

Well, is Example 6-2 valid? In short, yes, it *can* be valid.

The longer answer involves thinking about what kinds of T would make the code valid: What characteristics and abilities must a suitable T have? Let's do some detective work:

a) To make the expression &t[0] valid, T::operator[]() must exist and must return something that understands operator&(), which in turn must return a valid T::value_type* (or something that can be meaningfully converted to a valid T::value_type*).

In particular, this is true of containers that meet the standard's container and sequence requirements and implement the optional operator[](), because that operator must return a reference to the contained object. By definition, you can then take the contained object's address.

b) To make the expression &*t.begin() valid, T::begin() must exist, and it must return something that understands operator*(), which in turn must return something that understands operator&, which in turn must return a valid T::value_type* (or something that can be meaningfully converted to a valid T::value_type*).

In particular, this is true of containers whose iterators meet the standard's iterator requirements, because the iterator returned by begin() must, when dereferenced using operator*(), return a reference to the contained object. By definition, you can then take the contained object's address.

Which Brings Us to the Awkward Part

So here's the thing: The code in Example 6-2 will work for any container in the standard library that supports operator[](). If you take away the line containing "&t[0]", it will work for every container in the standard library, *except* for std::vector<bool>.

To see why, note that the following template works for every type T except bool.

```
// Example 6-3: Also works for every T except bool
//
```

```
template<typename T>
void g( vector<T>& v )
{
  T* p = &v.front();
  // ... do something with *p ...
}
```

Do you see why? At first (or even second and third) glance, it may seem odd that this is valid for all types but one. What makes vector<bool> so special?

The reason is as simple as it is unfortunate: Not all the templates defined in the C++ standard library that look like containers actually are containers. In particular, the standard library requires a specialization of vector for bool, and the specialization

vector<bool> is not a container

in that it does not meet the standard library's requirements for containers. True, vector<bool> does appear in the "containers and sequences" part of the standard; and, true, there's no note to indicate that it's really neither a container nor a sequence. But the fact is that vector<bool> is not a container, and so it should not be surprising that it cannot always be used as one.[7]

If this state of affairs seems a little strange to you, you're not alone, but there is a logical explanation.

The Life and Times of vector<bool>

The vector<bool> specialization is commonly (mis)used as an example right from the C++ standard showing how to write a proxied container. A "proxied container" is a container whose objects aren't accessed or manipulated directly. Instead of giving you pointers or references to a contained object, a proxied container gives you proxy objects that can be used to indirectly access or manipulate a contained object. Proxied collections can be useful in cases where the objects within the collection cannot always be reliably accessed directly as though they were in memory—as, for example, with a disk-based collection that automatically pages pieces of itself in and out of memory under the covers as needed. So the mistaken idea that many people have is that vector<bool> shows how to make such a proxied collection meet the requirements of a "container" in the sense defined by the standard library.

The fly in the ointment is that vector<bool> is *not* a "container" in the sense of meeting the standard's container and iterator requirements.[8] Proxied containers are

---

7. If anyone else had written vector<bool>, it would have been called "nonconforming" and "nonstandard." But it's in the standard, so it's harder to call it those names at this point. One correct solution to this discrepancy would be to remove clause 23.2.5, the vector<bool> specialization requirement, so that vector<bool> would be just another instantiation of the primary vector<> template, and so would really be what it claims to be — a vector of plain old bools. (Besides, many aspects of vector<bool> are redundant; std::bitset was designed for this kind of packed-representation work.)

8. Obviously it's a container in the general sense of being a collection that you can put things into and take things out of.

categorically disallowed by the standard's container and iterator requirements. For example, a `container<T>::reference` must be a true reference (T&), never a proxy. Iterators have similar requirements, so dereferencing a forward, bidirectional, or random-access iterator must yield a true reference (T&), never a proxy. These points preclude any proxy-based containers from meeting the standard's current container requirements.

The reason `vector<bool>` is of necessity nonconforming is that it attempts to do extra work invisibly, under the covers, in an attempt to optimize for space. A normal `bool` object is at least as big as a `char`; `sizeof(bool)` is implementation-defined and will vary from compiler to compiler, but it must be at least 1. Does that seem extravagant? Some people thought so, so `vector<bool>` tries to be more efficient about the amount of storage it uses. Instead of storing a full `char` or `int` for every contained "bool," it packs the `bool`s and stores them as individual bits (inside, say, `char`s or `int`s) in its internal representation. This gives `vector<bool>` a space advantage of at least 8:1 on platforms with 8-bit "normal" `bool`s, and possibly more. (By this point, some of you may already have noticed that this optimization makes the name `vector<bool>` rather misleading. The things inside aren't really normal `bool`s at all.)

One consequence of this packed representation is that `vector<bool>` clearly can't just return a normal `bool&` from its `operator[]` or its dereferenced iterators.[9] Instead, it has to return a "reference-like" proxy object that in many ways looks and smells like a `bool&` but which is not a `bool&`. Unfortunately, that can also make access into a `vector<bool>` slower, because we have to deal with proxies instead of direct pointers and references (not to mention the extra bit-fiddling). So `vector<bool>` is not a pure optimization, but a trade-off that favors "less space" at the expense of "potentially slower speed." More about this in a moment.

For example, whereas the functions `vector<T>::operator[]()` and `vector<T>:: front()` normally return simply a T& (a reference to the contained T), `vector<bool>::operator[]()` and `vector<bool>::front()` actually return a "reference-like" proxy object of type `vector<bool>::reference`. To make this proxy object look and feel as much like a real `bool&` as possible, `reference` provides an implicit conversion to `bool`, `operator bool()`, so that a `reference` can be used most anywhere a `bool` can be used, at least as a value. It also provides member functions `operator=(bool)`, `operator=(reference&)`, and `flip()`, which can be used to indirectly change the value of the `bool` that's actually inside the container, enabling natural coding styles such as `"v[0] = v[1];"`. (For greater amusement, note that the one service `vector<bool>::reference` can't ever provide is a `bool* operator&();`. That is, it can't provide a suitable address-of operator because there's no way to take the address of the individual bit inside the `vector<bool>` for which the `reference` object is serving as proxy.)

---

9. This is because there is no standard way to express a pointer or a reference to a bit.

Proxied Containers and STL Assumptions

Bottom line: `std::vector<bool>` may be standard, but it's not a container. (It's also not a particularly good bit vector, because it's missing a number of bit-twiddling operations that would be appropriate and which are present in `std::bitset`.)

Further, both the original STL's container requirements and the C++ standard's container requirements are based on the implicit assumption (among others) that dereferencing an iterator: (a) is a constant-time operation; and (b) requires negligible time compared to other operations. Neither of these assumptions is true for a disk-based container or a packed-representation container. For a disk-based container, access through the proxy object may require a disk seek, which can be orders of magnitude slower than main memory access. To illustrate, consider that you would be unlikely to apply a standard algorithm such as `std::find()` to a disk-based container; the performance would be abysmal compared with a special-purpose replacement, largely because the fundamental performance assumptions for in-memory containers do not apply to disk-based containers. (For similar reasons, even in-memory containers, such as `std::map`, provide their own `find()` as a member function.) For a packed-representation container like `vector<bool>`, access through the proxy object requires bitwise operations, which are generally much slower than manipulation of a native type like an `int`. Further, whenever the proxy object construction and destruction can't be completely optimized away by the compiler, managing the proxies themselves adds further overhead.

Although `vector<bool>` was in part intended to be an example of how to write a proxied container, so that other programmers could follow its example when writing disk-based or other containers whose contained objects cannot reliably be accessed directly, it also serves to demonstrate that the standard's current container requirements do not allow proxied containers.

Proxied collections are a useful tool and can often be appropriate, especially for collections that can become very large. Every programmer should know about them. They just don't fit as well into STL as many people thought, that's all. Even `vector<bool>` is still a perfectly good model for how to write a proxied collection; it's just not a "container" in the STL sense, and it should be called something else (some people asked for `"bitvector"`) so that people wouldn't think that it has anything to do with a conforming container.

Beware Premature Optimization

If you've read *Exceptional C++*, you're already familiar with my regular harangues against premature optimization.[10] The rules boil down to: "(1) Don't optimize early. (2) Don't optimize until you know that it's needed. (3) Even then, don't optimize until you know *what's needed, and where.*" As others have put it even more succinctly:

---

10. See also Item 12.

- The First Rule of Optimization: Don't do it.
- The Second Rule of Optimization: Don't do it yet.

By and large, programmers—that includes you and me—are notoriously bad at guessing the actual space/time performance bottlenecks in their own code. If you don't have performance profiles or other empirical evidence to guide you, you can easily spend days optimizing something that doesn't need optimizing and that won't measurably affect runtime space or time performance. What's even worse, however, is that when you don't understand *what* needs optimizing, you may actually end up pessimizing (degrading your program) by saving a small cost while unintentionally incurring a large cost.[11] Once you've run performance profiles and other tests, and you actually know that a particular optimization will help you in your situation, then it's the right time to optimize.

By now, you can probably see where I'm going with this: The most premature optimization of all is an optimization that's enshrined in the standard and that can't easily be avoided. In particular, vector<bool> intentionally favors "less space" at the expense of "slower speed," and forces this optimization choice on *all* programs. This optimization choice implicitly assumes that virtually all users of a vector of bools will prefer using less space at the expense of potentially slower speed, that they will be more space-constrained than performance-constrained, and so on. This is clearly untrue; on many popular implementations, a bool is the same size as an 8-bit char, and a vector of 1,000 bools consumes about 1K of memory. Saving that 1K is unimportant in many applications. (Yes, clearly a 1K space saving is important in some environments, such as embedded systems, and clearly some applications may manipulate vectors containing millions of bools, where the saved megabytes are real and significant.) The point is that *the correct optimization depends on the application.* If you are writing an application that manipulates a vector<bool> with 1,000 entries in an inner loop, it is much more likely that you would benefit from potentially faster raw performance due to reduced CPU workload (without the overhead of proxy objects and bit-fiddling) than from the marginal space savings, even if the space savings would reduce cache misses.

So What Should You Do?

If you are using vector<bool> in your code, you may be using it with algorithms that expect a real container (and that, hence, may or may not work portably), and you are using an optimization that favors space over time (possibly imperceptibly). Either

---

11. For an interesting example of this, see also Appendix A "Optimizations That Aren't (in a Multithreaded World)" for a case in point. That appendix dissects a popular optimization that turns out to be, quite unintentionally, an optimization principally for single-threaded environments, and which can actually be a distinct pessimization for (possibly) multithreaded code.

point might be inappropriate for your application. The easy way to discover the first is to use the code until it fails to compile; that day may never come. The only way to discover the second is by running empirical tests to measure your code's performance the way it uses vector<bool>. In many cases, the performance difference compared to something like vector<int>, if there is one, may well be negligible.

If you are being affected by vector<bool>'s noncontainerness, or *if* the measured performance difference is not negligible in your environment and the difference is material in your application, then don't use vector<bool>. You might at first think of using a vector<char> or vector<int> instead (that is, store a bool as a char or an int), and use casts when setting values in the container, but that's tedious. A superior workaround is to use a deque<bool>; it's a far simpler solution, and ties in with the advice about deque given in Item 7.

In summary:

1. vector<bool> is not a container.

2. vector<bool> attempts to illustrate how to write standard-conforming proxied containers that do extra work invisibly under the covers. Unfortunately, that's not a sound idea, because although a proxied collection can be an important and useful tool, by definition it must violate the standard's container requirements and therefore can never be a conforming container (see #1).

Corollary: Go ahead and write proxied collections, but don't attempt to write ones that still meet the standard's container or sequence requirements. First, it's not possible. Second, the main reason for collections to conform to the standard container requirements is to be used with the standard algorithms, yet the standard algorithms are typically inappropriate for proxied containers because proxied containers have different performance characteristics than do plain-and-in-memory containers.

3. vector<bool>'s name is a trifle misleading because the things inside aren't even standard bools. A standard bool is at least as big as a char so that it can be used "normally." So, in fact, vector<bool> does not even really store bools, despite the name.

4. vector<bool> forces a specific optimization on all users by enshrining it in the standard. That's probably not a good idea, even if the actual performance overhead turns out to be negligible for a given compiler for most applications; different users have different requirements.

A last word of advice: *Optimize wisely.* Never succumb to the temptation to perform premature optimizations until you have empirical evidence that the optimization is beneficial in your situation.

ITEM 7: USING vector AND deque   DIFFICULTY: 3

What is the difference between vector *and* deque*? When should you use each one? And how can you properly shrink such containers when you no longer need their full capacity? These answers and more, as we consider news updates from the standards front.*

1. In the standard library, vector and deque provide similar services. Which should you typically use? Why? Under what circumstances would you use the other?

2. What does the following code do?

```
vector<C> c( 10000 );
c.erase( c.begin()+10, c.end() );
c.reserve( 10 );
```

3. A vector or deque typically reserves extra internal storage as a hedge against future growth, to prevent too-frequent reallocation as new elements are added. Is it possible to completely clear a vector or deque (that is, not only remove all contained elements, but also free all internally reserved storage)? Demonstrate why or why not.

Warning: Answers 2 and 3 may be subtle. Each has a facile answer, but don't stop at the surface; try to be as detailed as possible.

SOLUTION

This Item answers the following questions:

- Can you use a vector interchangeably with a C-style array (say, with an existing function that expects an array)? How? What are the issues?
- Why would you usually prefer using a vector instead of a deque?
- How do you shrink a vector whose capacity has grown larger than you need? In particular, how do you "shrink-to-fit" (so that the vector's size is just big enough to hold only its current contents), or clear a vector's internal storage entirely (so that the vector is truly empty, with no contents and little or no under-the-covers preallocated storage)? Can the same technique be used for other containers?

Using a vector as an Array: A Motivating Example

C++ programmers are strongly encouraged to use the standard vector template instead of C-style arrays. Using a vector is easier and safer than using an array, because a vector is a better-abstracted and better-encapsulated form of container— for example, a vector can grow and shrink as needed, whereas an array has a fixed size.

Nonetheless, there's still a lot of code out there that is designed to work with C-style arrays. For example, consider the following code:

```
// Example 7-1(a): A function that operates
// on a C-style array
//
int FindCustomer(
  const char* szName,       // name to search for
  Customer*   pCustomers,   // pointer to beginning
                            //  of a Customer array
  size_t      nLength )     //  with nLength entries
{
  // performs a (possibly optimized) search and
  // returns the index at which the specified
  // name was found
}
```

To use the above function, we might create, populate, and pass in an array as follows:

```
// Example 7-1(b): Using an array
//
Customer c[100];
  //-- populate the contents of c somehow --
int i = FindCustomer( "Fred Jones", &c[0], 100 );
```

Example 7-1(b) is all well and good, but as modern C++ programmers aren't we supposed to use vectors instead of arrays? Indeed, wouldn't it be nice if we could have the best of both worlds—use a vector for its convenience and safety, yet still use the vector's contents with functions that expect an array? This desire comes up most often when an organization is migrating to C++ and people want to write new parts of the system in the "new and better" way while still tying in easily with a legacy code base.

So let's use a vector. Our first attempt could look something like this:

```
// Example 7-1(c): Using a vector -- will this work?
//
vector<Customer> c;
//-- populate the contents of c somehow --
int i = FindCustomer( "Fred Jones", &c[0], c.size() );
```

In Example 7-1(c), when it comes time to call FindCustomer(), the idea is to pass in the address of the first element, and the number of elements, which is pretty much just what we did in Example 7-1(b).

Before reading on, stop for a moment and consider these questions: What potential benefits does the code in Example 7-1(c) have over the code in Example 7-1(b)? Do you see any potential problems with Example 7-1(c), or do you think that it will work as intended?

A Fly in the Ointment?

I didn't just pull Example 7-1(c) out of a hat. It turns out there are a lot of real-world C++ programmers who have done exactly this, and with good reason, because code like that in Example 7-1(c) illustrates some of the important benefits that come from using a vector:

- We don't have to know the potential size of c in advance. In many C programs, arrays are allocated pessimistically so that they'll be big enough for most intended uses. Unfortunately, this means that space is needlessly wasted much of the time when the full size isn't needed, after all. (Worse, it means the program breaks if it ever ends up needing more space than we'd thought.) With a C++ vector, we can grow the container as needed instead of just guessing. Also, if we do happen to know in advance how many objects we're going to put into the vector, we can simply say so (by first calling c.reserve(100), if we want to reserve space for 100 elements), so there's no performance disadvantage with a vector compared to an array, because we have a way to avoid repeated reallocations as we insert new elements into the vector.
- We don't have to separately track the actual length of the array so that we can pass it as the final (nLength) parameter to FindCustomer(). Yes, you can use a C array and use workarounds that make remembering or recalculating the length easier,[12] but none of those workarounds are as easy and safe as just writing c.size().

In short, as far as I know, Example 7-1(c) has always worked on every implementation of std::vector that has ever existed.

Until 2001, a minor fly in the ointment was that the 1998 C++ standard [C++98] didn't actually guarantee that Example 7-1(c) would work portably on every C++ platform you might buy. This is because Example 7-1(c) assumes that the internal contents of the vector are stored contiguously in the same format as is an array, but the original C++ standard didn't require vendors to implement vector that way. If, for example, a vector implementation were to play games and store its contents in some other way (such as contiguously but in backwards order, or in sequential order but with an extra byte of housekeeping information between elements), then Example 7-1(c) would, in fact, fail miserably. This was fixed in 2001 as part of Technical Corrigendum #1 to the C++ standard, which now requires that the contents of a vector are stored contiguously, just like an array.

Even if your compiler doesn't include support for the Technical Corrigendum yet, though, Example 7-1(c) should work in practice today. Again, I don't know of a commercial vector implementation that doesn't store its elements contiguously.

Bottom line: Prefer using vector (or deque; see below) instead of arrays.

---

12. The most typical approaches are to use a const value or a #defined name for the size of the array, or else a macro that expands to sizeof(c)/sizeof(c[0]) to compute the size of the array.

In Most Cases, Prefer Using vector

1. In the standard library, vector and deque provide similar services. Which should you typically use? Why? Under what circumstances would you use the other?

The C++ standard [C++98], in section 23.1.1, offers some advice on which containers to prefer. It says:

> *vector is the type of sequence that should be used by default. ... deque is the data structure of choice when most insertions and deletions take place at the beginning or at the end of the sequence.*

vector and deque offer nearly identical interfaces and are generally interchangeable. deque also offers push_front() and pop_front(), which vector does not. (True, vector offers capacity() and reserve(), which deque does not, but that's no loss. Those functions are actually something of a weakness in vector, as I'll demonstrate in a moment.)

The main structural difference between vector and deque lies in the way the two containers organize their internal storage. Under the covers, a deque allocates its storage in pages, or "chunks," with a fixed number of contained elements in each page. This is why a deque is often compared to (and pronounced as) a "deck" of cards,[13] although its name originally came from "double-ended queue" because of its ability to insert elements efficiently at either end of the sequence. On the other hand, a vector allocates a contiguous block of memory, and can only insert elements efficiently at the end of the sequence.

The paged organization of a deque offers several benefits:

- A deque offers constant-time insert() and erase() operations at the front of the container, whereas a vector does not, hence the note in the standard about using a deque if you need to insert or erase at both ends of the sequence.
- A deque uses memory in a more operating system-friendly way. For example, a 10-megabyte vector uses a single 10-megabyte block of memory. On some operating systems that single block can be less efficient in practice than a 10-megabyte deque that can fit in a series of smaller blocks of memory. On other operating systems, a contiguous address space can be built of smaller blocks under the covers anyway. On such platforms, this deque noncontiguity advantage won't matter.
- A deque is somewhat easier to use, and inherently more efficient for growth, than a vector. The only operations supplied by vector that deque doesn't have are capacity() and reserve(). That's because deque doesn't need them! For vector, calling reserve() before a large number of push_back()s can elimi-

---

13. The first use I know of the "deck of cards" analogy for deque was by Donald Knuth in [Knuth97].

nate reallocating ever-larger versions of the same buffer every time it finds out that the current one isn't big enough, after all. A deque has no such problem, and having a deque::reserve() before a large number of push_back()s would not eliminate any allocations (or any other work), because none of the allocations is redundant. The deque has to allocate the same number of extra pages whether it does it all at once or as elements are actually appended.

Interestingly, note that within the C++ standard itself, the stack adapter prefers deque. Even though a stack can only grow in one direction and so never needs insertion in the middle or at the other end, the default implementation is required to be a deque:

```
namespace std
{
  template<typename T, typename Container = deque<T> >
  class stack
  {
    // ...
  };
}
```

Despite this, for readability and simplicity, prefer using vector by default in your programs unless you know you need to efficiently insert and erase at the beginning of the container and don't need the underlying objects to be stored contiguously. Note that vector is to C++ what the array is to C—the default container type to use in your programs, and one that does a reasonably good all-around job unless you know you need something different.

The Incredible Shrinking vector

As already noted, it's nice that vector manages its own storage, and that we can give it hints about how much capacity to keep ready under the covers as it grows. If we have a vector<T> c that we're about to grow to contain 100 elements, we can first call c.reserve(100) and incur, at most, a single reallocation hit. This allows optimally efficient growth.

But what if we're doing the opposite? What if we're using a vector that's pretty big, and then we remove elements we no longer need and want the vector to shrink to fit—that is, we want it to get rid of the now-unneeded extra capacity? You might think that the following would work:

2. What does the following code do?

```
// Example 7-2(a): A naïve attempt at shrinking a vector.
//
vector<C> c( 10000 );
```

Now `c.size() == 10000`, and `c.capacity() >= 10000`.
Next, we erase all but the first ten elements:

```
c.erase( c.begin()+10, c.end() );
```

Now `c.size() == 10`, and we know we don't need all that extra capacity, but the following line does *not* shrink c's internal buffer to fit:

```
c.reserve( 10 );
```

The reason that the last line in Example 7-2(a) does not do what one might expect is that calling `reserve()` will never shrink the `vector`'s capacity. Calling `reserve()` can only increase the capacity, or do nothing if the capacity is already sufficient.
Fortunately, there is a right way to get the intended effect:

```
// Example 7-2(b): The right way to shrink-to-fit a vector.
//
vector<Customer> c( 10000 );
// ...now c.capacity() >= 10000...

// erase all but the first 10 elements
c.erase( c.begin()+10, c.end() );

// the following line does shrink c's
// internal buffer to fit (or close)
vector<Customer>( c ).swap( c );

// ...now c.capacity() == c.size(), or
// perhaps a little more than c.size()
```

Do you see how the shrink-to-fit statement works? It's a little subtle:

1. First, we create a temporary (unnamed) `vector<Customer>` and initialize it to hold the same contents as c. The salient difference between the temporary `vector` and c is that, while c still carries around a lot of extra capacity in its oversize internal buffer, the temporary `vector` has just enough capacity to hold its copy of c's contents. (Some implementations may choose to round up the capacity slightly to their next larger internal "chunk size," with the result that the capacity actually ends up being slightly larger than the size of the contents.)

2. Next, we call `swap()` to exchange the internals of c with the temporary `vector`. Now the temporary `vector` owns the oversize buffer with the extra capacity that we're trying to get rid of, and c owns the "right-sized" buffer with the just-enough capacity.

3. Finally, the temporary `vector` goes out of scope, carrying away the old oversize buffer with it. The old buffer is deleted when the temporary `vector` is destroyed. All we're left with is c itself, but now c has a "right-sized" capacity.

Note that this procedure is not needlessly inefficient. Even if vector had a special-purpose shrink_to_fit() member function, it would have to do pretty much all the same work just described.

3. A vector or deque typically reserves extra internal storage as a hedge against future growth, to prevent too-frequent reallocation as new elements are added. Is it possible to completely clear a vector or deque (that is, not only remove all contained elements, but also free all internally reserved storage)? Demonstrate why or why not.

To completely clear a vector so that it has no contents and no extra capacity at all, the code is nearly identical. We just initialize the temporary vector to be empty instead of making it a copy of c:

```
// Example 7-3: The right way to clear out a vector.
//
vector<Customer> c( 10000 );
// ...now c.capacity() >= 10000...

// the following line makes
// c be truly empty
vector<Customer>().swap( c );

// ...now c.capacity() == 0, unless the
// implementation happens to enforce a
// minimum size even for empty vectors
```

Again, note that the vector implementation you use may choose to make even empty vectors have some slight capacity, but now you're guaranteed that c's capacity will be the smallest possible allowed by your implementation. It will be the same as the capacity of an empty vector.

These techniques work for deque, too, but you don't need to do this kind of thing for list, set, map, multiset, or multimap, because they allocate storage on an "exactly-as-needed" basis and so they should never have excess capacity.

Summary

It's safe to use vectors interchangeably with C-style arrays, and you should always prefer to use vectors or deques instead of arrays. Use a vector as your default container type, unless you know you need something different and you don't need all the contained elements to be contiguous in memory. Use the swap-with-a-temporary-container idiom if you want to shrink an existing vector or deque. Finally, as noted in

Item 6, unless you know that you really need the space optimization, always use deque<bool> instead of vector<bool>.

ITEM 8: USING set AND map   DIFFICULTY: 5

In Item 7, we considered vector and deque. This time, the focus is on more news about the associative containers set, multiset, map, and multimap.[14]

1. a) What's wrong with the following code? How would you correct it?

```
map<int,string>::iterator i = m.find( 13 );
if( i != m.end() )
{
   const_cast<int&>( i->first ) = 9999999;
}
```

b) To what extent are the problems fixed by writing the following instead?

```
map<int,string>::iterator i = m.find( 13 );
if( i != m.end() )
{
   string s = i->second;
   m.erase( i );
   m.insert( make_pair( 9999999, s ) );
}
```

2. Can you modify a set's contents through a set::iterator? Why or why not?

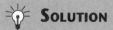 **SOLUTION**

Associative Containers: Review

First, a quick review: Here are some key points about what it means to iterate over an associative container, and about what associative containers' iterators do and are.

---

14. Note that set and multiset aren't really "associative" in the usual sense of relating a lookup key with another value, the way a dictionary does. That's the job of map and multimap. But all four of these containers appear in the C++ standard under the heading "Associative Containers," so I'll follow suit to be consistent.

The four standard associative containers are summarized in Figure 1. Each of these containers internally maintains its elements in a way that allows fast traversal in nondescending key order and fast retrieval by key, where the keys are always compared according to the provided Compare type (this defaults to less<Key>, which uses the operator<() provided for Key objects). Whenever a new key is inserted into a container, the container finds a proper place to insert the new key so that it maintains the proper ordering of its internal data structure.

Iterators are easy to implement, because they are supposed to traverse the entries in nondescending Key order, and the container already internally stores the elements in a way that naturally supports that ordering. Pretty basic, right?

```
set<Key, Compare>
multiset<Key, Compare>
map<Key, Value, Compare>
multimap<Key, Value, Compare>
```

Figure 1: The standard associative containers (minus the allocator parameters).

Which brings us to the "key" issue:

The Key Requirement

An essential requirement, without which associative containers could not work reliably at all, is this: Once a key has been inserted into the container, that key had better not be changed in any way that would change its relative position in the container. If that ever did happen, the container wouldn't know about it, and its assumptions about the ordering of its entries would be violated, searches for valid entries could fail, iterators would no longer be guaranteed to traverse the contents in key order, and in general Bad Things would happen.

I'll illustrate this issue in the context of an example, and then discuss what you can do about it.

A Motivating Example

Consider a map<int,string> named m that has the contents shown in Figure 2; each node within m is shown as a pair<const int,string>. I'm showing the internal structure as a binary tree because this is what all current standard library implementations actually use.

As the keys are inserted, the tree's structure is maintained and balanced such that a normal inorder traversal visits the keys in the usual less<int> ordering. So far, so good.

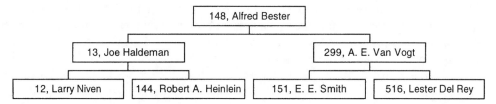

Figure 2: Sample internal contents of a map<int, string>.

But now say that, through an iterator, we could arbitrarily change the second entry's key, using code that looks something like the following:

1. a) What's wrong with the following code? How would you correct it?

```
// Example 8-1: Wrong way to change a
// key in a map<int,string> m.
//
map<int,string>::iterator i = m.find( 13 );
if( i != m.end() )
{
  const_cast<int&>( i->first ) = 9999999; // oops!
}
```

Note that we have to cast away const to get this code to compile. More on that in a moment. The problem here is that the code interferes with the map's internal representation by changing the map's internals in a way that the map isn't expecting and can't deal with.

Example 8-1 corrupts the map's internal structure (see Figure 3). Now, for example, an iterator traversal will not return the contents of the map in key order, as it should. For example, a search for key 144 will probably fail, even though the key exists in the map. In general, the container is no longer in a consistent or usable state. Note that it is not feasible to require the map to automatically defend itself against such illicit usage, because it can't even detect this kind of change when it occurs. In Example 8-1, the change was made through a reference into the container, without calling any map member functions.

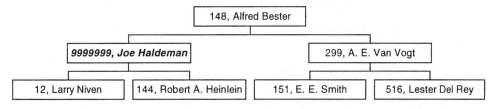

Figure 3:   Figure 2 after Example 8-1 executes. Problem!

If the Example 8-1 code had changed the key in such a way that the relative ordering remained unchanged, there would have been no problem for this implementation of map. The problem is only with code that attempts to change the relative ordering of keys once they are in the container.

What's the best way to deal with this? Ideally, we would like to prevent this through a suitable coding standard. What, then, should such a coding standard say?

Option #1: Say "const Means const!" (Insufficient)

In Example 8-1, we needed to cast away const in order to change the key. This is because standard C++ actively tries to prevent code that changes the relative ordering of keys. In fact, standard C++ enforces a (seemingly) stricter requirement—namely, that for both maps and multimaps, keys should not be modified at all. A map<Key, Value>::iterator points to a pair<const Key, Value> which, apparently, lets you modify the value part, but not the key part, of the pointed-at map entry. This, again apparently, prevents a key from changing at all, much less changing in a way that would alter its position in the map object's internal ordering.

One option, then, is to print large posters that say "const means const!" and hold rallies with celebrity speakers and incite mass media coverage to increase awareness of this deplorable problem. This would prevent code like that in Example 8-1, which doesn't work in practice anyway, wouldn't it?

It's a good idea, but unfortunately even telling people to respect const isn't enough. For example, if the Key type has a mutable member that affects the way Compare compares Key objects, then calling const member functions on a const key can still change the relative ordering of keys.

Option #2: Say "Always Change Keys Using Erase-Then-Insert" (Better, But Still Insufficient)

A better, but still insufficient, solution is to follow this discipline: To change a key, remove it and reinsert it. For example:

b) To what extent are the problems fixed by writing the following instead?

```
// Example 8-2: Better way to change a key
// in a map<int,string> m.
//
map<int,string>::iterator i = m.find( 13 );
if( i != m.end() )
{
  string s = i->second;
  m.erase( i );
  m.insert( make_pair( 9999999, s ) ); // OK
}
```

This is better, because it avoids any change to keys, even keys with mutable members that are significant in the ordering. It even works with our specific example. So this must be the solution, right?

Unfortunately, it's still not enough in the general case, because keys can still be changed while they are in the container. "What?" one might ask. "How can keys be changed while they're in the container, if we adopt the discipline of never changing key objects directly?" Here are two counterexamples:

1. Let's say the Key type has some externally available state that other code can get at—for example, a pointer to a shared buffer that can be modified by other parts of the system without going through the Key object. Let's also say that that externally available state participates in the comparison performed by Compare. Then making a change in the externally available state, even without the knowledge of the Key object and without the knowledge of the code that uses the associative container, can still change the relative ordering of keys. So in this case, even if the code owning the container tries to follow an erase-then-reinsert discipline, a key ordering change can happen at any time somewhere else and therefore without an erase-then-reinsert operation.

2. Consider a Key type of string and a Compare type that interprets the key as a file name and compares the *contents* of the files. It's obvious that even if the keys are never changed, the relative ordering of keys can still change if the files are modified by another *process*, or (if the file is shared on a network) even by a user on a different machine on the other side of the world.

What About set?

This brings us to set. Because we haven't found a good answer yet for map, we might as well look to see what set does about it.

2. Can you modify a set's contents through a set::iterator? Why or why not?

One way to think of a set is as just a map<Key, Value> with a Value type of void. You might expect that set would do much the same thing with its key type as does map, and that a set<Key>::iterator and a set<Key>::const_iterator would be the same thing—that is, they would both point to a const Key. This would prevent a programmer from modifying the pointed-at key.

Alas, the standard is not as clear about this for set as it is for map, but it's reasonable to want to change an object inside a set—after all, the contained object might well contain other information that does not affect comparison. There have been two distinct opinion camps, with differing ideas on the question of whether set::iterator ought to point at a non-const key, and so it should be no surprise that in some standard library implementations it does and in some it doesn't. In other words, in practice you can't portably rely on being able to modify an element of a set through a set::iterator without a const_cast. As this book goes to press, the current intent within the standards committee is to add wording to the standard that formally requires that both `set::iterator` and `set::const_iterator` be constant iterators, and that if you want to change an object in a `set`, you must use the `const_cast` bazooka.

There are, however, good reasons to want to use the bazooka. Remember that `set`s and `map`s are often intended to be used somewhat differently. For example, say you want to implement a lookup that, given a customer's name, finds the customer's address or phone number. Then you might implement a `map<string, CustData>`, where the key is the customer's name and the value is a `CustData` structure that contains address and telephone information.

But what if you already have a perfectly good `Customer` class that contains the customer's name and information? Then it might seem a waste of programmer time to add the needless complexity of yet another `CustData` structure that contains all the same information except for one name string. On the other hand, it would be wasteful of runtime resources to implement a `map<string, Customer>`, where the key is a redundant copy of the customer's name, which is already stored inside the `Customer` object. We really shouldn't have to store that name twice. Instead, you would naturally think of implementing a `set<Customer>` which needs no new data structure and incurs no redundant `string` overhead. A `map<string, Customer>` will let you change the `Customer` object once it's in the container—and so should `set<Customer>`, but in reality (and probably soon in legality) you will have to do it with a `const_cast`. Some current implementations of `set` will let you change it without a cast; some won't. If you're using one that will let you change it, and/or are deliberately using `const_cast` to change it, remember that implementations of `set` still require that you not change a `Customer` object in such a way that would change its relative ordering in the container.

Noting that our first two attempts to write a more specific rule didn't cover all the cases, and noting that even `set` and `map` handle things a little differently, perhaps we can do no better than a general rule.

The Key Requirement (Reprise)

What rule should we follow to ensure that we're using associative containers correctly? Although it would be nice to codify a more-specific discipline, `const` alone won't do it (and, at any rate, `set` and `map` have divergent "key `const`ness" policies in practice today), and simple coding rules alone won't do it. So we can't really be much more specific than to simply state the requirement and add: "You have to know what you're doing."

The Associative Container Key Rule

Once a key has been inserted into an associative container,
that key must never change its relative position in the container.

Be aware of the direct and indirect ways by which a key might change its relative order, and avoid those practices. You'll be avoiding needless problems with the standard associative containers.

ITEM 9: EQUIVALENT CODE?   DIFFICULTY: 5

Can subtle code differences really matter, especially in something as simple as postincrementing a function parameter? This Item explores an interesting interaction that becomes important in STL-style code.

1. Describe what the following code does:

```
// Example 9-1
//
f( a++ );
```

Be as complete as you can about all possibilities.

2. What is the difference, if any, between the following two code fragments?

```
// Example 9-2(a)
//
f( a++ );
```

```
// Example 9-2(b)
//
f( a );
a++;
```

3. In Question #2, make the simplifying assumption that f() is a function that takes its argument by value, and that a is an object of class type that has an operator++(int) with natural semantics. Now what is the difference, if any, between Example 9-2(a) and Example 9-2(b)?

☀️ SOLUTION

1. Describe what the following code does:

```
// Example 9-1
//
f( a++ );
```

Be as complete as you can about all possibilities.

A comprehensive list would be daunting, but here are the main possibilities.

First, f could be any of the following:

1. A macro.

In this case, the statement could mean just about anything, and a++ could be evaluated many times or not at all. For example:

```
#define f(x) x                       // once
#define f(x) (x,x,x,x,x,x,x,x,x)     // 9 times
#define f(x)                         // not at all
```

↗ Guideline

Avoid using macros. They usually make code more difficult to understand and, therefore, more troublesome to maintain.

---

2. A function.

In this case, first a++ is evaluated and then the result is passed to the function as its parameter. Normally, postincrement returns the previous value of a in the form of a temporary object, so f() could take its parameter either by value or by reference to const, but not by reference to non-const, because a reference to non-const cannot be bound to a temporary object.

3. An object.

In this case, f would be a function object, that is, an object for which operator()() is defined. Again, if postincrement returns the previous value of a (as postincrement always should) then f's operator()() could take its parameter either by value or by reference to const.

4. A type name.

In this case, the statement first evaluates a++ and uses the result of that expression to initialize a temporary object of type f.

* * * * *

Next, a could be:

1. A macro.

In this case, again, a could mean just about anything.

2. An object (possibly of a built-in type).

In this case, it must be a type for which a suitable `operator++(int)` postincrement operator is defined.

Normally, postincrement should be implemented in terms of preincrement and should return the previous value of a:

```
// Canonical form of postincrement:
T T::operator++(int)
{
  T old( *this ); // remember our original value

  ++*this;        // always implement postincrement
                  //  in terms of preincrement

  return old;     // return our original value
}
```

When you overload an operator, of course, you do have the option of changing its normal semantics to do "something unusual." For example, the following is likely to break the Example 9-1 code for most kinds of f, assuming a is of type A:

```
void A::operator++(int) // doesn't return anything
```

Don't do that. Instead, follow this sound advice:

⤢ Guideline

Always preserve natural semantics for overloaded operators. "Do as the `ints` do"; that is, follow the semantics of the built-in types. [Meyers96, Item 32]

---

3. A value, such as an address.

For example, a could be a pointer.

Some Effects of Side Effects

For the remaining questions, I will make the simplifying assumptions that f() is not a macro, and that a is an object with natural postincrement semantics.

2. What is the difference, if any, between the following two code fragments?

```
// Example 9-2(a)
//
f( a++ );
```

Example 9-2(a) performs these steps:

1. a++: Increment a and return the old value.
2. f(): Execute f(), passing it the old value of a.

Example 9-2(a) ensures that the postincrement is performed, and therefore a gets its new value, before f() executes. As already noted, f() could still be a function, a function object, or a type name that leads to a constructor call.

Some coding standards state that operations like ++ should always appear on separate lines, on the grounds that it can be dangerous to perform multiple operations like ++ in the same statement because of sequence points (more about this in Items 20 and 21). Instead, such coding standards would recommend Example 9-2(b):

```
// Example 9-2(b)
//
f( a );
a++;
```

This example performs the following steps:

1. f(): Execute f(), passing it the old value of a.
2. a++: Increment a and return the old value, which is then ignored.

In both cases, f() gets the old value of a. "So what's the big difference?" you may ask. Well, Example 9-2(b) will not always have the same effect as Example 9-2(a), because Example 9-2(b) ensures that the postincrement is performed, and therefore a gets its new value, after f() executes.

This has two major consequences. First, in the case in which f() emits an exception, Example 9-2(a) ensures that a++ and all its side effects have already been completed successfully; whereas Example 9-2(b) ensures that a++ has not been performed, and none of its side effects has occurred.

Second, even in non-exceptional cases, if f() and a.operator++(int) have visible side effects, the order in which they are executed can matter. More specifically, consider what happens if f() has a side effect that affects the state of a itself. That's neither farfetched nor unlikely, and it can happen even if f() doesn't and can't directly change a, as we'll now illustrate with an example.

Scissors, Traffic, and Iterators

3. In Question #2, make the simplifying assumption that f() is a function that takes its argument by value, and that a is an object of class type that has an operator++(int) with natural semantics. Now what is the difference, if any, between Example 9-2(a) and Example 9-2(b)?

The difference is that, for perfectly normal C++ code, Example 9-2(a) can be legal when Example 9-2(b) is not. This is because in Example 9-2(a) there is a period of time during which objects exist simultaneously with the old and new values of a. In Example 9-2(b), there is no such overlap.

Consider what happens when we replace f() with list::erase(), and a with a list::iterator. Now the first form is valid:

```
// Example 9-3(a)
//
// l is a list<int>
// i is a valid non-end iterator into l
//
l.erase( i++ ); // OK, incrementing a valid iterator
```

But the second form is not:

```
// Example 9-3(b)
//
// l is a list<int>
// i is a valid non-end iterator into l
//
l.erase( i );
i++;            // error, i is not a valid iterator
```

The reason that Example 9-3(b) is incorrect is that the call to l.erase(i) invalidates i, so you can no longer call operator++() on i afterward.

Warning: Some programmers do write code like Example 9-3(b), perhaps because of coding guidelines that have a blanket policy of discouraging operations like ++ in function call statements. Programmers who write code like Example 9-3(b) may even be routinely getting away with it (and not realizing the danger) just because it happens to work on the current version of their compiler and library. But let them be warned: Code like Example 9-3(b) is not portable; it is not sanctioned by the standard; and it's likely to turn and bite them when they port to another compiler platform, or even just upgrade the one they're working on today. When it does bite, it will bite hard, because "using-an-invalid-iterator" bugs can be very difficult to find—unless you have the joy of working with a good checked library implementation during debugging, but then you'd already have been warned about such errors.

Some mothers (who are also software engineers) give the following three pieces of good advice, and we should always strive to follow them for our own good:

1. Don't run with scissors.
2. Don't play in traffic.
3. Don't use invalid iterators.

Having said that, with the exception of examples like the above, we'll see in Items 20 and 21 why it's still a good idea in general to avoid writing operations like ++ in function calls.

ITEM 10: TEMPLATE SPECIALIZATION AND OVERLOADING   DIFFICULTY: 6

How do you specialize and overload templates? When you do, how do you determine which template gets called? Try your hand at analyzing these 12 examples.

1. What is template specialization? Give an example.

2. What is partial specialization? Give an example.

3. Consider the following declarations:

```
template<typename T1, typename T2>
void g( T1, T2 );                        // 1
template<typename T> void g( T );        // 2
template<typename T> void g( T, T );     // 3
template<typename T> void g( T* );       // 4
template<typename T> void g( T*, T );    // 5
template<typename T> void g( T, T* );    // 6
template<typename T> void g( int, T* );  // 7
template<> void g<int>( int );           // 8
void g( int, double );                   // 9
void g( int );                           // 10
```

Which of the above functions are invoked by each of the following? Identify the template parameter types, where appropriate.

```
int             i;
double          d;
float           f;
complex<double> c;

g( i );         // a
g<int>( i );    // b
g( i, i );      // c
g( c );         // d
g( i, f );      // e
g( i, d );      // f
g( c, &c );     // g
g( i, &d );     // h
g( &d, d );     // i
```

```
g( &d );        // j
g( d, &i );     // k
g( &i, &i );    // l
```

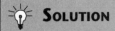

Solution

Templates provide C++'s most powerful form of genericity. They allow you to write generic code that works with many kinds of unrelated objects—for example, strings that contain various kinds of characters, containers that can hold arbitrary types of objects, and algorithms that can operate on arbitrary types of sequences.

1. What is template specialization? Give an example.

Template specialization lets templates deal with special cases. Sometimes, a generic algorithm can work much more efficiently for a certain kind of sequence (for example, when given random-access iterators), so it makes sense to specialize it for that case while using the slower but more generic approach for all other cases. Performance is a common reason to specialize, but it's not the only one. For example, you might also specialize a template to work with certain objects that don't conform to the normal interface expected by the generic template.

These special cases can be handled using two forms of template specialization: explicit specialization and partial specialization.

Explicit Specialization

Explicit specialization lets you write a specific implementation for a particular combination of template parameters. For example, consider the following function template:

```
template<typename T> void sort( Array<T>& v ) { /*...*/ };
```

If we have a faster (or other specialized) way we want to deal with Arrays of char*'s, we could explicitly specialize sort() for that case:

```
template<> void sort<char*>( Array<char*>& );
```

The compiler will then choose the most appropriate template. For example:

```
Array<int>   ai;
Array<char*> apc;

sort( ai );     // calls sort<int>
sort( apc );    // calls specialized sort<char*>
```

Partial Specialization

2. What is partial specialization? Give an example.

For class templates only, you can define partial specializations that don't have to fix all the primary (unspecialized) class template's parameters.

Here is an example from the C++ standard [C++98], in 14.5.4 [temp.class.spec]. The first template is the primary class template:

```
template<typename T1, typename T2, int I>
class A                { };              // #1
```

We can specialize this for the case when T2 is a T1*:

```
template<typename T, int I>
class A<T, T*, I>   { };              // #2
```

Or for the case when T1 is any pointer:

```
template<typename T1, typename T2, int I>
class A<T1*, T2, I> { };              // #3
```

Or for the case when T1 is int and T2 is any pointer and I is 5:

```
template<typename T>
class A<int, T*, 5> { };              // #4
```

Or for the case when T2 is any pointer:

```
template<typename T1, typename T2, int I>
class A<T1, T2*, I> { };              // #5
```

Declarations 2 through 5 declare partial specializations of the primary template. The compiler will then choose the appropriate template. From [C++98] section 14.5.4.1 comes the following:

```
A<int, int, 1>   a1;  // uses #1

A<int, int*, 1>  a2;  // uses #2, T is int,
                      //          I is 1

A<int, char*, 5> a3;  // uses #4, T is char

A<int, char*, 1> a4;  // uses #5, T1 is int,
                      //          T2 is char,
                      //          I is 1

A<int*, int*, 2> a5;  // ambiguous:
                      // matches #3 and #5
```

Function Template Overloading

Now let's consider function template overloading. It isn't the same as specialization, but it's related to it.

C++ lets you overload functions, yet makes sure the right one is called:

```
int  f( int );
long f( double );

int    i;
double d;

f( i );   // calls f(int)
f( d );   // calls f(double)
```

Similarly, you can also overload function templates, which brings us to the final question:

3. Consider the following declarations:

```
template<typename T1, typename T2>
void g( T1, T2 );                       // 1
template<typename T> void g( T );       // 2
template<typename T> void g( T, T );    // 3
template<typename T> void g( T* );      // 4
template<typename T> void g( T*, T );   // 5
template<typename T> void g( T, T* );   // 6
template<typename T> void g( int, T* ); // 7
template<> void g<int>( int );          // 8
void g( int, double );                  // 9
void g( int );                          // 10
```

First, let's simplify things a little by noticing that there are two groups of overloaded g()'s here: those that take a single parameter and those that take two parameters.

```
template<typename T1, typename T2>
void g( T1, T2 );                       // 1
template<typename T> void g( T, T );    // 3
template<typename T> void g( T*, T );   // 5
template<typename T> void g( T, T* );   // 6
template<typename T> void g( int, T* ); // 7
void g( int, double );                  // 9

template<typename T> void g( T );       // 2
template<typename T> void g( T* );      // 4
template<> void g<int>( int );          // 8
void g( int );                          // 10
```

Note that I deliberately didn't muddy the waters by including an overload with two parameters where the second parameter had a default. Had there been such a function, then for the purposes of determining the correct ordering, it should be considered in both lists—once as a single-parameter function (using the default), and once as a two-parameter function (not using the default).

Now let's consider each of the calls in turn:

Which of the above functions are invoked by each of the following? Identify the template parameter types, where appropriate.

```
int              i;
double           d;
float            f;
complex<double>  c;

g( i );          // a
```

A. This calls #10, because it's an exact match for #10 and such non-templates are always preferred over templates (see 13.3.3).

```
g<int>( i );     // b
```

B. This calls #8, because g<int>() is being explicitly requested.

```
g( i, i );       // c
```

C. This calls #3 (T is int), because that is the best match.

```
g( c );          // d
```

D. This calls #2 (T is complex<double>), because no other g() can match.

```
g( i, f );       // e
```

E. This calls #1 (T1 is int, T2 is float).
You might think that #9 is very close—and it is—but a nontemplate function is preferred only if it is an exact match. In this case, #9 is only close, not exact.

```
g( i, d );       // f
```

F. This one does call #9, because this time #9 is an exact match and the nontemplate is preferred.

```
g( c, &c );      // g
```

G. This calls #6 (T is complex<double>), because #6 is the closest overload. Template #6 provides an overload of g(), where the second parameter is a pointer to the same type as the first parameter.

```
g( i, &d );      // h
```

H. This calls #7 (T is double), because #7 is the closest overload.

```
g( &d, d );      // i
```

I. This calls #5 (T is double). #5 provides an overload of g(), where the first parameter is a pointer to the same type as the second parameter.

Only a few more to go:

```
g( &d );          // j
```

J. Clearly (by now), we're asking for #4 (T is double).

```
g( d, &i );       // k
```

K. Several other overloads are close, but only #1 fills the bill here (T1 is double, T2 is int*).

And finally:

```
g( &i, &i );      // l
```

L. This calls #3 (T is int*), which is the closest overload even though some of the others explicitly mention a pointer parameter.

The good news is that modern compilers generally have good template support so that you can make use of features like the above more reliably and portably than in the past.

The (potential) bad news is that if you got all the answers right, you may know the rules better than your current compiler does.

ITEM 11: MASTERMIND   DIFFICULTY: 8

To conclude this section, this puzzle offers some fun and lighthearted code techniques, but also gives you practice building your own function objects and reusing the standard library's built-in algorithm facilities.

Write a program that plays simplified Mastermind, using only standard library containers, algorithms, and streams. Usually, this book's goal is to demonstrate strict and sound software engineering. This time, just for some fun, the challenge is a bit more lighthearted. Use as few ifs, whiles, fors, and other keywords as possible, and have the program take up as few statements as possible. For this one Item, dense code is okay.

Simplified Rules Summary

To start the game, the program randomly chooses a string of four pegs in some internal order. Each peg can be one of three colors: red (R), green (G), or blue (B). For example, the program might pick "RRBB" or "GGGG" or "BGRG."

The player makes successive guesses until he figures out the order. For each guess, the program tells the player two numbers. The first is the number of pegs that are the correct color, independent of order. The second is the number of pegs having both the correct color and the correct location.

The following is an example session, in which the program chose the combination "RRBB":

```
guess--> RBRR
3 1
guess--> RBGG
2 1
guess--> BBRR
4 0
guess--> RRBB
4 4 - solved!
```

SOLUTION

The solutions presented here are not the only right answers. Both are nicely extensible to additional colors and pegs, because they avoid hardcoding peg-color and combination-size restrictions within the algorithm. Peg colors can be extended simply by changing the `colors` string; the combination length can be changed directly by changing the length of the `comb` string. On the downside, both solutions do insufficient error checking.

One of the requirements of the problem was to minimize the number of statements, so wherever possible these solutions use a comma instead of a semicolon as a statement separator. Most of us aren't used to seeing so many commas in C or C++ code, but it's possible to use commas in more places than one might at first think. Another requirement was to avoid the built-in control keywords, so for our purposes the ternary `?:` operator will understudy for `if`/`else`.

Solution #1

The idea of the first solution is to evaluate each guess by making only a single pass through the guess string input by the player. This first solution does still use one `while`. In the second solution, we'll replace it with `find_if` (although at some further cost of clarity).

To see the basic structure of this code, let's start with the mainline:

```
typedef map<int,int> M;

int main() {
  const string colors("BGR");  // possible colors
  string comb(4, '.'),         // combination
         guess;                // current guess
```

Extending this program to handle more colors, or more pegs per combination, is easy: To change the colors, change `colors`. To make the guess length longer or shorter, make comb longer or shorter.

```
int cok, pok = 0;           // right color & place
M cm, gm;                   // helper structures
```

We need a string to hold the combination to be found, and another to hold the guess. The rest are working data used to process each guess.

The first thing we need to do is to generate the combination:

```
srand( time(0) ),
  generate( comb.begin(), comb.end(),
            ChoosePeg( colors ) );
```

After seeding the built-in random number generator, we use the standard library's `generate()` facility to make up a combination. Here `generate()` uses a function object of type `ChoosePeg` to generate a combination by invoking `ChoosePeg`'s function call operator, `operator()()`, once for each peg position to determine the color at that position. We'll see how `ChoosePeg` works later on.

Now all we need is the main loop, to print prompts and process guesses:

```
while( pok < comb.size() )
  cout << "\n\nguess--> ",
    cin >> guess,
    guess.resize( comb.size(), ' ' ),
```

We do some basic input-error handling. If the player's guess is too long, the guess is truncated; if it's too short, it's padded with spaces. Padding short guesses lets the player cheat by simply trying one-letter guesses until he or she finds the right letter, then two-letter guesses to find the second letter, and so on to incrementally guess the solution. This code doesn't bother to prevent that.

Next, we need to clear our working area and process the guess:

```
cm = gm = M(),
```

We have to process the guess in two ways: First, we determine the number of pegs that are the right color and in the right place (pok, or "place okay"). Separately, we determine the number of pegs that are the right color but not necessarily in the right location (cok, or just "color okay"). To avoid making two passes through the guess, we first use `transform()` to process the two ranges and let the `CountPlace` function object accumulate information about how many pegs of each color appear in the combination and in the guess:

```
transform( comb.begin(), comb.end(),
          guess.begin(), guess.begin(),
          CountPlace( cm, gm, pok ) ),
```

The standard library's `transform()` algorithm operates on two input ranges—here, the combination and guess strings viewed as sequences of characters. Now, `transform()` actually does more than we need; it can also generate output, and we don't care about the output. The easiest way to ignore the output is to make sure the supplied `CountPlace` function object doesn't actually change anything and then put the output back into the guess string, which is thus a no-op.

Note that the `CountPlace` function object also populates our `cm` and `gm` maps, in addition to its primary purpose of calculating `pok`. These helper maps are then used in the second phase, where the `for_each` loop loops through the colors (not the guess) and counts how many pegs of each color will match:

```
for_each ( colors.begin(), colors.end(),
          CountColor( cm, gm, cok ) ),
```

The `for_each()` algorithm is probably the best-known algorithm in the standard library. All it does is iterate over a range and apply the supplied function object to each element in the range. In this case, the `CountColor` object is responsible for counting and then totaling how many pegs of each color match up in the two strings.

Having done all the work to process the guess, we report our results:

```
cout << cok << ' ' << pok;
```

Note that no braces are needed around the `while` loop's body because the whole body is one statement, thanks to all those commas.

Finally, when the loop ends, we're done:

```
    cout << " - solved!\n";
}
```

Having seen how the whole program is intended to work, let's take a look at the three helper function objects.

ChoosePeg

The simplest of the helpers is `ChoosePeg`, which is used to generate the combination:

```
class ChoosePeg
{
public:
  ChoosePeg( const string& colors )
    : colors_(colors) { }

  char operator()() const
```

```
  { return colors_[rand() % colors_.size()]; }

private:
  const string& colors_;
};
```

Each invocation of `operator()()` generates another peg's color.

If it weren't for the fact that `ChoosePeg` remembers a reference to the string of valid colors, it could be a plain function. We could have made `colors` a global string and polluted the global namespace. This solution prefers avoiding global data and making `ChoosePeg` better encapsulated rather than making the `colors` string global and having `ChoosePeg` depend on knowledge of the global data.

CountPlace

Next, `CountPlace` is responsible for calculating `pok`, the number of pegs that are the right color and in the right place. It's also responsible for populating statistical information about the guess and combination strings for later tallying by `CountColor`.

```
class CountPlace
{
public:
  CountPlace( M& cm, M& gm, int& pok )
    : cm_(cm), gm_(gm), pok_(pok=0) { }

  char operator()( char c, char g )
  {
    return ++cm_[c],
           ++gm_[g],
           pok_ += (c == g),
           g;
  }

private:
  M &cm_, &gm_;
  int& pok_;
};
```

Each invocation of `operator()()` compares one of the combination's pegs, c, with the corresponding peg from the guess, g. If they're equal, we increment `pok_`. Now the purpose of the maps is clearer. Each map stores the number of pegs of a given color (the color's `char` value converted to an `int`) appearing in the given string.

Because of `transform()`'s semantics, `operator()()` has to return some `char`. It doesn't really matter what we return because, although the output is directed back into the `guess` string, the `guess` string won't be used again. For simplicity and general cleanliness, though, we just return the guess's peg color so that the `guess` string remains unmodified.

CountColor

Finally, `CountColor` is responsible for calculating cok, using the statistical information generated by `CountPlace`. It does so in the obvious way: For each possible color, it adds the number of matching pegs regardless of location, which is to say the minimum of the number of pegs of that color in the combination and in the guess.

```
class CountColor {
public:
  CountColor( M& cm, M& gm, int& cok )
    : cm_(cm), gm_(gm), cok_(cok=0) { }

  void operator()( char c ) const
    { cok_ += min( cm_[c], gm_[c] ); }

private:
  M &cm_, &gm_;
  int& cok_;
};
```

Summary

Putting it all together into a complete program, we get the following:

```
#include <iostream>
#include <algorithm>
#include <map>
#include <string>
#include <ctime>
#include <cstdlib>
using namespace std;

typedef map<int,int> M;

class ChoosePeg
{
public:
  ChoosePeg( const string& colors )
    : colors_(colors) { }

  char operator()() const
    { return colors_[rand() % colors_.size()]; }

private:
  const string& colors_;
};

class CountPlace
{
public:
  CountPlace( M& cm, M& gm, int& pok )
    : cm_(cm), gm_(gm), pok_(pok=0) { }
```

```
    char operator()( char c, char g )
    {
      return ++cm_[c],
             ++gm_[g],
             pok_ += (c == g),
             g;
    }
private:
  M &cm_, &gm_;
  int& pok_;
};

class CountColor {
public:
  CountColor( M& cm, M& gm, int& cok )
    : cm_(cm), gm_(gm), cok_(cok=0) { }

  void operator()( char c ) const
    { cok_ += min( cm_[c], gm_[c] ); }

private:
  M &cm_, &gm_;
  int& cok_;
};

int main() {
  const string colors("BGR"); // possible colors
  string comb(4, '.'),        // combination
         guess;               // current guess
  int cok, pok = 0;           // right color & place
  M cm, gm;                   // helper structures

  srand( time(0) ),
   generate( comb.begin(), comb.end(),
             ChoosePeg( colors ) );

  while( pok < comb.size() )
    cout << "\n\nguess--> ",
    cin >> guess,
    guess.resize( comb.size(),' '),
    cm = gm = M(),
    transform( comb.begin(), comb.end(),
               guess.begin(), guess.begin(),
               CountPlace( cm, gm, pok ) ),
    for_each ( colors.begin(), colors.end(),
               CountColor( cm, gm, cok ) ),
    cout << cok << ' '<< pok;

  cout << " - solved!\n";
}
```

Solution #2

The idea of the second solution is to make the mainline dead simple by simply saying "find the combination in the input." Here's the mainline:

```
int main()
{
  srand( time(0) ),
    find_if( istream_iterator<string>(cin),
             istream_iterator<string>(),
             Combination() );
}
```

That's it. The Combination predicate has to do all the work.

Combination

Clearly, we expect that Combination's default constructor will invent a combination:

```
class Combination
{
public:
  Combination()
    : comb_(4, '.')
  {
    generate( comb_.begin(), comb_.end(), ChoosePeg ),
      Prompt();
  }
```

Note that this ChoosePeg() is different from the one in the first solution; more on that in a moment. After generating the combination, the constructor emits the first prompt, and that's all it needs to do.

Next, Combination::operator()() will compare each input guess string with the combination and return true if it matches the combination, and false otherwise:

```
bool operator()( string guess ) const // one round
{
  int cok, pok;    // right color & place

  return
    guess.resize( comb_.size(), ' '),
```

Again, we do some basic error handling by adjusting the size of the guess, if necessary.

The major work will, again, be done in two stages. The difference is that this time the two states are reversed, and we don't bother limiting ourselves to just one pass through the input. First, we determine cok, the number of pegs that are the right color but may or may not be in the right place:

```
cok = accumulate( colors.begin(), colors.end(),
                  ColorMatch( 0, &comb_, &guess ),
                  ColorMatch::Count ),
```

We'll look at the `ColorMatch` helper in a moment.

Phase 2 is to calculate `pok`, the number of pegs with the right color and position. To do this, we're going to use what may seem like an inappropriate algorithm:

```
pok = inner_product( comb_.begin(), comb_.end(),
                     guess.begin(), 0,
                     plus<int>(),
                     equal_to<char>() ),
```

We're not performing mathematical matrix calculations here, so why use `inner_product()`? The short answer is, because it's there.

The longer answer is that it's the algorithm whose behavior is the closest to what's wanted. The `inner_product()` algorithm:

- Takes two input ranges
- Performs a specified operation (let's call it *op2*) on the two first elements of the ranges, then on the two second elements of the ranges, and so on; and
- Performs another specified operator (let's call it *op1*) to combine the results.

It happens that the defaults for *op1* and *op2*, respectively, are addition and multiplication. But what we want is only slightly different. For *op1*, addition is fine, and we just want *op2* to return 1 if the two characters are equal, and 0 otherwise, which happens to be what you get when you use equality comparison *à la* `equal_to<char>` and let the resulting `bool` promote to an `int`.

If the name `inner_product()` still worries you, think of this standard algorithm as a kind of *mélange* of `accumulate()`, which counts things in a single input range, and `transform()`, which processes two input ranges, with a dash of flexibility to customize what to do with the elements from the two ranges. A mathematical inner product calculation is a special case of the same description, but the `inner_product()` algorithm is specified more generally and can adapt to different ways of combining and tallying input sequences, as we've just seen.

```
        cout << cok <<' '<< pok,
        (pok == comb_.size())
          ? (cout << " - solved!\n", true)
          : (Prompt(), false);
    }
```

Finally, the operator also generates the user interface, including guess feedback and the subsequent prompt or completion message.

When it comes to nonstatic data members, we need only the obvious one:

```
private:
  string comb_;  // actual combination
```

That's it for the nonstatic members. The rest of `Combination`'s members are static:

```
static char ChoosePeg() { return colors[rand() % colors.size()]; }
```

Note that because of the changed encapsulation—with the `colors` string in the same scope as `ChoosePeg()`—we can simplify `ChoosePeg()` and make it just a stateless function.

```
static void Prompt()    { cout << "\n\nguess--> "; }
static const string colors;       // possible colors
};
```

```
const string Combination::colors = "BGR";
```

Since `Combination` is now the only class that needs to know about the possible colors and the length of guesses, we can nicely hide that information by tucking it away inside `Combination`'s scope.

ColorMatch

The only thing we still need is a `ColorMatch` function object. Remember, it is intended to be used like this:

```
cok = accumulate( colors.begin(), colors.end(),
                  ColorMatch( 0, &comb_, &guess ),
                  ColorMatch::Count ),
```

There are a couple of wrinkles here. Note that `ColorMatch` is actually the type of value being accumulated. For one thing, this means that `accumulate()` will return the final `ColorMatch` value, whereas we're looking for an `int`. That's pretty easy—we'll just provide a conversion to `int`:

```
class ColorMatch {
public:
  ColorMatch( int i, const string* s1, const string* s2 )
    : cok_(i), s1_(s1), s2_(s2) { }

  operator int() const { return cok_; }
```

Now, when we use `accumulate()` as above, instead of adding plain values such as `int`s, we'll be `Count()`-ing using `ColorMatch` objects. That is, for each `char` in `colors`, `accumulate()` will apply the function `ColorMatch::Count()`, which takes a `ColorMatch` value representing the tally so far and the next `colors` character to process:

```
static ColorMatch Count( ColorMatch& cm, char c )
{
  return
    ColorMatch(
      cm.cok_ +
        min( count( cm.s1_->begin(), cm.s1_->end(), c ),
              count( cm.s2_->begin(), cm.s2_->end(), c ) ),
      cm.s1_, cm.s2_ );
}
```

Count()'s job is to figure out how many pegs of color c exist in both strings (although not necessarily in the same positions), and add that to the current ColorMatch tally. It does this by simply using another standard algorithm, count(), to determine the number of pegs with color c in each string, and adding the lower number. Count() then returns a new ColorMatch object that contains the new tally. Because Count() will be called once for each possible color, the final ColorMatch object's cok_ value will be exactly the number we want: the number of pegs with the right color but not necessarily in the right place.

Finally, the function object keeps some private state:

```
private:
  int cok_;
  const string *s1_, *s2_;
};
```

Summary

Again, putting it all together into a complete program makes it easier to see how the various parts fit and coexist:

```
#include <iostream>
#include <algorithm>
#include <numeric>
#include <functional>
#include <string>
#include <ctime>
#include <cstdlib>
using namespace std;

class ColorMatch {
public:
  ColorMatch( int i, const string* s1, const string* s2 )
    : cok_(i), s1_(s1), s2_(s2) { }

  operator int() const { return cok_; }
```

```
    static ColorMatch Count( ColorMatch& cm, char c )
    {
      return
        ColorMatch(
          cm.cok_ +
            min( count( cm.s1_->begin(), cm.s1_->end(), c ),
                 count( cm.s2_->begin(), cm.s2_->end(), c ) ),
          cm.s1_, cm.s2_ );
    }

private:
  int cok_;
  const string *s1_, *s2_;
};

class Combination
{
public:
  Combination()
    : comb_(4, '.')
  {
    generate( comb_.begin(), comb_.end(), ChoosePeg ),
     Prompt();
  }

  bool operator()( string guess ) const // one round
  {
    int cok, pok;    // right color & place

    return
      guess.resize( comb_.size(),' ' ),
      cok = accumulate( colors.begin(), colors.end(),
                   ColorMatch( 0, &comb_, &guess ),
                   ColorMatch::Count ),
      pok = inner_product( comb_.begin(), comb_.end(),
                     guess.begin(), 0,
                     plus<int>(),
                     equal_to<char>() ),
      cout << cok <<' '<< pok,
      (pok == comb_.size())
        ? (cout << " - solved!\n", true)
        : (Prompt(), false);
  }

private:
  string comb_;   // actual combination

  static char ChoosePeg() { return colors[rand() % colors.size()]; }
  static void Prompt()    { cout << "\n\nguess--> "; }
  static const string colors;        // possible colors
};
```

```
const string Combination::colors = "BGR";

int main()
{
  srand( time(0) ),
    find_if( istream_iterator<string>(cin),
             istream_iterator<string>(),
             Combination() );
}
```

Comparing the Solutions

This Item has two purposes. One purpose is to have some fun with some C++ features, so we've enjoyed some creative use of comma operators that should be used rarely, if ever, in real-world production code.

The other purpose, however, and the more serious one, is to get better acquainted with generic programming and with what the C++ standard library has to offer, pre-packaged and ready-to-use. Each solution approached this purpose in a different way, with different goals. The main goal shaping Solution 1 was to avoid multiple passes through the input. That's not a performance consideration in this simple program whose runtime is dominated by user input, not by the program's processing, but avoiding multiple passes is a useful technique worth knowing for real-world code. When might you want to avoid multiple passes through data? One common example is when the input data is very large, and multiple passes may be prohibitively expensive if the data is larger than memory and needs to be read from disk twice or more—clearly, it can be desirable to avoid needless access to slow secondary storage. Another example is when multiple passes might be impossible—you may get only one chance at the data, such as when the input comes from an input iterator.

The main goal shaping Solution 2 was to have a clean and expressive mainline and better-encapsulated internal code. Although a bit longer than Solution 1, Solution 2 is clearer because it avoids Solution 1's possibly mysterious indirect coordination between the main loop's two phases via helper structures. Those structures aren't needed when we allow two passes through the input data, and so the two passes become distinct instead of interdependent. Therefore, they're easier to understand.

Both solutions have given us some exercise reusing the standard library, and both have demonstrated techniques that can be useful in production code. (But, yes, in production code, I'd stay away from all those commas; those were just for fun.)

Optimization and Performance

Efficiency has always been important to programmers. It is one of the key pillars in the tradition of C and C++, in which the guiding principle of "you shouldn't pay for what you don't use"—also known as the zero-cost principle—has always been at the forefront of the language's and library's design, and has been largely achieved.

This section, along with the two appendixes at the end of the book, takes a hard look at a few key C++ optimization issues selected for their real-world impact. When and how should you optimize your code? What does `inline` do, really? Why can (and do) fancy optimizations get us into trouble? Finally, and to me most interestingly, how can some of these answers change if you're writing multithread-safe code? After all, we're interested in efficiency issues in the real world, and although the C++ standard is silent about threads, more and more programmers in the trenches are writing multi-threaded C++ code every day. And they will care about the answers.

ITEM 12: `inline`   **DIFFICULTY: 4**

Contrary to popular opinion, the keyword `inline` *is not some sort of magic bullet. It is, however, a useful tool when employed properly. The question is: When should you use it?*

1. What does `inline` do?
2. Does making a function `inline` increase efficiency?
3. When and how should you decide to `inline` a function?

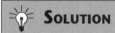 **SOLUTION**

1. What does `inline` do?

Making a function `inline` directs the compiler that it may choose to place a copy of the function's code directly into each place the code is used. In the cases where the compiler does so, it avoids generating a function call.

2. Does making a function `inline` increase efficiency?

Not necessarily.

First off, if you tried to answer this question without first asking what you want to optimize, you fell into a classic trap. The first question has to be: "What do you mean by efficiency?" Does the above question mean program size? Memory footprint? Execution time? Development speed? Build time? Or something else?

Second, contrary to popular opinion, inlining can improve *or* worsen any of those aspects of efficiency:

a) *Program size.* Many programmers assume that inlining increases program size, because instead of having one copy of a function's code, the compiler creates a copy in every place that function is used. This is often true, but not always. If the function size is smaller than the code the compiler has to generate to perform the function call, inlining will reduce program size.

b) *Memory footprint.* Inlining usually has little or no effect on a program's memory usage, apart from the basic program size (above).

c) *Execution time.* Many programmers assume that inlining a function will improve execution time because it avoids the function call overhead, and because "seeing through the veil" of the function call gives the compiler's optimizer more opportunities to work its craft. This can be true, but often isn't. If the function is not called extremely frequently, there will usually be no visible improvement in overall program execution time. In fact, just the opposite can happen. If inlining increases a calling function's size, it will reduce that caller's locality of reference, which means that overall program speed can actually worsen if the caller's inner loop no longer fits in the processor's cache.

   To put this point in perspective, don't forget that most programs are not CPU-bound. Probably the most common bottleneck is being I/O-bound, which can include anything from network bandwidth or latency to file or database access.

d) *Development speed, build time.* To be most useful, `inlined` code has to be visible to the caller, which means that the caller has to depend on the internals of the `inlined` code. Depending on another module's internal implementation details increases the practical coupling of modules (it does not, however, increase their theoretical coupling, because the caller doesn't actually use any of the callee's internals). Usually, when functions change, callers do not need to be recompiled, only relinked. When `inlined` functions change, callers are forced to recompile. What's more, there's a completely separate hit on development speed that appears at debugging time, because stepping into inlined functions and managing breakpoints inside them tends to be more difficult for most debuggers.

   There is one case in which inlining a function can arguably be viewed as an optimization for development speed—when the cost of writing an accessor function (see below) would otherwise be too high to justify the good practice of providing an accessor function to avoid making a data member public. In this case, some would argue that inline encourages good coding style and better module insulation.

Finally, if you're looking to improve efficiency in some way, always look to your algorithms and data structures first. They will give you the order-of-magnitude overall improvements, whereas process optimizations, such as inlining, generally (note, generally) yield less-dramatic results.

Just Say "No for Now"

3. When and how should you decide to inline a function?

The answer is the same as when to apply any other optimization: after a profiler tells you to, and not a minute sooner. There are a few valid exceptions to this guideline for cases in which you would reasonably inline right away, such as for an empty function that's likely to stay empty, or when you're absolutely forced to—for example, when writing a non-exported template.

↗ Guideline

The first rule of optimization: Don't do it.
The second rule of optimization: Don't do it yet.

Bottom line, inlining always costs something, if only increased coupling, and you should never pay for something until you know you're going to turn a profit—that is, get something better in return.

"But I can always tell where the bottlenecks are," you may think. Don't worry, you're not alone. Most programmers think this at one time or another, but they're still wrong. Dead wrong. Programmers are notoriously poor guessers about where their code's true bottlenecks lie. Sometimes, we get lucky and are right. Most of the time, we're not.

Usually, only experimental evidence (a.k.a. profiling output) helps to tell you where the true hot spots are. Nine times out of ten, a programmer cannot identify the number-one hot-spot bottleneck in his or her code without some sort of profiling tool. In my years in this business, I've come across several programmers who have protested until they (or their colleagues) were blue in the face that this didn't apply to them, that they could consistently "feel" where the hot spots were in their code. In those same years, I've never seen such a claim turn out to be consistently true. We're good at fooling ourselves.

Finally, note another practical reason for this: Profilers are a lot less good at identifying which inlined functions should *not* be inlined.

What About Computation-Intensive Tasks (Such as Numeric Libraries)?

Some people write small, tight library code, such as advanced scientific and engineering numerical libraries, and can do reasonably well with seat-of-the-pants inlining. Even those developers, however, tend to `inline` judiciously and to tune later rather than earlier. Note that writing a module and then comparing performance with "inlining on" and "inlining off" is generally an unsound idea, because "all on" or "all off" is a coarse measure that tells you only about the average case. It doesn't tell you which functions benefited, nor how much each one benefited. Even in these cases, you're usually better off to use a profiler and to optimize based on its advice.

What About Accessors?

There are people who will argue that one-line accessor functions (like "`X& Y::f()
{ return myX_; }`") are a reasonable exception and could or should be automatically inlined. I understand the reasoning, but be careful. At the very least, all inlined code increases coupling. So, unless you're certain in advance that inlining will help, there's no harm in deferring that decision to profiling time. If at that point, a profiler does point out that inlining will help, at least you know that what you're doing is worth doing, and you've deferred the coupling and possible build overhead until you know it will really matter. Not a bad deal, that.

 Guideline

Avoid inlining or detailed tuning until performance profiles prove the need.

ITEM 13: LAZY OPTIMIZATION, PART 1: A PLAIN OLD STRING   DIFFICULTY: 2

Copy-on-write (also called "lazy copy") is a common optimization that uses reference counting. Do you know how to implement it? In this first Item, we consider a simple plain-vanilla String that's not reference-counted at all. In the rest of the miniseries, we'll see what impact adding copy-on-write semantics can have on the class.

Consider the following simplified `String` class. (Note: This is not intended to be a complete string facility. It's been distilled to serve as an example, and is missing many common operations that you would otherwise see in a real string class. In particular, I don't show `operator=()` because its code is essentially the same as that of copy construction.)

```cpp
namespace Original
{
  class String
  {
  public:
    String();                     // start off empty
   ~String();                     // free the buffer
    String( const String& );      // take a full copy
    void Append( char );          // append one character

    // ... operator=() etc. omitted ...

  private:
    char*    buf_;                // allocated buffer
    size_t   len_;                // length of buffer
    size_t   used_;               // # chars actually used
  };
}
```

This is a simple `String` that does not contain any fancy optimizations. When you copy an `Original::String`, the new object immediately allocates its own buffer and you immediately have two completely distinct objects.

Your assignment: Implement `Original::String`.

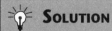 **SOLUTION**

Implementing `Original::String`

Here is a straightforward implementation. The default constructor and destructor are simple to write:

```cpp
namespace Original {

  String::String() : buf_(0), len_(0), used_(0) { }

  String::~String() { delete[] buf_; }
```

Next, to implement copy assignment, we just make a new buffer and use the standard `copy()` algorithm to make a copy of the original's contents:

```cpp
  String::String( const String& other )
    : buf_(new char[other.len_]),
      len_(other.len_),
      used_(other.used_)
```

```
{
  copy( other.buf_, other.buf_ + used_, buf_ );
}
```

I've chosen to implement an additional `Reserve()` helper function for code clarity because it will be needed by other mutators besides `Append()`. `Reserve()` ensures that our internal buffer is at least n bytes long, and allocates additional space using an exponential-growth strategy:

```
void String::Reserve( size_t n )
{
  if( len_ < n )
  {
    size_t newlen = max( len_ * 1.5, n );
    char*  newbuf = new char[ newlen ];
    copy( buf_, buf_+used_, newbuf );

    delete[] buf_;  // now all the real work is
    buf_ = newbuf;  //  done, so take ownership
    len_ = newlen;
  }
}
```

Finally, `Append()` just makes sure there's enough space, then tacks on the new character:

```
void String::Append( char c )
{
  Reserve( used_+1 );
  buf_[used_++] = c;
}
```

Aside: What's the Best Buffer Growth Strategy?

When a `String` object runs out of room in its currently allocated buffer, it needs to allocate a larger one. The key question is: How big should the new buffer be? Note that the question is important because the analysis we're about to do holds for other structures and containers that use allocated buffers, such as a standard `vector`.

There are several popular buffer growth strategies. I'll note each strategy's complexity in terms of the number of allocations required, and the average number of times a given character must be copied, for a string of eventual length N.

a) *Exact growth.* In this strategy, the new buffer is made exactly as large as required by the current operation. For example, appending one character and then appending another will force two allocations. First, a new buffer is allocated, with space for the existing string and the first new character. Next, another new buffer is allocated, with space for that and the second new character.

- Advantage: no wasted space.
- Disadvantage: poor performance. This strategy requires O(N) allocations and an average of O(N) copy operations per char, but with a high constant factor in the worst case (same as option (b) below with an increment size of 1). Control of the constant factor is in the hands of the user code, not controlled by the String implementer.

b) *Fixed-increment growth.* The new buffer should be a fixed amount larger than the current buffer. For example, a 64-byte increment size would mean that all string buffers would be an integer multiple of 64 bytes long.

- Advantage: little wasted space. The amount of unused space in the buffer is bounded by the increment size, and does not vary with the length of the string.
- Disadvantage: moderate performance. This strategy requires both O(N) allocations and an average of O(N) copy operations per char. That is, both the number of allocations and the average number of times a given char is copied vary linearly with the length of the string. However, control of the constant factor is in the hands of the String implementer.

Exponential growth. The new buffer is a factor of F larger than the current buffer. For example, with F = .5, appending one character to a full string that is already 100 bytes long will allocate a new buffer of length 150 bytes.

Advantage: good performance. This strategy requires O(logN) allocations and an average of O(1) copy operations per char. That is, the number of allocations varies as the log of the length of the string, but the average number of times a given char is copied is *constant*, which means that the amount of copying work to create a string using this strategy is at most a constant factor greater than the amount of work that would have been required had the size of the string been known in advance.

Disadvantage: some wasted space. The amount of unused space in the buffer will always be strictly less than N×F bytes, but that's still O(N) average space wastage.

The following chart summarizes the trade-offs:

Growth Strategy	Allocations	Char Copies	Wasted Space
Exact	O(N) with high const.	O(N) with high const.	none
Fixed-increment	O(N)	O(N)	O(1)
Exponential	O(logN)	O(1)	O(N)

In general, the best-performing strategy is exponential growth. Consider a string that starts empty and grows to 1,200 characters long. Fixed-increment growth requires

O(N) allocations and, on average, requires copying each character O(N) times (in this case, using 32-byte increments, that's 38 allocations and, on average, 19 copies of each character). Exponential growth requires O(logN) allocations and, on average, requires making only O(1)—one or two—copies of each character (yes, really; see the reference below). In this case, using a factor of 1.5, that's 10 allocations and on average 2 copies of each character.

	1,200-char string		12,000-char string	
	Fixed-incr growth (32 bytes)	Exponential growth (1.5x)	Fixed-incr growth (32 bytes)	Exponential growth (1.5x)
# of memory allocations	38	10	380	16
avg # of copies made of each char	19	2	190	2

This result can be surprising. For more information, see Andrew Koenig's column in the September 1998 issue of *JOOP* (*Journal of Object-Oriented Programming*). Koenig also shows why, again in general, the best growth factor is not 2 but probably about 1.5. He also shows why the average number of times a given character is copied is constant—that is, it doesn't depend on the length of the string.

ITEM 14: LAZY OPTIMIZATION, PART 2: INTRODUCING LAZINESS   DIFFICULTY: 3

Copy-on-write is a common optimization. Do you know how to implement it?

`Original::String` (from Item 13) is all very well, but sometimes copies of string objects are taken, used without modification, and then discarded.

"It seems a shame," the implementer of `Original::String` from Item 13 might frown to herself, "that I always do all the work of allocating a new buffer (which can be expensive) when it may turn out that I never needed to if all the user does is read from the new string and then destroy it. I could have simply let the two string objects share a buffer under the covers, avoiding the copy for a while, and only really take a copy when I know I need to because one of the objects is going to try to modify the string. That way, if the user never modifies the copy, I never need to do the extra work!"

With a smile on her face and determination in her eyes, the implementer designs an `Optimized::String` that uses a copy-on-write implementation (also called "lazy copy"), implemented by reference-counting the underlying string representations:

```
namespace Optimized
{
  class StringBuf
  {
  public:
    StringBuf();              // start off empty
    ~StringBuf();             // delete the buffer
    void Reserve( size_t n );// ensure len >= n

    char*    buf;             // allocated buffer
    size_t   len;             // length of buffer
    size_t   used;            // # chars actually used
    unsigned refs;            // reference count

  private:
    // No copying...
    //
    StringBuf( const StringBuf& );
    StringBuf& operator=( const StringBuf& );
  };

  class String
  {
  public:
    String();                 // start off empty
    ~String();                // decrement reference count
                              //   (delete buffer if refs==0)
    String( const String& );  // point at same buffer and
                              //   increment reference count
    void    Append( char );   // append one character

    // ... operator=() etc. omitted ...

  private:
    StringBuf* data_;
  };
}
```

Your assignment: Implement `Optimized::StringBuf` and `Optimized::String`.[1] You may want to add a private `String::AboutToModify()` helper function to simplify the logic.

---

1. This Item incidentally illustrates another use for namespaces—namely clearer exposition. It makes code easy and natural both to read as code and to talk about in human language. Writing the above description was much nicer than writing about differently named `Original String` and `OptimizedString` classes, never mind that those longer names would have made reading and writing the example code a little harder. Using namespaces judiciously can likewise improve readability in your production code and "talkability" during design meetings and code reviews.

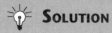 **SOLUTION**

First, let's consider StringBuf. Note that the default memberwise copying and assignment don't make sense for StringBufs, so both operations are suppressed (declared as private and not defined).

Optimized::StringBuf now does part of the work that the Original::String did for itself. StringBuf's default construction and destruction are just what you'd expect:

```
namespace Optimized
{

  StringBuf::StringBuf()
    : buf(0), len(0), used(0), refs(1) { }

  StringBuf::~StringBuf() { delete[] buf; }
```

Reserve() too is familiar from our Original::String:

```
  void StringBuf::Reserve( size_t n )
  {
    if( len < n )
    {
      size_t newlen = max( len * 1.5, n );
      char*  newbuf = new char[ newlen ];
      copy( buf, buf+used, newbuf );

      delete[] buf;    // now all the real work is
      buf = newbuf;    //  done, so take ownership
      len = newlen;
    }
  }
```

That's it for StringBuf.

Next, consider String itself. The default constructor is easy to implement:

```
String::String() : data_(new StringBuf) { }
```

In the destructor, we have to remember to manage the reference count because there might be other String objects sharing the same StringBuf representation. If other Strings are still using the StringBuf, we leave it alone and just go away after decrementing the usage count to note that we don't care about it anymore. But if we're the last client of the StringBuf, we clean it up:

```
String::~String()
{
  if( --data_->refs < 1 )  // last one out ...
  {
    delete data_;  // ... turns off the lights
  }
}
```

The only other place we have to change the reference count is in the copy constructor, which we'll write to implement the lazy copy semantics by simply pointing at the
other String's existing StringBuf and bumping the count to record our presence.
This is a "shallow" copy. We will only split off the shared representation (that is, make
a deep copy) if we discover that we need to modify one of the strings that share this
buffer:

```
String::String( const String& other )
  : data_(other.data_)
{
  ++data_->refs;
}
```

I've chosen to implement an additional AboutToModify() helper function for code
clarity, because it will be needed by other mutators besides Append(). AboutTo
Modify() ensures that we have an unshared copy of the internal buffer—it lazily performs the deep copy if it has not already been performed. For convenience, About
ToModify() also takes a minimum buffer size hint so that we won't needlessly take
our own copy of a full string only to turn around and immediately perform a second
allocation to get more space.

```
void String::AboutToModify( size_t n )
{
  if( data_->refs > 1 )
  {
    auto_ptr<StringBuf> newdata( new StringBuf );
    newdata->Reserve( max( data_->len, n ) );
    copy( data_->buf, data_->buf+data_->used, newdata->buf );
    newdata->used = data_->used;

    --data_->refs;              // now all the real work is
    data_ = newdata.release(); //  done, so take ownership
  }
  else
  {
    data_->Reserve( n );
  }
}
```

Now that all the other machinery is in place, Append() is simple. As before, it just
declares that it's about to modify the string, thereby ensuring both that the physical

string buffer is unshared and that it's big enough to hold an additional character. Then it goes ahead and makes the change:

```
void String::Append( char c ) {
  AboutToModify( data_->used+1 );
  data_->buf[data_->used++] = c;
}

}
```

That's all there is to it. In our next step, we'll make the interface just a little richer and see what happens.

Item 15: Lazy Optimization, Part 3: Iterators and References   Difficulty: 6

In the third part of this miniseries, we examine the effect of references and iterators into a copy-on-write string. Can you spot the issues?

Consider the copy-on-write Optimized::String class from Item 14, but with two new functions: Length() and operator[]().

```
namespace Optimized
{
  class StringBuf
  {
  public:
    StringBuf();           // start off empty
   ~StringBuf();           // delete the buffer
    void Reserve( size_t n ); // ensure len >= n

    char*   buf;           // allocated buffer
    size_t  len;           // length of buffer
    size_t  used;          // # chars actually used
    unsigned refs;         // reference count

  private:
    // No copying...
    //
    StringBuf( const StringBuf& );
    StringBuf& operator=( const StringBuf& );
  };

  class String
  {
  public:
    String();              // start off empty
```

```
  ~String();                 // decrement reference count
                             //   (delete buffer if refs==0)
  String( const String& );   // point at same buffer and
                             //   increment reference count
  void   Append( char );     // append one character

  size_t Length() const;     // string length

  char&  operator[](size_t);// element access
  const char operator[](size_t) const;

  // ... operator=() etc. omitted ...

private:
  void AboutToModify( size_t n );
                             // lazy copy, ensure len>=n
  StringBuf* data_;
};
}
```

This allows code such as the following:

```
if( s.Length() > 0 )
{
  cout << s[0];
  s[0] = 'a';
}
```

Implement the new members of Optimized::String. Do any of the other members need to be changed because of the new member functions? Explain.

SOLUTION

Consider the copy-on-write Optimized::String class from Item 14, but with two new functions: Length() and operator[]().

The point of this Item is to demonstrate why adding functionality like operator[] changes Optimized::String's semantics enough to affect other parts of the class. But first things first:

Implement the new members of Optimized::String.

The Length() function is simple:

```
namespace Optimized
{

  size_t String::Length() const
  {
    return data_->used;
  }
```

There's more to `operator[]`, however, than meets the casual eye. In the following, what I want you to notice is that what `operator[]` does (the non-const version returns a reference into the string) is really no different from what `begin()` and `end()` do for standard `string`s (they return iterators that "point into" the `string`). Any copy-on-write implementation of `std::basic_string` will run into the same considerations that we do below.

Writing `operator[]` for Shareable Strings

Here's a naïve first attempt:

```
// BAD: Naïve attempt #1 at operator[]
//
char& String::operator[]( size_t n )
{
  return data_->buf[n];
}

const char String::operator[]( size_t n ) const
{
  return data_->buf[n];
}
```

This isn't good enough by a long shot. Consider:

```
// Example 15-1: Why attempt #1 doesn't work
//
void f( const Optimized::String& s )
{
  Optimized::String s2( s ); // take a copy of the string
  s2[0] = 'x';               // oops: also modifies s!
}
```

You might be thinking that the poor programmer of Example 15-1 could be a little unhappy about this side effect. You would be right. After all, not only is he changing two strings at once when he only meant to change one, but that other invisibly changed string was actually supposed to be `const`! Now the poor author of `f()` has been turned into something of a liar in that he ended up by inadvertently changing something he promised would be `const`. But he didn't mean to lie, for there's not the slightest bit of casting or other subversion/perversion going on here. That things went badly wrong anyway is just not a good scene, except perhaps to a few strange people who also enjoy watching car wrecks.

So let's go back to `String::operator[]()` and try again. At the very least, we'd better make sure the string isn't shared, or else the caller might inadvertently be modifying what looks to him like two unrelated `String`s. "Aha," thinks the once-naïve programmer, "I'll call `AboutToModify()` to ensure I'm using an unshared representation." And so he does the following:

```
// BAD: Inadequate attempt #2 at operator[]
//
char& String::operator[]( size_t n )
{
  AboutToModify( data_->len );
  return data_->buf[n];
}

const char String::operator[]( size_t n ) const
{
  // no need to check sharing status this time
  return data_->buf[n];
}
```

This looks good, but it's still not enough. The problem is that we only need to rearrange the Example 15-1 problem code slightly to get back into the same situation as before:

```
// Example 15-2: Why attempt #2 doesn't work either
//
void f( Optimized::String& s )
{
  char& rc = s[0];   // take a reference to the first char
  Optimized::String s2( s ); // take a copy of the string
  rc = 'x';                  // oops: also modifies s2!
}
```

You might be thinking that the poor programmer of Example 15-2 could be a little perturbed about this surprise, too. You would again be right, but as of this writing certain popular implementations of `basic_string` have precisely this copy-on-write-related bug.

The problem is that the reference was taken while the original string was unshared, but then the string became shared and the single update through the reference modified both `String` objects' visible state.

Key Notion: An "Unshareable" String

When the non-`const` `operator[]()` is called, besides taking an unshared copy of the `StringBuf`, we also need to mark the string "unshareable" just in case the user remembers the reference (and later tries to use it).

Now, marking the string "unshareable for all time" will work, but that's actually a little excessive. It turns out that all we really need to do is mark the string "unshareable for a while." To see what I mean, consider that it's already true that references returned by `operator[]()` into the string must be considered invalid after the next mutating operation. That is, code like this:

```
// Example 15-3: Why references are
// invalidated by mutating operations
//
void f( Optimized::String& s )
{
  char& rc = s[0];
  s.Append( 'i' );
  rc = 'x';    // error: oops, buffer may have
}              // moved if s did a reallocation
```

should already be documented as invalid, whether or not the string uses copy-on-write. In short, calling a mutator clearly invalidates references into the string because you never know if the underlying memory may move—and move invisibly, from the point of view of the calling code.

Given that fact, in Example 15-2, `rc` would be invalidated anyway by the next mutating operation on `s`. So instead of marking `s` as "unshareable for all time" just because someone might have remembered a reference into it, we could just mark it "unshareable until after the next mutating operation," when any such remembered reference would be invalidated anyway. To the user, the documented behavior is the same.

Do any of the other members need to be changed because of the new member functions? Explain.

As we can now see, the answer is yes.

First, we need to be able to remember whether a given string is currently unshareable so that we won't use reference counting when copying it. We could just throw in a Boolean flag. To avoid even that overhead, though, let's just encode the "unshareable" state directly in the `refs` count by agreeing that "`refs` == the biggest `unsigned int` there can possibly be" means "unshareable." We'll also add a flag to `AboutToModify()` that advises whether to mark the string unshareable.

```
// GOOD: Correct attempt #3 at operator[]
//
// Add a new static member for convenience, and
// change AboutToModify() appropriately. Because
// now we'll need to clone a StringBuf in more than
// one function (see the String copy constructor,
// below), we'll also move that logic into a
// single function... it was time for StringBuf to
// have its own copy constructor, anyway.
//
const size_t String::Unshareable = numeric_limits<size_t>::max();
```

```
StringBuf::StringBuf( const StringBuf& other, size_t n )
  : buf(0), len(0), used(0), refs(1)
{
  Reserve( max( other.len, n ) );
  copy( other.buf, other.buf+other.used, buf );
  used = other.used;
}

void String::AboutToModify(
  size_t n,
  bool   markUnshareable /* = false */
)
{
  if( data_->refs > 1 && data_->refs != Unshareable )
  {
    StringBuf* newdata = new StringBuf( *data_, n );
    --data_->refs;   // now all the real work is
    data_ = newdata; //  done, so take ownership
  }
  else
  {
    data_->Reserve( n );
  }
  data_->refs = markUnshareable ? Unshareable : 1;
}

char& String::operator[]( size_t n )
{
  AboutToModify( data_->len, true );
  return data_->buf[n];
}

const char String::operator[]( size_t n ) const
{
  return data_->buf[n];
}
```

Note that all the other calls to AboutToModify() continue to work as originally written.

Now all we need to do is make String's copy constructor respect the unshareable state, if it's set:

```
String::String( const String& other )
{
  // If possible, use copy-on-write.
  // Otherwise, take a deep copy immediately.
  //
  if( other.data_->refs != Unshareable )
  {
    data_ = other.data_;
    ++data_->refs;
  }
```

```
     else
     {
       data_ = new StringBuf( *other.data_ );
     }
   }
```

String's destructor needs a small tweak, too:

```
String::~String()
{
  if( data_->refs == Unshareable || --data_->refs < 1 )
  {
    delete data_;
  }
}
```

The other String functions work as originally written:

```
String::String() : data_(new StringBuf) { }

void String::Append( char c )
{
  AboutToModify( data_->used+1 );
  data_->buf[data_->used++] = c;
}

}
```

That's about it… in a single-threaded environment, that is. In the final Item of this lazy-optimization miniseries, we'll consider how multithreading affects our copy-on-write string. See Item 16 for the juicy details.

Summary

Here's all the code together. Note that I've also taken this opportunity to implement a slight change to StringBuf::Reserve(); it now rounds up the chosen "new buffer size" to the next multiple of four, in order to ensure that the size of the memory buffer's size is always a multiple of 4 bytes. This is in the name of efficiency, because many popular operating systems don't allocate memory in chunks smaller than this, anyway. For small strings, this code is also a bit faster than the original version. (The original code would allocate a 1-byte buffer, then a 2-byte buffer, then a 3-byte buffer, then a 4-byte buffer, and then a 6-byte buffer before the exponential-growth strategy would really kick in. The code below goes straight to a 4-byte buffer, then an 8-byte buffer, and so on.)

```
namespace Optimized {

class StringBuf
{
public:
```

```cpp
    StringBuf();              // start off empty
   ~StringBuf();              // delete the buffer
    StringBuf( const StringBuf& other, size_t n = 0 );
                              // initialize to copy of other,
                              //  and ensure len >= n

    void Reserve( size_t n ); // ensure len >= n

    char*   buf;              // allocated buffer
    size_t  len;              // length of buffer
    size_t  used;             // # chars actually used
    unsigned refs;            // reference count

private:
    // No copying...
    //
    StringBuf( const StringBuf& );
    StringBuf& operator=( const StringBuf& );
};

class String
{
public:
    String();                 // start off empty
   ~String();                 // decrement reference count
                              //  (delete buffer if refs==0)
    String( const String& );  // point at same buffer and
                              //  increment reference count
    void    Append( char );   // append one character
    size_t Length() const;    // string length
    char&  operator[](size_t);// element access
    const char operator[](size_t) const;

    // ... operator=() etc. omitted ...

private:
    void AboutToModify( size_t n, bool bUnshareable = false );
                              // lazy copy, ensure len>=n
                              //  and mark if unshareable
    static size_t Unshareable;// ref-count flag for "unshareable"
    StringBuf* data_;
};

StringBuf::StringBuf()
  : buf(0), len(0), used(0), refs(1) { }

StringBuf::~StringBuf() { delete[] buf; }

StringBuf::StringBuf( const StringBuf& other, size_t n )
  : buf(0), len(0), used(0), refs(1)
{
    Reserve( max( other.len, n ) );
    copy( other.buf, other.buf+other.used, buf );
    used = other.used;
}
```

```
void StringBuf::Reserve( size_t n )
{
  if( len < n )
  {
    // Same growth code as in Item 14, except now we round
    // the new size up to the nearest multiple of 4 bytes.
    size_t needed = max<size_t>( len*1.5, n );
    size_t newlen = needed ? 4 * ((needed-1)/4 + 1) : 0;
    char*  newbuf = newlen ? new char[ newlen ] : 0;
    if( buf )
    {
      copy( buf, buf+used, newbuf );
    }

    delete[] buf;   // now all the real work is
    buf = newbuf;   //  done, so take ownership
    len = newlen;
  }
}


const size_t String::Unshareable = numeric_limits<size_t>::max();

String::String() : data_(new StringBuf) { }

String::~String()
{
  if( data_->refs == Unshareable || --data_->refs < 1 )
  {
    delete data_;
  }
}

String::String( const String& other )
{
  // If possible, use copy-on-write.
  // Otherwise, take a deep copy immediately.
  //
  if( other.data_->refs != Unshareable )
  {
    data_ = other.data_;
    ++data_->refs;
  }
  else
  {
    data_ = new StringBuf( *other.data_ );
  }
}

void String::AboutToModify(
  size_t n,
  bool   markUnshareable /* = false */
```

```
)
{
  if( data_->refs > 1 && data_->refs != Unshareable )
  {
    StringBuf* newdata = new StringBuf( *data_, n );
    --data_->refs;   // now all the real work is
    data_ = newdata; //  done, so take ownership
  }
  else
  {
    data_->Reserve( n );
  }
  data_->refs = markUnshareable ? Unshareable : 1;
}

void String::Append( char c )
{
  AboutToModify( data_->used+1 );
  data_->buf[data_->used++] = c;
}

size_t String::Length() const
{
  return data_->used;
}

char& String::operator[]( size_t n )
{
  AboutToModify( data_->len, true );
  return data_->buf[n];
}

const char String::operator[]( size_t n ) const
{
  return data_->buf[n];
}

}
```

ITEM 16: LAZY OPTIMIZATION, PART 4:
MULTITHREADED ENVIRONMENTS   DIFFICULTY: 8

In this final chapter of the miniseries, we consider the effects of thread safety on copy-on-write strings. Is lazy copy really an optimization? The answer may surprise you.

1. Why is Optimized::String (from Item 15) not thread-safe? Give examples.

2. Demonstrate how to make Optimized::String thread-safe:

a) assuming there are atomic operations to get, set, and compare integer values; and

b) assuming there aren't.

3. What are the effects on performance? Discuss.

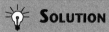

SOLUTION

Thread-Safety Problems with Copy-on-Write (COW)

Standard C++ is silent on the subject of threads. Unlike Java, C++ has no built-in support for threads, and does not attempt to address thread-safety issues through the language. So why an Item on thread- and concurrency-related issues? Simply because more and more of us are writing multithreaded (MT) programs, and no discussion of copy-on-write `String` implementations is complete if it does not cover thread-safety issues. Good C++ threading classes and frameworks have existed nearly as long as C++ itself. Today, they include facilities such as those in ACE,[2] the omnithread library available as part of omniORB,[3] and many commercial libraries. Chances are that today you're already using one of these libraries, or using your own in-house wrapper around your operating system's native services.

In conjunction with this Item, see also *Appendix A: Optimizations That Aren't (In a Multithreaded World)*. That appendix overlaps with and builds upon the results we'll see in this Item. It demonstrates not only the effects that mistaken optimizations can have on you and your production code, but also how to detect them and protect yourself against them. This Item presents a summary of results for which more details are shown in *Appendix B: Test Results for Single-Threaded Versus Multithread-Safe String Implementations*.

1. Why is Optimized::String (from Item 15) not thread-safe? Give examples.

It is the responsibility of code that uses an object to ensure that access to the object is serialized as needed. For example, if a certain `String` object could be modified by two different threads, it's not the poor `String` object's job to defend itself from abuse. It's the job of the code that uses the `String` to make sure that two threads never try to modify the same `String` object at the same time.

The problem with the code in Item 15 is twofold. First, the copy-on-write (COW) implementation is designed to hide the fact that two different visible `String` objects could be sharing a common hidden state. Hence, it's the `String` class's responsibility to ensure that the calling code never modifies a `String` whose representation is

---

2. See *http://www.gotw.ca/publications/mxc++/ace.htm*.
3. See *http://www.gotw.ca/publications/mxc++/omniorb.htm*.

shared. The String code shown already does precisely that, by performing a deep copy (unsharing the representation), if necessary, the moment a caller tries to modify the String. This part is fine in general.

Unfortunately, it now brings us to the second problem, which is that the code in String that unshares the representation isn't thread-safe. Imagine two String objects s1 and s2 such that:

a) s1 and s2 happen to share the same representation under the covers (okay, because String is designed for this);

b) Thread 1 tries to modify s1 (okay, because thread 1 knows that no one else is trying to modify s1);

c) Thread 2 tries to modify s2 (okay, because thread 2 knows that no one else is trying to modify s2);

d) At the same time (error)

The problem is (d). At the same time, both s1 and s2 will attempt to unshare their shared representation, and the code to do that is not thread-safe. Specifically, consider the very first line of code in String::AboutToModify():

```
void String::AboutToModify(
  size_t n,
  bool   markUnshareable /* = false */
)
{
  if( data_->refs > 1 && data_->refs != Unshareable )
  {
    /* ... etc. ... */
```

This if-condition is not thread-safe. For one thing, evaluating even data_->refs > 1 may not be atomic. If so, it's possible that if thread 1 tries to evaluate data_->refs > 1 while thread 2 is updating the value of refs, the value read from data_->refs might be anything—1, 2, or even something that's neither the original value nor the new value. The problem is that String isn't following the basic thread-safety requirement that code that uses an object must ensure that access to the object is serialized as needed. Here, String has to ensure that no two threads are going to use the same refs value in a dangerous way at the same time. The traditional way to accomplish this is to serialize access to the shared StringBuf (or just its refs member) using a mutex or semaphore. In this case, at minimum the "comparing an int" operation must be guaranteed to be atomic.

This brings us to the second issue: Even if reading and updating refs were atomic, and even if we knew we were running on a single-CPU machine so that the threads were interleaved rather than truly concurrent, there are still two parts to the if condition. The problem is that the thread executing the above code could be interrupted after it evaluates the first part of the condition, but before it evaluates the second part. In our example:

Thread 1	Thread 2
enter s1's AboutToModify() evaluate "data_->refs > 1" (true, because data_->refs is 2)	
context switch	
	enter s2's AboutToModify() (runs to completion, including decrementing data_->refs to the value 1) **exit** s2's AboutToModify()
context switch	
evaluate "data_->refs != Unshareable" (true, because data_->refs is now 1) enters AboutToModify()'s "I'm shared and need to unshare" block, which clones the representation, decrements data_->refs to the value 0, and gives up the last pointer to the StringBuf. Poof, we have a memory leak, because the StringBuf that had been shared by s1 and s2 can now never be deleted **exit** s1's AboutToModify()	

Having covered that, we're ready to see how to solve these safety problems.

Protecting COW Strings

In all that follows, remember that the goal is not to protect Optimized::String against every possible abuse. After all, the code using the String object is still responsible for knowing whether any given visible String object could be used by different threads and doing the proper concurrency control if it is—that's just normal. The problem here is that because of the extra sharing going on under the covers, the calling code *can't* just perform its normal duty of care because it doesn't know which String objects really are completely distinct and which only look distinct but are actually invisibly joined. The goal, then, is simply for Optimized::String to get back up to the level at which it's safe enough so that other code that uses String can assume that distinct String objects really are distinct, and therefore do the usual proper concurrency control as needed.

2. Demonstrate how to make `Optimized::String` thread-safe:

   a) assuming that there are atomic operations to get, set, and compare integer values; and

   b) assuming that there aren't.

I'm going to answer (b) first because it's more general. What's needed here is a lock-management device such as a mutex.[4] The key to what we're about to do is quite simple. It turns out that if we do things right, we need only lock access to the reference count itself.

Before doing anything else, we need to add a `Mutex` member object into `Optimized::StringBuf`. Let's call the member m:

```
namespace Optimized
{

    class StringBuf
    {
    public:
        StringBuf();              // start off empty
        ~StringBuf();             // delete the buffer
        StringBuf( const StringBuf& other, size_t n = 0 );
                                  // initialize to copy of other,
                                  //  and ensure len >= n

        void Reserve( size_t n ); // ensure len >= n

        char*    buf;             // allocated buffer
        size_t   len;             // length of buffer
        size_t   used;            // # chars actually used
        unsigned refs;            // reference count
        Mutex    m;               // serialize work on this object

    private:
        // No copying...
        //
        StringBuf( const StringBuf& );
        StringBuf& operator=( const StringBuf& );
    };
```

The only function that necessarily operates on two `StringBuf` objects at once is the copy constructor. `String` only calls `StringBuf`'s copy constructor from two places (from `String`'s own copy constructor and from `AboutToModify()`). Note that `String` only needs to serialize access to the reference count, because by definition no `String` will do any work on a `StringBuf` that's shared. (If it is shared, it will be read

---

4. If you're using Win32, what's called a "critical section" (a slight hijacking of the term) is a lot more efficient than a mutex, and should be used unless you really need the Win32 mutex's heavyweight facilities.

in order to take a copy. But we don't need to worry about anyone else trying to change
or `Reserve()` or otherwise alter/move the buffer.)

The default constructor needs no locks:

```
String::String() : data_(new StringBuf) { }
```

The destructor need only lock its interrogation and update of the `refs` count:

```
String::~String()
{
  bool bDelete = false;
  data_->m.Lock(); //---------------------------
  if( data_->refs == Unshareable || --data_->refs < 1 )
  {
    bDelete = true;
  }
  data_->m.Unlock(); //------------------------
  if( bDelete )
  {
    delete data_;
  }
}
```

For the `String` copy constructor, note that we can assume the other `String`'s data
buffer won't be modified or moved during this operation, because it's the responsibility of the caller to serialize access to visible objects. We must still, however, serialize
access to the reference count itself, as we did above:

```
String::String( const String& other )
{
  bool bSharedIt = false;
  other.data_->m.Lock(); //--------------------
  if( other.data_->refs != Unshareable )
  {
    bSharedIt = true;
    data_ = other.data_;
    ++data_->refs;
  }
  other.data_->m.Unlock(); //------------------

  if( !bSharedIt )
  {
    data_ = new StringBuf( *other.data_ );
  }
}
```

So making the `String` copy constructor safe wasn't very hard at all. This brings us
to `AboutToModify()`, which turns out to be very similar. But notice that this sample
code actually acquires the lock during the entire deep copy operation—really, the lock
is strictly needed only when looking at the `refs` value and again when updating the
`refs` value at the end. But let's go ahead and lock the whole operation instead of get-

ting slightly better concurrency by releasing the lock during the deep copy and then reacquiring it just to update refs:

```
void String::AboutToModify(
  size_t n,
  bool   markUnshareable /* = false */
)
{
  data_->m.Lock(); //--------------------------
  if( data_->refs > 1 && data_->refs != Unshareable )
  {
    StringBuf* newdata = new StringBuf( *data_, n );
    --data_->refs;   // now all the real work is
    data_->m.Unlock(); //----------------------
    data_ = newdata; //  done, so take ownership
  }
  else
  {
    data_->m.Unlock(); //----------------------
    data_->Reserve( n );
  }
  data_->refs = markUnshareable ? Unshareable : 1;
}
```

None of the other functions need to be changed. Append() and operator[]() don't need locks because once AboutToModify() completes, we're guaranteed that we're not using a shared representation. Length() doesn't need a lock because by definition, we're okay if our StringBuf is not shared (there's no one else to change the used count on us), and we're okay if it is shared (the other thread would take its own copy before doing any work and hence still wouldn't modify our used count on us):

```
void String::Append( char c )
{
  AboutToModify( data_->used+1 );
  data_->buf[data_->used++] = c;
}

size_t String::Length() const
{
  return data_->used;
}

char& String::operator[]( size_t n )
{
  AboutToModify( data_->len, true );
  return data_->buf[n];
}

const char String::operator[]( size_t n ) const
{
  return data_->buf[n];
}
}
```

Again, note the interesting thing in all of this: The only locking we needed to do involved the refs count itself.

With that observation and the above general-purpose solution under our belts, let's look back to the (a) part of the question:

a) assuming that there are atomic operations to get, set, and compare integer values; and

Some operating systems provide these kinds of functions.

Note: These functions are usually significantly more efficient than general-purpose synchronization primitives such as mutexes. It is, however, a fallacy to say that we can use atomic integer operations "instead of locks" because locking is still required—the locking is just generally less expensive than other alternatives, but it's not free by a long shot, as we will see.

Here is a thread-safe implementation of String that assumes we have three functions: an IntAtomicGet(), and IntAtomicDecrement() and IntAtomicIncrement() that safely return the new value. We'll do essentially the same thing we did above, but use only atomic integer operations to serialize access to the refs count:

```
namespace Optimized
{

  String::String() : data_(new StringBuf) { }

  String::~String()
  {
    if( IntAtomicGet( data_->refs ) == Unshareable ||
        IntAtomicDecrement( data_->refs ) < 1 )
    {
      delete data_;
    }
  }

  String::String( const String& other )
  {
    if( IntAtomicGet( other.data_->refs ) != Unshareable )
    {
      data_ = other.data_;
      IntAtomicIncrement( data_->refs );
    }
    else
    {
      data_ = new StringBuf( *other.data_ );
    }
  }
```

```
void String::AboutToModify(
    size_t n,
    bool   markUnshareable /* = false */
)
{
    int refs = IntAtomicGet( data_->refs );
    if( refs > 1 && refs != Unshareable )
    {
        StringBuf* newdata = new StringBuf( *data_, n );
        if( IntAtomicDecrement( data_->refs ) < 1 )
        {                          // just in case two threads
            delete newdata;   //  are trying this at once
        }
        else
        {                          // now all the real work is
            data_ = newdata; //  done, so take ownership
        }
    }
    else
    {
        data_->Reserve( n );
    }
    data_->refs = markUnshareable ? Unshareable : 1;
}

void String::Append( char c )
{
    AboutToModify( data_->used+1 );
    data_->buf[data_->used++] = c;
}

size_t String::Length() const
{
    return data_->used;
}

char& String::operator[]( size_t n )
{
    AboutToModify( data_->len, true );
    return data_->buf[n];
}

const char String::operator[]( size_t n ) const
{
    return data_->buf[n];
}

}
```

3. What are the effects on performance? Discuss.

Without atomic integer operations, copy-on-write typically incurs a significant performance penalty. Even with atomic integer operations, COW can make common String operations take nearly 50% longer, even in single-threaded programs.

In general, copy-on-write is often a bad idea in multithread-ready code. That's because the calling code can no longer know whether two distinct String objects actually share the same representation under the covers, so String must incur overhead to do enough serialization so that calling code can take its normal share of responsibility for thread safety. Depending on the availability of more-efficient options such as atomic integer operations, the impact on performance ranges from moderate to profound.

Some Empirical Results

In this test environment, I tested the following six main flavors of string implementations.

```
           Name   Description (refined versions of
                                code shown earlier)
----------------   ----------------------------------------
          Plain   Non-use-counted string; all others are
                  modeled on this

     COW_Unsafe   Plain + COW, not thread-safe

  COW_AtomicInt   Plain + COW + thread-safe

 COW_AtomicInt2   COW_AtomicInt + StringBuf in same
                  buffer as the data

     COW_CritSec   Plain + COW + thread-safe (Win32
                  critical sections)

      COW_Mutex   Plain + COW + thread-safe (Win32
                  mutexes) (COW_CritSec with Win32 mutexes
                  instead of Win32 critical sections)
```

I also threw in a seventh flavor to measure the result of optimizing memory allocation instead of optimizing copying:

```
Plain_FastAlloc   Plain + an optimized memory allocator
```

I focused on comparing Plain with COW_AtomicInt. COW_AtomicInt was generally the most efficient thread-safe COW implementation. The results were as follows:

1. For all mutating and possibly-mutating operations, COW_AtomicInt was always worse than Plain. This is natural and expected.

2. COW should shine when there are many unmodified copies. But for an average string length of 50:

a) When 33% of all copies were never modified and the rest were modified only once each, COW_AtomicInt was still slower than Plain.

b) When 50% of all copies were never modified and the rest were modified only thrice each, COW_AtomicInt was still slower than Plain.

This second result may be the more surprising one to many—particularly the result that COW_AtomicInt is slower in cases in which there are more copy operations than mutating operations in the entire system!

Note that in both cases traditional thread-unsafe COW did perform better than Plain. This shows that COW can be an optimization for purely single-threaded environments, but it is less often appropriate for thread-safe code.

3. It is a myth that COW's principal advantage lies in avoiding memory allocations. Especially for longer strings, COW's principal advantage is that it avoids copying the characters in the string.

4. Optimized allocation, not COW, was a consistent true speed optimization in all cases (but note that it does trade off space). Here is perhaps the most important conclusion from the Detailed Measurements section in the appendixes:

> *Most of COW's primary advantage for small strings could be gained without COW by using a more efficient allocator. (Of course, you could also do both—use COW and an efficient allocator.)*

Let's briefly raise and answer two natural questions.

First, why measure something as inefficient as COW_CritSec? The answer is simple: Because at least one popular commercial basic_string implementation used this method as recently as 2000 (and perhaps still does, I haven't seen their code lately), despite the fact that COW_CritSec is nearly always a pessimization. Be sure to check whether your library vendor is doing this, because if the library is built for possible multithreaded use, you will bear the performance cost all the time, even if your program is single-threaded.

Second, what's COW_AtomicInt2? It's the same as COW_AtomicInt except that instead of allocating a StringBuf and then separately allocating the data buffer, the StringBuf and data are in the same allocated block of memory. Note that all other COW_* variants use a fast allocator for the StringBuf object (so that there's no unfair double allocation cost), and the purpose of COW_AtomicInt2 is mainly to demonstrate that I have actually addressed that concern. COW_AtomicInt2 is actually slightly slower than COW_AtomicInt for most operations, because of the extra logic.

I also tested the relative performance of various integer operations (incrementing int, incrementing volatile int, and incrementing int using the Win32 atomic integer operations) to ensure that COW_AtomicInt results were not unfairly skewed by poor implementations or function call overhead.

Summary

A few important points about this test harness and these results:

1. *Caveat lector:* Take this for what it is, a first cut at a test harness. Comments and corrections are welcome. I'm showing raw performance numbers here. I haven't inspected the compiled machine code, and I've made no attempt to determine the impact of cache hits/misses and other secondary effects.

2. *TANSTAAFL.* ("There ain't no such thing as a free lunch."—Robert A. Heinlein) Even with atomic integer operations, it is incorrect to say "there's no locking required," because the atomic integer operations clearly do perform serialization and do incur significant overhead.

3. *Tanj.* ("There ain't no justice."—Larry Niven) The test harness itself is *single-threaded*. A thread-safe COW implementation incurs overhead even in programs that are not themselves multithreaded. At best, COW could be a true optimization only when the COW code does not need to be made thread-safe at all (even then, see [Murray93] pages 70–72 for more empirical tests that show COW is beneficial only in certain situations). If thread safety is required, COW imposes a significant performance penalty on all users, even users running only single-threaded code.

Exception Safety Issues and Techniques

It's pretty near impossible to write robust code in modern C++ without knowing about exception safety issues. Period.

If you use the C++ standard library, including even just new, you have to be prepared for exceptions. This section builds on the corresponding section of *Exceptional C++* and considers new issues and techniques, such as, What's std:: uncaught_exception(), and does it help you to write more-robust code? Does exception safety affect a class's design, or can it just be retrofitted as an afterthought? Why use manager objects to encapsulate resource ownership, and why is the "resource acquisition is initialization" idiom so important for writing safe code?

But first, let's get our feet wet by considering an exception safety lesson that also demonstrates the deeper meaning of key fundamental C++ concepts: What does construction mean, and what is an object's lifetime?

ITEM 17: CONSTRUCTOR FAILURES, PART 1: OBJECT LIFETIMES   DIFFICULTY: 4

What exactly happens when a constructor emits an exception? What if the exception comes from an attempt to construct a subobject or member object?

1. Consider the following class:

```
// Example 17-1
//
class C : private A
{
  B b_;
};
```

In the C constructor, how can you catch an exception thrown from the constructor of a base subobject (such as A) or a member object (such as b_)?

2. Consider the following code:

```
// Example 17-2
//
{
  Parrot p;
}
```

When does the object's lifetime begin? When does it end? Outside the object's lifetime, what is the status of the object? Finally, what would it mean if the constructor threw an exception?

SOLUTION

Function try blocks were added to C++ to slightly enlarge the scope of exceptions that a function can catch. This Item covers

- What object construction and construction failure mean in C++; and
- That function try blocks are useful to translate (not suppress) an exception thrown from a base or member subobject constructor—and that's pretty much it.

For convenience, throughout this Item, *member* means "nonstatic class data member" unless otherwise noted.

Function Try Blocks

1. Consider the following class:

```
// Example 17-1
//
class C : private A
{
  B b_;
};
```

In the C constructor, how can you catch an exception thrown from the constructor of a base subobject (such as A) or a member object (such as b_)?

That's what function try blocks are for:

```
// Example 17-1(a): Constructor function try block
//
C::C()
```

```
try
  : A ( /*...*/ )    // optional initialization list
  , b_( /*...*/ )
{
}
catch( ... )
{
  // We get here if either A::A() or B::B() throws.

  // If A::A() succeeds and then B::B() throws, the
  // language guarantees that A::~A() will be called
  // to destroy the already-created A base subobject
  // before control reaches this catch block.
}
```

The more interesting question, though, is: Why would you want to do this? That question brings us to the first of two key points in this Item.

Object Lifetimes and What a Constructor Exception Means

In a moment, we'll consider the question of whether the above C constructor can, or should, absorb an A or B constructor exception and emit no exception at all. But before we can answer that question correctly, we need to make sure we fully understand object lifetimes[1] and what it means for a constructor to throw an exception.

2. Consider the following code:

```
// Example 17-2
//
{
  Parrot p;
}
```

When does the object's lifetime begin? When does it end? Outside the object's lifetime, what is the status of the object? Finally, what would it mean if the constructor threw an exception?

Let's take the questions one at a time:

Q: When does an object's lifetime begin?

A: When its constructor completes successfully and returns normally. That is, when control reaches the end of the constructor body or completes an earlier return statement.

Q: When does an object's lifetime end?

---

1. For simplicity, I'm speaking only of the lifetime of an object of class type that has a constructor.

A: When its destructor begins. That is, when control reaches the beginning of the destructor body.

Q: What is the state of the object after its lifetime has ended?

A: As a well-known software guru once put it while speaking about a similar code fragment and anthropomorphically referring to the local object as a "he":

```
// Example 17-3
//
{
  Parrot& perch = Parrot();
  // ...
}
// <-- the soliloquy takes place here
```

He's not pining! He's passed on! This Parrot *is no more! He has ceased to be! He's expired and gone to meet his maker! He's a stiff! Bereft of life, he rests in peace! If you hadn't nailed him to the* perch *he'd be pushing up the daisies [even earlier, before the end of the block]! His metabolic processes are now history! He's off the twig! He's kicked the bucket, he's shuffled off his mortal coil, run down the curtain and joined the bleedin' choir invisible!* This is an ex-Parrot!

— Dr. M. Python, B.Math, MA.Sc., Ph.D. (CompSci)[2]

Kidding aside, the important point here is that the state of the object before its lifetime begins is exactly the same as after its lifetime ends: There is no object, period. This observation brings us to the next key question:

Q: What does emitting an exception from a constructor mean?

A: It means that construction has failed, the object never existed, its lifetime never began. Indeed, the only way to report the failure of construction—namely, the inability to correctly build a functioning object of the given type—is to throw an exception. (Yes, there is a now-obsolete programming convention that said: "If you get into trouble, just set a status flag to 'bad' and let the caller check it via an IsOK() function." I'll comment on that presently.)

Incidentally, this is why a destructor will never be called if the constructor didn't succeed—there's nothing to destroy. It cannot die, for it never lived. Note that this makes the phrase "an object whose constructor threw an exception" really an oxymoron. Such a thing is even less than an ex-object. It never lived, never made it to objecthood. It is a non-object.

---

2.   With apologies to Monty Python.

We might summarize the C++ constructor model as follows:
Either:

a) The constructor returns normally by reaching its end or a `return` statement, and the object exists, or

b) The constructor exits by emitting an exception, and the object not only does not now exist, but it never existed as an object.

There are no other possibilities. Armed with this information, we can now better tackle the next Item's question: What about absorbing exceptions?

ITEM 18: CONSTRUCTOR FAILURES, PART 2: ABSORPTION?   DIFFICULTY: 7

This Item analyzes constructor failures in detail, shows why the C++ rules should work the way they do, and demonstrates the implications for constructor exception specifications.

1. In Item 17 Example 17-1, if the A or B constructor throws an exception, is it possible for the C constructor to absorb the exception and emit no exception at all? Justify your answer, explaining by example why this is as it should be.

2. What are the minimal requirements that A and B must meet in order for us to safely put an empty throw-specification on C's constructor(s)?

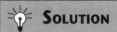 **SOLUTION**

I Can't Keep No Caught Exceptions[3]

1. In Item 17 Example 17-1, if the A or B constructor throws an exception, is it possible for the C constructor to absorb the exception and emit no exception at all?

If we didn't consider the object lifetime rules, we might have tried something like the following:

---

3. A double pun, can be sung to the chorus of the Rolling Stones' "Satisfaction" or to the opening bars of Pink Floyd's "Another Brick in the Wall, Part *N*."

```
// Example 18-1(a): Absorbing exceptions?
//
C::C()
try
  : A ( /*...*/ )    // optional initialization-list
  , b_( /*...*/ )
{
}
catch( ... )
{
  // ?
}
```

How will the try block handler exit? Consider:

- The handler cannot simply "`return;`" because that's illegal.
- If the handler just says "`throw;`" it will rethrow whatever exception `A::A()` or `B::B()` originally emitted.
- If the handler throws some other exception, that exception is emitted instead of whatever the base or member subobject constructor originally threw.
- What's less obvious, but clearly stated in the C++ standard, is that if the handler does not exit by throwing an exception (either by rethrowing the original exception or by throwing something new), and control reaches the end of the catch block of a constructor or destructor, then the original exception is automatically rethrown as if the handler's last statement had been `throw;`.

Think about what this means: A constructor or destructor function try block's handler code *must* finish by emitting some exception. There's no other way. As long as you don't try to violate exception specifications, the language doesn't care what exception it is that gets emitted—it can be the original one or some other translated exception—but an exception there must be! It is impossible to keep any exceptions thrown by base or member subobject constructors from causing some exception to leak beyond their containing constructors.

In fewer words, it means that:

> *In C++, if construction of any base or member subobject fails,*
> *the whole object's construction* must *fail.*

A constructor cannot possibly recover and do something sensible after one of its base or member subobjects' constructors throws. It cannot even put its own object into a "construction failed" state recognizable to the compiler. Its object *is not* constructed; it never will be constructed no matter what Frankensteinian efforts the handler attempts in order to breathe life into the nonobject. And whatever destruction can be done has already been done automatically by the language; that includes all base and member subobjects.

What if your class can honestly have a sensible "construction partially failed" state—that is, it really does have some "optional" members that aren't strictly required and the object can limp along without them, possibly with reduced functionality? Then use the Pimpl idiom (described in *Exceptional C++* [Sutter00] Items 27–30) to hold the possibly-bad parts of the object at arm's length. For similar reasoning, see *Exceptional C++* Items 31–34 about abuses of inheritance. Incidentally, this "optional parts of an object" idea is another great reason to use delegation instead of inheritance whenever possible. Base subobjects can never be made optional because you can't put base subobjects into a Pimpl.[4]

In the past, I've sometimes had a love/hate relationship with exceptions. Even so, I've always had to agree that exceptions are the right way to signal constructor failures, given that constructors cannot report errors via return codes (ditto for most operators). I have found the "if a constructor encounters an error, set a status bit and let the user call `IsOK()` to see if construction actually worked" method to be outdated, dangerous, tedious, and in no way better than throwing an exception. Ditto for its fraternal twin, the two-phase construction approach. I'm not the only one who views these approaches as odious. For a thorough debunking of these outmoded styles by none other than Stroustrup, including juicy sound bites like "bogus" and "this style is a relic of pre-exception C++," see section E.3.5 of [Stroustrup00].

A Step Toward Morality

Incidentally, this also means that the only (repeat only) possible use for a constructor function try block is to translate an exception thrown from a base or member subobject. That's Moral #1. Moral #2 says that destructor function try blocks are entirely usele—

"—But wait!" I hear someone interrupting from the middle of the room. "I don't agree with Moral #1. I can think of another possible use for constructor function try blocks—to free resources allocated in the initializer list or in the constructor body!"

Sorry, no. Remember that once you get into your constructor try block's handler, any local variables in the constructor body are also already out of scope, and you are guaranteed that no base subobjects or member objects exist anymore, period. You can't even refer to their names. Either the parts of your object were never constructed, or those that were constructed have already been destroyed. So you can't be cleaning up anything that relies on referring to a base or member of the class (and anyway, that's what the base and member destructors are for, right?).

---

4. Convergence is funny sometimes. Long after I started pushing the Pimpl idiom and bashing needless inheritance, I kept coming across new problems that were solved by using Pimpl or removing needless inheritance, especially to improve exception safety. I guess it shouldn't have been a surprise, because it's just this whole coupling thing again. Higher coupling means greater exposure to failure in a related component. To this comment, Bobby Schmidt responded in private correspondence: "And maybe that's the core lesson to pull out of this— we've really just rediscovered and amplified the old minimal-coupling-maximum-cohesion axiom."

Aside: Why Does C++ Do It That Way?

To understand why it's good that C++ does it this way, let's put that restriction aside for the moment and imagine that C++ did let you mention member names in constructor try block handlers. Then imagine the following case, and try to decide: Should the handler delete t_ or z_? (Again, ignore for the moment that, in real C++, it can't even refer to t_ or z_.)

```
// Example 18-1(b): Very Buggy Class
//
class X : Y
{
  T* t_;
  Z* z_;
public:
  X()
  try
    : Y(1)
    , t_( new T( static_cast<Y*>(this) ) )
    , z_( new Z( static_cast<Y*>(this), t_ ) )
  {
    /*...*/
  }
  catch(...)  // Y::Y() or T::T() or Z::Z()
              // or X::X()'s body has thrown
  {
    // Q: should I delete t_ or z_?
    // (Note: NOT legal C++!)
  }
};
```

The first problem is that we cannot possibly know whether t_ or z_ were ever allocated. Therefore deleting either might not be safe.

Second, even if we did know that we had reached one of the allocations, we probably can't destroy *t_ or *z_ because they refer to a Y (and possibly a T) that no longer exists, and they may try to use that Y (and possibly T). Incidentally, this means that not only can't we destroy *t_ or *z_, but they can never be destroyed by anyone.

If that didn't just sober you up, it should have. I have seen people write code similar in spirit to the above, never imagining that they were creating objects that, should the wrong things happen, could never be destroyed! The good news is that there's a simple way to avoid the problem. These difficulties would largely go away if the T* members were instead held by auto_ptrs or similar manager objects. (For more about the dangers of auto_ptr members and how to avoid them, turn to Items 30 and 31.)

Finally, if Y::~Y() can throw, it is not possible to reliably create an X object at any time! If you haven't been sobered yet, this should definitely do it. If Y::~Y() can throw, even writing "X x;" is fraught with peril. This reinforces the dictum that destructors must never be allowed to emit an exception under any circumstances, and writing a destructor that could emit an exception is simply an error. Destruction and emitting exceptions don't mix.

All right, enough about that. The preceding side discussion was just to get a better understanding of why it's good that the rules are as they are. In real C++, you can't refer to t_ or z_ inside the handler in the first place. I've refrained from quoting standardese so far, so here's your dose, from the C++ standard [C++98], clause 15.3, paragraph 10: "Referring to any non-static member or base class of an object in the handler for a function try block of a constructor or destructor for that object results in undefined behavior."

Morals About Function Try Blocks

Therefore, the status quo can be summarized as follows:

Moral #1: Constructor function try block handlers are only good for translating an exception thrown from a base or member subobject constructor (and maybe to do related logging or some other side effects in response to such failures). They are not useful for any other purpose.

Moral #2: Destructor function try blocks have little or no practical use, because destructors should never emit an exception.[5] Thus there should never be anything for a destructor function try block to detect that couldn't be detected with a normal try block. Even if there were something to detect because of evil code (namely a member subobject whose destructor could throw), the handler would not be useful for dealing with it because it couldn't suppress the exception. The best it could do is log something, or otherwise complain.

Moral #3: All other function try blocks have no practical use. A regular function try block can't catch anything that a regular try block within the function couldn't catch just as well.

Morals About Safe Coding

Moral #4: Always perform unmanaged resource acquisition in the constructor body, never in initializer lists. In other words, either use "resource acquisition is initialization" (thereby avoiding unmanaged resources entirely) or else perform the resource acquisition in the constructor body.[6]

For example, building on Example 18-1(b), say T was char and t_ was a plain old char* that was new[]'d in the initializer list. Then there would be no way to delete[] it in the handler or anywhere else. The fix would be either to wrap the dynamically allocated memory resource (for example, change char* to string) or to new[] it in

---

5. Not even for logging or other side effects, because there shouldn't be any exceptions from base or member subobject destructors. Therefore, anything you could catch in a destructor function try block could be caught equally well using a normal try block inside the destructor body.

6. See [Stroustrup94] Section 16.5 and [Stroustrup00] Section 14.4.

the constructor body where it can be safely cleaned up using a local try block or otherwise.

Moral #5: Always clean up unmanaged resource acquisition in local try block handlers within the constructor or destructor body, never in constructor or destructor function try block handlers.

Moral #6: If a constructor has an exception specification, that exception specification must allow for the union of all possible exceptions that could be thrown by base and member subobjects. As Holmes might add, "It really must, you know." (Indeed, this is the way the implicitly generated constructors are declared; see [GotW] #69.[7])

Moral #7: Use the Pimpl idiom to hold "optional parts" of a class's internals. If a constructor of a member object can throw but you can get along without said member, hold it by pointer and use the pointer's nullness to remember whether you've got one, as usual. Use the Pimpl idiom to group such "optional" members, so you have to allocate only once.

And finally, one last moral that overlaps with the rest but is worth restating in its own right:

Moral #8: Prefer using "resource acquisition is initialization" to manage resources. Really, really, really. It will save you more headaches than you can probably imagine, including hard-to-see ones, similar to some we've already dissected.

That's Just the Way It Is

From legality, we now turn to morality:

Justify your answer, explaining by example why this is as it should be.

The way the language works is entirely correct and easily defensible, once you think about the meaning of C++'s object lifetime model and philosophy.

A constructor exception must be propagated. There is no other way to signal that the constructor failed. Two cases spring to mind:

```
// Example 18-1(c): Auto object
//
{
  X x;
  g( x ); // do something else
}
```

If X's construction fails—whether it's due to X's own constructor body code or to some X base subobject or member object construction failure—control must not continue within the scope of this code block. After all, there is no x object! The only way for control not to continue here is to emit an exception. Therefore, a failed construction of an auto object must result in some sort of exception, whether it is the same

---

7. Available online at *http://www.gotw.ca /gotw/069.htm*.

exception that caused the base or member subobject construction failure or some translated exception emitted from an X constructor function try block.

Similarly:

```
// Example 18-1(d): Array of objects
//
{
  X ax[10];
  // ...
}
```

Say the fifth X object construction fails—whether it's due to X's own constructor body code failing, or to some X base or member subobject construction failing. Then control must not continue within the scope of this code block. After all, if you tried to continue, you'd end up with a "holey array"—an array not all of whose objects really exist. (Even that would probably be better than leaving things in a holy disarray, but I digress.)

A Final Word: Failure-Proof Constructors?

2. What are the minimal requirements that A and B must meet in order for us to safely put an empty throw-specification on C's constructor(s)?

Consider: Is it possible to write and enforce an empty throw-specification for a constructor of a class (like C in Item 17 Example 17-1) if some base or member constructor could throw? The answer is no; you could write the "I won't throw anything" empty throw-specification, but it would be a lie because there's no way to enforce it. To enforce a "throws nothing" guarantee for any function, we must be able to absorb any possible exceptions that come our way from lower-level code to avoid accidentally trying to emit them to our own caller. If you really want to write a constructor that promises not to throw, you can work around possibly-throwing member subobjects (for example, if you can hold them by pointer or Pimpl because they truly are optional), but you can't work around possibly-throwing base subobjects—another reason to avoid unnecessary inheritance, which always implies gratuitous coupling.

For a constructor to have an empty throw-specification, all base and member subobjects must be known to never throw, whether they have throw-specifications that say so or not. An empty throw-specification on a constructor declares to the world that construction cannot fail. If for whatever reason it can indeed fail, then the empty throw-specification is inappropriate.

What happens if you wrote an empty throw-specification on a constructor, and a base or member subobject constructor really does throw? The short answer: "Go to terminate(). Go directly to terminate(). Do not pass try, do not collect $200." The slightly longer answer: The function unexpected() gets called, which has two choices—to throw or rethrow an exception allowed by the exception specification (impossible, because it's empty and won't allow anything) or to call `terminate()`. `terminate()`, in turn, immediately aborts the program.[8] In automobile terms: screech, crunch.

Summary

A C++ object's lifetime begins only after its constructor completes successfully. Therefore, throwing an exception from a constructor always means (and is the only way of reporting) that construction failed. There is no way to recover from failed construction of a base or member subobject, so if construction of any base or member subobject fails, the whole object's construction must fail.

Avoid function try blocks, not because they're evil but because they offer few or no benefits over plain try blocks—and when you're hiring, you'll find that more people understand the latter than the former. This follows the principles of picking the simplest solution that's effective, and of writing for clarity first. Constructor function try blocks are useful only to translate exceptions emitted from base or member constructors. All other function try blocks are rarely if ever useful at all.

Finally, as pointed out repeatedly in *Exceptional C++* Items 8 to 19, use owning objects and "resource acquisition is initialization" to manage resources, and you'll usually avoid having to write `try` and `catch` at all in your code, never mind in function try blocks.

ITEM 19: UNCAUGHT EXCEPTIONS   DIFFICULTY: 6

What is the standard function `uncaught_exception()`, *and when should it be used? The answer given here isn't one that most people expect.*

1. What does `std::uncaught_exception()` do?

2. Consider the following code:

```
T::~T()
{
  if( !std::uncaught_exception() )
  {
    // ... code that could throw ...
  }
  else
    {
```

---

8. You can use `set_unexpected()` and `set_terminate()` to get your own handlers invoked, which gives you a chance to do a bit of extra logging or cleanup, but they'll end up doing much the same things.

```
         // ... code that won't throw ...
      }
   }
```

Is this a good technique? Present arguments for and against.

3. Is there any other good use for `uncaught_exception()`? Discuss and draw conclusions.

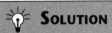 **SOLUTION**

Recapping `uncaught_exception()`

1. What does `std::uncaught_exception()` do?

The standard `uncaught::exception()` function provides a way of knowing whether there is an exception currently active. An important thing to note is that this is *not* the same thing as knowing whether it is safe to throw an exception.

To quote directly from the standard (15.5.3/1):

> *The function* `bool uncaught_exception()` *returns* `true` *after completing evaluation of the object to be thrown until completing the initialization of the exception-declaration in the matching handler. This includes stack unwinding. If the exception is rethrown,* `uncaught_exception()` *returns* `true` *from the point of rethrow until the rethrown exception is caught again.*

As it turns out, this specification is deceptively close to being useful.

Background: The Problem with Throwing Destructors

If a destructor throws an exception, Bad Things can happen. Specifically, consider code like the following:

```
// Example 19-1: The problem
//
class X {
public:
  ~X() { throw 1; }
};

void f() {
  X x;
  throw 2;
} // calls X::~X (which throws), then calls terminate()
```

If a destructor throws an exception while another exception is already active (that is, during stack unwinding), the program is terminated. This is usually not a good thing.

For more information, see also *Exceptional C++* [Sutter00] Item 16, which discusses "Destructors That Throw and Why They're Evil."

The Wrong Solution

"Aha," many people, including many experts, have said, "let's use uncaught_ exception() to figure out whether we can throw!" And that's where the code in Question 2 comes from. It's an attempt to solve the illustrated problem:

2. Consider the following code:

```
// Example 19-2: The wrong solution
//
T::~T()
{
  if( !std::uncaught_exception() )
  {
    // ... code that could throw ...
  }
  else
  {
    // ... code that won't throw ...
  }
}
```

Is this a good technique? Present arguments for and against.

In short: No, this is not a good technique, even though it attempts to solve a problem. There are technical grounds why this technique shouldn't be used. But I'm more interested in arguing against this idiom on moral grounds.

The idea behind the idiom in Example 19-2 is simple: We'll use the path that could throw as long as it's safe to throw. This philosophy is wrong on two counts. First, this code doesn't do that. Second (and more important, in my opinion), the philosophy itself is in error. Let's investigate these two points separately.

Why the Wrong Solution Is Unsound

The first problem is that the idiom in Example 19-2 won't actually work as intended in some situations. That's because it can end up using the path that doesn't throw even when it would be safe to throw.

```
// Example 19-2(a): Why the wrong solution is wrong
//
U::~U()
{
  try
  {
    T t;
    // do work
  }
  catch( ... )
  {
    // clean up
  }
}
```

If a U object is destroyed because of stack unwinding during exception propagation, T::~T() will fail to use the "code that could throw" path even though it safely could. T::~T() doesn't know that in this case it's already protected by a catch(...) block external to itself, up in U::~U().

Note that none of this is materially different from the following:

```
// Example 19-3: Variant, another wrong solution
//
Transaction::~Transaction()
{
  if( uncaught_exception() )
  {
    RollBack();
  }
  else
  {
    // ...
  }
}
```

Again, note that this doesn't do the right thing if a transaction is attempted in a destructor that might be called during stack unwinding:

```
// Example 19-3(a): Why the variant wrong solution
// is still wrong
//
U::~U() {
  try {
    Transaction t( /*...*/ );
    // do work
  } catch( ... ) {
    // clean up
  }
}
```

So Example 19-2 doesn't work the way it's intended to work. That's fine, but it's not the main issue.

Why the Wrong Solution Is Immoral

The second and more fundamental problem with this solution is not technical, but moral. It is poor design to give T::~T() two different "modes" of operation for its error reporting semantics. The reason is that it is always poor design to allow an operation to report the same error in two different ways. Making the interface not merely modal, but modal in a way that the calling code can't easily control or account for, has two major failings. It complicates the interface and the semantics. And it makes the caller's life harder because the caller must be able to handle both flavors of error reporting—and this when far too many programmers don't check errors well in the first place.

Sometimes, when I'm driving my car, I find myself behind another driver who's partly in one lane and partly in the next. After several seconds have passed and the driver is still (from my point of view) behaving erratically, I feel the urge to roll down the window and call out, in a loud, but kind, thoughtful, and caring voice: "C'mon, buddy! Pick a lane! Any lane!" As long as the other driver continues to straddle the line, I have to be ready to handle the possibility of his moving into either lane at any time. This is not only annoying, but it slows down my own progress.

Sometimes, when we're writing code, we find ourselves using another programmer's class or function that has a schizophrenic interface, such as indecisively trying to report the same failure in more than one way, instead of just picking one set of semantics and running with those semantics consistently. We should all feel the urge to walk over to the offender's office or cube and help this poor unenlightened person to make a decision that would simplify life for us and other users.

The Right Solution

The right answer to the Example 19-1 problem is much simpler:

```
// Example 19-4: The right solution
//
T::~T() /* throw() */
{
  // ... code that won't throw ...
}
```

Example 19-4 demonstrates how to make a design decision instead of waffling.

Note that the throw() throws-nothing exception specification is only a comment. That's the style I've chosen to follow, in part because it turns out that exception specifications confer a lot less benefit than they're worth. Whether or not you decide to actually write the specification is a matter of taste. The important thing is that this function won't emit an exception. For a discussion about the possibility of exceptions thrown by destructors of members of T, turn to Item 18.

If necessary, T can provide a "pre-destructor" function (for example, T::Close()), which can throw and which performs all shutdown of the T object and any resources it owns. That way, the calling code can call T::Close() if it wants to detect hard errors, and T::~T() can be implemented in terms of T::Close() plus a try/catch block:

```
// Example 19-5: Alternative right solution
//
T::Close()
{
  // ... code that could throw ...
}

T::~T() /* throw() */
{
  try
  {
    Close();
  }
  catch( ... ) { }
}
```

This nicely follows the principle of "one function, one responsibility." A problem in the original code was that it had the same function responsible for both destroying the object and final cleanup/reporting.

See also Items 17 and 18 about why this try block is inside the destructor body and should not be a destructor function try block.

> **↗ Guideline**
>
> *Never allow an exception to be emitted from a destructor. Write destructors as though they had an exception specification throw() (whether the throw-specification actually appears in the code is a matter of personal taste).*

> **↗ Guideline**
>
> *If a destructor calls a function that might throw, always wrap the call in a try/catch block that prevents the exception from escaping.*

3. **Is there any other good use for uncaught_exception()? Discuss and draw conclusions.**

Unfortunately, I do not know of any good and safe use for uncaught_exception(). My advice: Don't use it.

ITEM 20: AN UNMANAGED POINTER PROBLEM, PART 1: PARAMETER EVALUATION   DIFFICULTY: 6

Readers of Exception C++ *and this book know that exception safety is anything but trivial. This Item points out an exception safety problem that was discovered fairly recently, and shows how best to avoid it in your own code.*

1. In each of the following statements, what can you say about the order of evaluation of the functions f, g, and h and the expressions expr1 and expr2? Assume that expr1 and expr2 do not contain more function calls.

```
// Example 20-1(a)
//
f( expr1, expr2 );

// Example 20-1(b)
//
f( g( expr1 ), h( expr2 ) );
```

2. In your travels through the dusty corners of your company's code archives, you find the following code fragment:

```
// Example 20-2
//

// In some header file:
void f( T1*, T2* );

// In some implementation file:
f( new T1, new T2 );
```

Does this code have any potential exception safety problems? Explain.

☀ SOLUTION

Recap: Evaluation Orders and Disorders

1. In each of the following statements, what can you say about the order of evaluation of the functions f, g, and h and the expressions expr1 and expr2? Assume that expr1 and expr2 do not contain more function calls.

Ignoring threads, which are not mentioned in the C++ standard, the answer to the first question hinges on the following basic rules:

1. All of a function's arguments must be fully evaluated before the function is called. This includes the completion of any side effects of expressions used as function arguments.
2. Once the execution of a function begins, no expressions from the calling function begin or continue to be evaluated until execution of the called function has completed. Function executions never interleave with each other.
3. Expressions used as function arguments may generally be evaluated in any order, including interleaved, except as otherwise restricted by the other rules.

Given those rules, let's see what happens in our opening examples:

```
// Example 20-1(a)
//
f( expr1, expr2 );
```

In Example 20-1(a), all we can say is that both `expr1` and `expr2` must be evaluated before `f()` is called.

That's it. The compiler may choose to perform the evaluation of `expr1` before, after, *or interleaved with* the evaluation of `expr2`. There are enough people who find this surprising that it comes up as a regular question on the newsgroups, but it's just a direct result of the C and C++ rules about sequence points.

```
// Example 20-1(b)
//
f( g( expr1 ), h( expr2 ) );
```

In Example 20-1(b), the functions and expressions may be evaluated in any order that respects the following rules:

- `expr1` must be evaluated before `g()` is called.
- `expr2` must be evaluated before `h()` is called.
- both `g()` and `h()` must complete before `f()` is called.
- The evaluations of `expr1` and `expr2` may be interleaved with each other, but nothing may be interleaved with any of the function calls. For example, no part of the evaluation of `expr2` nor the execution of `h()` may occur from the time `g()` begins until it ends.

That's it. For example, this means that any one or more of the following are possible:

- Either `g()` or `h()` could be called first.
- Evaluation of `expr1` could begin, then be interrupted by `h()` being called, then complete. (Likewise for `expr2` and `g()`.)

Some Function Call Exception Safety Problems

2. In your travels through the dusty corners of your company's code archives, you find the following code fragment:

```
// Example 20-2
//

// In some header file:
void f( T1*, T2* );

// In some implementation file:
f( new T1, new T2 );
```

Does this code have any potential exception safety problems? Explain.

Yes, there are several potential exception safety problems.

Brief recap: An expression such as new T1 is called, simply enough, a new-expression. Recall what a new-expression really does (ignoring in-place and array forms for simplicity, because they're not very relevant here):

- It allocates memory;
- It constructs a new object in that memory; and
- If the construction fails because of an exception the allocated memory is freed.

So each new-expression is essentially a series of two function calls: one call to operator new() (either the global one, or one provided by the type of the object being created), and then a call to the constructor.

For Example 20-1, consider what happens if the compiler decides to generate code as follows:

1: allocate memory for the T1
2: construct the T1
3: allocate memory for the T2
4: construct the T2
5: call f()

The problem is this: If either step 3 or step 4 fails because of an exception, the C++ standard does not require that the T1 object be destroyed and its memory deallocated. This is a classic memory leak, and clearly Not a Good Thing.

Another possible sequence of events is the following:

1: allocate memory for the T1
2: allocate memory for the T2
3: construct the T1
4: construct the T2
5: call f()

This sequence has not one, but two exception safety problems with different effects:

a) If step 3 fails because of an exception, then the memory allocated for the T1 object is automatically deallocated (step 1 is undone), but the standard does not require that the memory allocated for the T2 object be deallocated. The memory is leaked.

b) If step 4 fails because of an exception, then the T1 object has been allocated and fully constructed, but the standard does not require that it be destroyed and its memory deallocated. The T1 object is leaked.

"Hmm," you might wonder, "then why does this exception safety loophole exist at all? Why doesn't the standard just prevent the problem by requiring compilers to Do the Right Thing when it comes to cleanup?"

Following the spirit of C in the matter of efficiency, the C++ standard allows the compiler some latitude with the order of evaluation of expressions, because this allows the compiler to perform optimizations that might not otherwise be possible. To permit this, the expression evaluation rules are specified in a way that is not exception-safe, so if you want to write exception-safe code you need to know about, and avoid, these cases. Fortunately, you can do just that and prevent this problem. Perhaps a managed pointer like `auto_ptr` could help? We'll see the answer in Item 21.

ITEM 21: AN UNMANAGED POINTER PROBLEM, PART 2: WHAT ABOUT auto_ptr?   DIFFICULTY: 8

Does using `auto_ptr` help to solve the problem in Item 20?

1. As you continue to root through the archives, you see that someone must not have liked Item 20 Example 20-2 because later versions of the files in question were changed as follows:

```
// Example 21-1
//

// In some header file:
void f( auto_ptr<T1>, auto_ptr<T2> );

// In some implementation file:
f( auto_ptr<T1>( new T1 ), auto_ptr<T2>( new T2 ) );
```

What improvements does this version offer over Item 20 Example 20-2, if any? Do any exception safety problems remain? Explain.

2. Demonstrate how to write an `auto_ptr_new` facility that solves the safety problems in Question 1 and can be invoked as follows:

```
// Example 21-2
//

// In some header file:
void f( auto_ptr<T1>, auto_ptr<T2> );

// In some implementation file:
f( auto_ptr_new<T1>(), auto_ptr_new<T2>() );
```

💡 SOLUTION

1. As you continue to root through the archives, you see that someone must not have liked Item 20 Example 20-2 because later versions of the files in question were changed as follows:

```
// Example 21-1
//

// In some header file:
void f( auto_ptr<T1>, auto_ptr<T2> );

// In some implementation file:
f( auto_ptr<T1>( new T1 ), auto_ptr<T2>( new T2 ) );
```

What improvements does this version offer over Item 20 Example 20-2, if any? Do any exception safety problems remain? Explain.

This code attempts to "throw[9] auto_ptr at the problem." Many people believe that a smart pointer like auto_ptr is an exception-safety panacea, a touchstone or amulet that by its mere presence somewhere nearby can help ward off compiler indigestion.

It is not. Nothing has changed. Example 21-1 is still not exception-safe, for exactly the same reasons as before.

Specifically, the problem is that the resources are safe only if they really make it into a managing auto_ptr, but the same problems already noted can still occur before either auto_ptr constructor is ever reached. This is because both of the two problematic execution orders mentioned earlier are still possible, but now with the auto_ptr constructors tacked onto the end before f(). For one example:

1: allocate memory for the T1
2: construct the T1
3: allocate memory for the T2
4: construct the T2
5: construct the auto_ptr<T1>
6: construct the auto_ptr<T2>
7: call f()

---

9. Pun intended.

In the above case, the same problems are still present if either of steps 3 or 4 throws. Similarly:

1: allocate memory for the T1
2: allocate memory for the T2
3: construct the T1
4: construct the T2
5: construct the auto_ptr<T1>
6: construct the auto_ptr<T2>
7: call f()

Again, the same problems are present if either step 3 or step 4 throws.

Fortunately, though, this is not a problem with `auto_ptr`; `auto_ptr` is being used the wrong way, that's all. In a moment, we'll see several ways to use it better.

Aside: A Non-Solution

Note that the following is not a solution:

```
// In some header file:
void f( auto_ptr<T1> = auto_ptr<T1>( new T1 ),
        auto_ptr<T2> = auto_ptr<T2>( new T2 ) );

// In some implementation file:
f();
```

Why is this code not a solution? Because it's identical to Example 21-1 in terms of expression evaluation. Default arguments are considered to be created in the function call expression, even though they're written somewhere else entirely (in the function declaration).

A Limited Solution

2. Demonstrate how to write an `auto_ptr_new` facility that solves the safety problems in Question 1 and can be invoked as follows:

```
// Example 21-2
//

// In some header file:
void f( auto_ptr<T1>, auto_ptr<T2> );

// In some implementation file:
f( auto_ptr_new<T1>(), auto_ptr_new<T2>() );
```

The simplest solution is to provide a function template like the following:

```
// Example 21-2(a): Partial solution
//
template<typename T>
auto_ptr<T> auto_ptr_new()
{
  return auto_ptr<T>( new T );
}
```

This solves the exception safety problems. No sequence of generated code can cause resources to be leaked, because now all we have is two functions, and we know that one must be executed entirely before the other. Consider the following evaluation order:

1: call `auto_ptr_new<T1>()`
2: call `auto_ptr_new<T2>()`

If step 1 throws, there are no leaks because the `auto_ptr_new()` template is itself strongly exception-safe.

If step 2 throws, then is the temporary `auto_ptr<T1>` created by step 1 guaranteed to be cleaned up? Yes, it is. One might wonder: Isn't this pretty much the same as the `new T1` object created in the corresponding case in Item 20 Example 20-2, which isn't correctly cleaned up? No, this time it's not quite the same, because here the `auto_ptr<T1>` is actually a temporary object, and cleanup of temporary objects is correctly specified in the standard. From the standard, in 12.2/3:

> *Temporary objects are destroyed as the last step in evaluating the full-expression that (lexically) contains the point where they were created. This is true even if that evaluation ends in throwing an exception.*

But Example 21-2(a) is a limited solution: It only works with a default constructor, which breaks if a given type T doesn't have a default constructor, or if you don't want to use it. A more general solution is still needed.

Generalizing the `auto_ptr_new()` Solution

As pointed out by Dave Abrahams, we can extend the solution to support non-default constructors by providing a family of overloaded function templates:

```
// Example 21-2(b): Improved solution
//
template<typename T>
auto_ptr<T> auto_ptr_new()
{
  return auto_ptr<T>( new T );
}

template<typename T, typename Arg1>
```

```
auto_ptr<T> auto_ptr_new( const Arg1& arg1 )
{
  return auto_ptr<T>( new T( arg1 ) );
}

template<typename T, typename Arg1, typename Arg2>
auto_ptr<T> auto_ptr_new( const Arg1& arg1,
                          const Arg2& arg2 )
{
  return auto_ptr<T>( new T( arg1, arg2 ) );
}

// etc.
```

Now `auto_ptr_new()` fully and naturally supports non-default construction.

A Better Solution

Although `auto_ptr_new()` is nice, is there any way we could have avoided all the exception-safety problems without writing such helper functions? Could we have avoided the problems with better coding standards? Yes, and here is one possible standard that would have eliminated the problem: *Never allocate resources (for example, via new) in the same expression as any other code that could throw an exception. This applies even if the new'd resource will immediately be managed (for example, passed to an auto_ptr constructor) in the same expression.*

In the Example 21-1 code, the way to satisfy this guideline is to move one of the temporary `auto_ptr`s into a separate named variable:

```
// Example 21-1(a): A solution
//

// In some header file:
void f( auto_ptr<T1>, auto_ptr<T2> );

// In some implementation file:
{
  auto_ptr<T1> t1( new T1 );
  f( t1, auto_ptr<T2>( new T2 ) );
}
```

This satisfies guideline #1 because, although we are still allocating a resource, it can't be leaked because of an exception, because it's not created in the same expression as any other code that could throw.[10]

Here is another possible coding standard, which is even simpler and easier to get right (and easier to catch in code reviews): *Perform every explicit resource allocation*

---

10. I'm being deliberately, but only slightly, fuzzy, because although the body of f() is included in the expression evaluation, we don't care whether it throws.

(for example, new) in its own code statement, which immediately gives the new'd resource to a manager object (for example, auto_ptr).

In Example 21-1, the way to satisfy the second alternative guideline is to move both of the temporary auto_ptrs into separate named variables:

```
// Example 21-1(b): A simpler solution
//

// In some header file:
void f( auto_ptr<T1>, auto_ptr<T2> );

// In some implementation file:
{
  auto_ptr<T1> t1( new T1 );
  auto_ptr<T2> t2( new T2 );
  f( t1, t2 );
}
```

This satisfies guideline #2, and it required a lot less thought to get it right. Each new resource is created in its own expression and is immediately given to a managing object.

Summary

My recommendation is:

↗ Guideline

Perform every explicit resource allocation (for example, new) in its own code statement, which immediately gives the new'd resource to a manager object (for example, auto_ptr).

This guideline is easy to understand and remember, it neatly avoids all the exception safety problems in the original problem, and by mandating the use of manager objects, it helps to avoid many other exception safety problems as well. This guideline is a good candidate for inclusion in your team's coding standards.

Acknowledgments

This Item was prompted by a discussion thread on comp.lang.c++.moderated. This solution draws on observations presented by James Kanze, Steve Clamage, and Dave Abrahams in that and other threads, and in private correspondence.

ITEM 22: EXCEPTION-SAFE CLASS DESIGN, PART 1: COPY ASSIGNMENT   DIFFICULTY: 7

Is it possible to make any C++ class strongly exception-safe, for example, for its copy assignment operator? If so, how? What are the issues and consequences? To illustrate, this Item explains and then solves the Cargill Widget Example.

1. What are the three common levels of exception safety? Briefly explain each one and why it is important.
2. What is the canonical form of strongly exception-safe copy assignment?
3. Consider the following class:

```
// Example 22-1: The Cargill Widget Example
//
class Widget
{
public:
  Widget& operator=( const Widget& ); // ???
  // ...
private:
  T1 t1_;
  T2 t2_;
};
```

   Assume that any T1 or T2 operation might throw. Without changing the structure of the class, is it possible to write a strongly exception-safe Widget::operator= (const Widget&)? Why or why not? Draw conclusions.
4. Describe and demonstrate a simple transformation that works on any class in order to make (nearly) strongly exception-safe copy assignment possible and easy for that class. Where have we seen this transformation technique before in other contexts?

🔆 SOLUTION

This Item answers the following questions:

- Can any arbitrary class be made exception-safe—that is, without modifying its structure?
- If not (that is, if exception safety does affect a class's design), is there any simple change that always works to let us make any arbitrary class exception-safe?
- Are there exception safety consequences to the way we choose to express relationships among classes? Specifically, does it matter whether we choose to express a relationship using inheritance or using delegation?

Review: Exception Safety Canonical Forms

1. What are the three common levels of exception safety? Briefly explain each one and why it is important.

The canonical Abrahams Guarantees are as follows.

- *Basic guarantee:* If an exception is thrown, no resources are leaked, and objects remain in a destructible and usable, but not necessarily predictable, state. This is the weakest usable level of exception safety and is appropriate when calling code can cope with failed operations that have already made changes to objects' states.
- *Strong guarantee:* If an exception is thrown, program state remains unchanged. This level always implies commit-or-rollback semantics, including that no references or iterators into a container be invalidated if an operation fails.

In addition, certain functions must provide an even stricter guarantee in order to make the above exception safety levels possible:

- *Nothrow guarantee:* The function will not emit an exception under any circumstances. It turns out that it is sometimes impossible to implement the strong or even the basic guarantee unless certain functions are guaranteed not to throw (for example, destructors, deallocation functions). As we will see below, an important feature of the standard `auto_ptr` is that no `auto_ptr` operation will throw.

2. What is the canonical form of strongly exception-safe copy assignment?

The canonical form for copy assignment involves two steps. First, provide a nonthrowing `Swap()` function that swaps the guts, or internal state, of two objects:

```
void T::Swap( T& other ) /* throw() */
{
  // ...swap the guts of *this and other...
}
```

Second, implement `operator=()` using the "create a temporary and swap" idiom:

```
T& T::operator=( const T& other )
{
  T temp( other ); // do all the work off to the side
  Swap( temp );    // then "commit" the work using
  return *this;    //  nonthrowing operations only
}
```

Analyzing the Cargill Widget Example

This brings us to an exception safety challenge proposed by Tom Cargill:

3. Consider the following class:

```
// Example 22-1: The Cargill Widget Example
//
```

```
class Widget
{
public:
  Widget& operator=( const Widget& ); // ???
  // ...
private:
  T1 t1_;
  T2 t2_;
};
```

Assume that any T1 or T2 operation might throw. Without changing the structure of the class, is it possible to write a strongly exception-safe Widget::operator=(const Widget&)? Why or why not? Draw conclusions.

In short: Exception safety cannot be achieved in general without changing the structure of Widget. In Example 22-1, it's not possible to write a safe Widget::operator=() at all. We cannot guarantee the Widget object will even be in a consistent final state if an exception is thrown, because there's no way we can change the state of both of the t1_ and t2_ members atomically, or even reliably back out to a consistent (same or different) state if things go wrong partway through. Say our Widget::operator=() attempts to change t1_, then attempts to change t2_ (one or the other member has to be done first, it doesn't really matter which, in this case). The problem is twofold:

If the attempt to change t1_ throws, t1_ must be unchanged. That is, to make Widget::operator=() exception-safe relies fundamentally on the exception safety guarantees provided by T1, namely that T1::operator=()—or whatever mutating function we are using—either succeeds or does not change its target. This comes close to requiring the strong guarantee of T1::operator=(). The same reasoning applies to T2::operator=().

If the attempt to change t1_ succeeds, but the attempt to change t2_ throws, we've entered a "halfway" state and cannot, in general, roll back the change already made to t1_. For example, what if our attempt to reassign t1_'s original value, or any other reasonable value, also fails? Then the Widget object can't even guarantee recovery to a consistent state that maintains Widget's invariants.

Therefore, the way Widget is structured in Example 22-1, its operator=() cannot be made strongly exception-safe. (See the accompanying sidebar, "A Simpler but Still Difficult Widget," for a simpler example that has a subset of the above problems.)

Our goal is to write a Widget::operator=() that is strongly exception-safe, without making any assumptions about the exception safety of any T1 or T2 operation. Can it be done? Or is all lost?

A Simpler But Still Difficult Widget

Note that Cargill's Widget Example isn't all that different from the following simpler case.

```
class Widget2
{
  // ...
private:
  T1 t1_;
};
```

Even for the simplified Widget2, problem #1 in the main text still exists. If T1::operator=() can throw in such a way that it has already started to modify the target, there is no way to write a strongly exception-safe Widget2::operator=(), unless T1 provides suitable facilities through some other function. But if T1 can do that, why doesn't it do so for T1::operator=()?

A General Technique: Using the Pimpl Idiom

4. Describe and demonstrate a simple transformation that works on any class in order to make (nearly) strongly exception-safe copy assignment possible and easy for that class. Where have we seen this transformation technique before in other contexts?

The good news is that even though Widget::operator=() can't be made strongly exception-safe without changing Widget's structure, the following simple transformation always works to enable an *almost* strongly exception-safe assignment. Hold the member objects by pointer instead of by value, preferably all behind a single pointer with a Pimpl transformation. (For more details, including an analysis of the costs of using Pimpls and how to minimize those costs, see *Exceptional C++* [Sutter00] Items 26 to 30.)

Example 22-2 illustrates the general exception safety-promoting transformation (alternatively, the pimpl_ could be held as a bald pointer or you can use some other pointer-managing object):

```
// Example 22-2: The general solution to
// Cargill's Widget Example
//
class Widget
{
public:
  Widget();  // initializes pimpl_ with new WidgetImpl

  ~Widget(); // must be provided, because the implicit
             // version causes usage problems
             // (see Items 30 and 31)
```

```
Widget& operator=( const Widget& );

// ...

private:
  class WidgetImpl;
  auto_ptr<WidgetImpl> pimpl_;
  // ... provide copy construction that
  //     works correctly, or suppress it ...
};

// Then, typically in a separate
// implementation file:
//
class Widget::WidgetImpl
{
public:
  // ...
  T1 t1_;
  T2 t2_;
};
```

Aside: Note that if you use an `auto_ptr` member, then: (a) you must either provide the definition of `WidgetImpl` with the definition of `Widget`, or if you want to keep hiding `WidgetImpl` you must write your own destructor for `Widget` even if it's a trivial destructor;[11] and (b) you should also provide your own copy construction and assignment for `Widget`, because you usually don't want transfer-of-ownership semantics for class members. If you have a different kind of smart pointer available, consider using that instead of `auto_ptr`, but the principles described here remain important.

Now we can easily implement a nonthrowing `Swap()`, which means we can easily implement exception-safe copy assignment that *nearly* meets the strong guarantee. First, provide the nonthrowing `Swap()` function that swaps the guts (state) of two objects. Note that this function can provide the no-throw guarantee that no exceptions will be thrown under any circumstances, because no `auto_ptr` operation is permitted to throw exceptions:[12]

```
void Widget::Swap( Widget& other ) /* throw() */
{
  auto_ptr<WidgetImpl> temp( pimpl_ );
  pimpl_ = other.pimpl_;
  other.pimpl_ = temp;
}
```

---

11. If you use the automatically compiler-generated destructor, that destructor will be defined in every translation unit, and therefore the definition of `WidgetImpl` must be visible in every translation unit.

12. Note that replacing the three-line body of `Swap()` with the single line "`swap( pimpl_, other.pimpl_ );`" is not guaranteed to work correctly, because `std::swap()` will not necessarily work correctly for `auto_ptrs`.

Second, implement the common exception-safe form of operator=() using the "create a temporary and swap" idiom:

```
Widget& Widget::operator=( const Widget& other )
{
  Widget temp( other ); // do all the work off to the side
  Swap( temp );    // then "commit" the work using
  return *this;    //  nonthrowing operations only
}
```

This is nearly strongly exception-safe. It doesn't quite guarantee that if an exception is thrown program state will remain entirely unchanged. Do you see why? It's because, when we create the temporary Widget object and therefore its pimpl_'s t1_ and t2_ members, the creation of those members (and/or their destruction if we fail) may cause side effects, such as changing a global variable, and there's no way we can know about or control that.

A Potential Objection, and Why It's Unreasonable

Some may leap upon this with the ardent battle cry: "Aha, so this proves exception safety is unattainable in general, because you can't solve the general problem of making any arbitrary class strongly exception-safe without changing the class." I raise this point because some people have indeed raised this objection.

Such a conclusion seems unreasonable. The Pimpl transformation, a minor structural change, is indeed the solution to the general problem. Like most implementation goals, exception safety affects a class's design, period. Just as one wouldn't expect to make a class work polymorphically without accepting the slight change to inherit from the necessary base class, one wouldn't expect to make a class work in an exception-safe way without accepting the slight change to hold its members at arm's length. To illustrate, consider three statements:

- Unreasonable statement #1: Polymorphism doesn't work in C++ because you can't make an arbitrary class usable in place of a Base& without changing it (to derive from Base).
- Unreasonable statement #2: STL containers don't work in C++ because you can't make an arbitrary class usable in an STL container without changing it (to provide an assignment operator).
- Unreasonable statement #3: Exception safety doesn't work in C++ because you can't make an arbitrary class exception-safe without changing it (to put the internals in a Pimpl class).

The above arguments are equally fruitless, and the Pimpl transformation is indeed the general solution to writing classes that give useful exception safety guarantees (indeed, nearly the strong guarantee) without requiring any knowledge of the safety of class data members.

So, what have we learned?

Conclusion 1: Exception Safety Affects a Class's Design

Exception safety is never "just an implementation detail." The Pimpl transformation is a straightforward structural change, but still a change.

Conclusion 2: You Can Always Make Your Code (Nearly) Strongly Exception-Safe

There's an important principle here:

> *Just because a class you use isn't in the least exception-safe is no reason why code that uses it can't be strongly exception-safe (except for side effects).*

Anybody can use a class that lacks a strongly exception-safe copy assignment operator and make that use strongly exception-safe, except that of course if Widget operations cause side effects (such as changing a global variable), there's no way we can know about or control it. In other words, we can achieve what might be called the local strong guarantee:

- *Local strong guarantee:* If an exception is thrown, program state remains unchanged with respect to the objects being manipulated. This level always implies local commit-or-rollback semantics, including that no references or iterators into a container be invalidated if an operation fails.

The "hide the details behind a pointer" technique can be done equally well by either the Widget implementer or the Widget user. If it's done by the Widget implementer, however, it's always safe, and the user won't have to do the following:

```
// Example 22-3: What the user has to do if
// the Widget author doesn't
//
class MyClass
{
  auto_ptr<Widget> w_; // hold the unsafe-to-copy
                       //  Widget at arm's length
public:
  void Swap( MyClass& other ) /* throw() */
  {
    auto_ptr<Widget> temp( w_ );
    w_ = other.w_;
    other.w_ = temp;
  }
```

```
MyClass& operator=( const MyClass& other )
{
  MyClass temp( other ); // do all the work off to the side
  Swap( temp );    // then "commit" the work using
  return *this;    //  nonthrowing operations only
}

// ... provide destruction, copy construction
//     and assignment that work correctly, or
//     suppress them ...
};
```

Conclusion 3: Use Pointers Judiciously

Scott Meyers writes[13]:

> When I give talks on EH, I teach people two things:
>
> 1. POINTERS ARE YOUR ENEMIES because they lead to the kinds of problems that auto_ptr is designed to eliminate.

To wit, bald pointers should normally be owned by manager objects that own the pointed-at resource and perform automatic cleanup. Then Scott continues:

> 2. POINTERS ARE YOUR FRIENDS because operations on pointers can't throw.
>
> Then I tell them to have a nice day.

Scott captures a fundamental dichotomy well. Fortunately, in practice you can and should get the best of both worlds.

- *Use pointers because they are your friends,* because operations on pointers can't throw.
- *Keep them friendly by wrapping them* in manager objects such as auto_ptrs, because this guarantees cleanup. This doesn't compromise the nonthrowing advantages of pointers, because auto_ptr operations never throw either (and you can always get at the real pointer inside an auto_ptr whenever you need to—for example by calling auto_ptr::get()).

Often, the best way to implement the Pimpl idiom is as shown in Example 22-2 above, by using a pointer (in order to take advantage of nonthrowing operations) while still wrapping the dynamic resource safely in a manager object (in this example, an auto_ptr). Just remember that if you do use auto_ptr, your class must provide its own destruction, copy construction, and copy assignment with the right semantics, or you can disable copy construction and assignment if those don't make sense for the class.

---

13. Scott Meyers, private communication.

In the next Item, we'll apply what we've learned by using the above to analyze the best way to express a common class relationship.

ITEM 23: EXCEPTION-SAFE CLASS DESIGN, PART 2: INHERITANCE   DIFFICULTY: 6

What does Is-Implemented-In-Terms-Of mean? It may surprise you to learn there are definite exception-safety consequences when choosing between inheritance and delegation. Can you spot them?

1. What does Is-Implemented-In-Terms-Of mean?
2. In C++, Is-Implemented-In-Terms-Of can be expressed by either nonpublic inheritance or by containment/delegation. That is, when writing a class T that is implemented in terms of a class U, the two main options are to inherit privately from U or to contain a U member object.

Does the choice between these techniques have exception safety implications? Explain. (Ignore any issues not related to exception safety.)

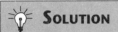 **SOLUTION**

Is-Implemented-In-Terms-Of

By coining expressions like Has-A, Is-A, and Uses-A, we have developed a convenient shorthand for describing many types of code relationships.

"Is-A," or more precisely "Is-Substitutable-For-A," must follow Barbara Liskov's Substitutability Principle (LSP), in which she defines what it means for a type S to be substitutable for a type T:

> *If for each object o1 of type S there is an object o2 of type T such that for all programs P defined in terms of T, the behavior of P is unchanged when o1 is substituted for o2, then S is a subtype of T. [Liskov88]*

Is-A is usually used to describe public inheritance that preserves substitutability according to the LSP, as all public inheritance ought to do. For example, "D Is-A B" means that code that accepts objects of the base class B by pointer or reference can seamlessly use objects of the publicly derived class D instead.

It's important to remember, however, that there are more ways to spell "Is-A" in C++ than are dreamt of in inheritance alone. Is-A can also describe unrelated (by inheritance) classes that support the same interface and can therefore be used inter-changeably in templated code that uses that common interface. The LSP applies to this form of substitutability just as much as it does to other forms. In this context, for example, "X Is-A Y"—or, "X Is-Substitutable-For-A Y"—communicates that tem-plated code that accepts objects of type Y will also accept objects of type X because both X and Y support the same interface. For an enjoyable treatise on substitutability, a good place to begin is Kevlin Henney's article "Substitutability" [Henney00].

Clearly, both kinds of substitutability depend on the context in which the objects are actually used, but the point is that Is-A can be implemented in different ways. So, as it turns out, can Is-Implemented-In-Terms-Of, as we shall now see.

1. What does Is-Implemented-In-Terms-Of mean?

An equally common code relationship is Is-Implemented-In-Terms-Of, or IIITO for short. A type T IIITO another type U if T uses U in its implementation in some form. Saying "uses... in some form" certainly leaves a lot of latitude, and this can run the gamut from T being an adapter or proxy or wrapper for U, to T simply using U inci-dentally to implement some details of T's own services.

Typically "T IIITO U" means that either T Has-A U, as shown in Example 23-1(a):

```
// Example 23-1(a): "T IIITO U" using Has-A
//
class T
{
  // ...
private:
  U* u_;  // or by value or by reference
};
```

or that T is derived from U nonpublicly, as shown in Example 23-1(b):[14]

```
// Example 23-1(b): "T IIITO U" using derivation
//
class T : private U
{
  // ...
};
```

This brings us to the natural questions: When we have a choice, which is the better way to implement IIITO? What are the trade-offs? When should we consider using each one?

---

14. Arguably, public derivation also models IIITO, but the primary meaning of public derivation is still Is-Substitutable-For-A.

How to Implement IIITO: Inheritance or Delegation?

2. In C++, Is-Implemented-In-Terms-Of can be expressed by either nonpublic inheritance or by containment/delegation. That is, when writing a class T that is implemented in terms of a class U, the two main options are to inherit privately from U or to contain a U member object.

As I've argued before, inheritance is often overused, even by experienced developers. A sound rule of software engineering is to minimize coupling. If a relationship can be expressed in more than one way, use the weakest relationship that's practical. Given that inheritance is nearly the strongest relationship we can express in C++, second only to friendship,[15] it's only really appropriate when there is no equivalent weaker alternative. If you can express a class relationship using delegation alone, you should always prefer that.

The principle of minimum coupling clearly has a direct effect on the robustness (or fragility) of your code, of how long your compile times are, and other observable consequences. What's interesting is that the choice between inheritance and delegation for IIITO turns out to have exception safety implications. In hindsight, that the principle of minimum coupling should also relate to exception safety should not be surprising, because a design's coupling has a direct impact on its possible exception safety.

The coupling principle states:

> *Lower coupling promotes program correctness (including exception safety), and tight coupling reduces the maximum possible program correctness (including exception safety).*

This is only natural. After all, the less tightly real-world objects are related, the less effect they have on each other. That's why we put firewalls in buildings and bulkheads in ships. If there's a failure in one compartment, the more we've isolated the compartments, the less likely the failure is to spread to other compartments before things can be brought back under control.

Now let's return to Examples 23-1(a) and 23-1(b) and consider again a class T that IIITO another type U. Consider the copy assignment operator: How does the choice of how to express the IIITO relationship affect how we write T::operator=()?

Exception Safety Consequences

Does the choice between these techniques have exception safety implications? Explain. (Ignore any issues not related to exception safety.)

---

15. A friend of a class X has the strongest possible relationship because it has access to and can depend upon all the members of X. A class derived from X only has access to and can only depend upon X's public and protected members.

First, consider how we would have to write T::operator=() if the IIITO relationship is expressed using Has-A. We of course have the good habit of using the common "do all the work off to the side, then commit using nonthrowing operations only" technique to maximize exception safety, and so we would write something like the following:

```
// Example 23-2(a): "T IIITO U" using Has-A
//
class T
{
  // ...
private:
  U* u_;
};

T& T::operator=( const T& other )
{
  U* temp = new U( *other.u_ );   // do all the work
                                  //  off to the side

  delete u_;       // then "commit" the work using
  u_ = temp;       //  nonthrowing operations only
  return *this;
}
```

This is pretty good. Without making any assumptions about U, we can write a T::operator=() that is "nearly" strongly exception-safe except for possible side effects of U.

Even if the U object were contained by value instead of by pointer, it could be easily transformed to be held by pointer as above. The U object could also be put into a Pimpl using the transformation described in the first part of this Item. It is precisely the fact that delegation (Has-A) gives us this flexibility that allows us to easily write a fairly exception-safe T::operator=() without making any assumptions about U.

Next, consider how the problem changes once the relationship between T and U involves any kind of inheritance:

```
// Example 23-2(b): "T IIITO U" using derivation
//
class T : private U
{
  // ...
};
T& T::operator=( const T& other )
{
  U::operator=( other );   // ???
  return *this;
}
```

The problem is the call to `U::operator=()`. As alluded to in the Item 22 sidebar (speaking of a similar case), if `U::operator=()` can throw in such a way that it has already started to modify the target, there is no way to write a strongly exception-safe `T::operator=()` unless `U` provides suitable facilities through some other function. (But if `U` can do that, why doesn't it do so for `U::operator=()`?)

In other words, now `T`'s ability to make an exception safety guarantee for its own member function `T::operator=()` depends implicitly on `U`'s own safety and guarantees. Again, should this be surprising? No, because Example 23-2(b) uses the tightest possible relationship, and hence the highest possible coupling, to express the connection between `T` and `U`.

Summary

Looser coupling promotes program correctness (including exception safety), and tight coupling reduces the maximum possible program correctness (including exception safety).

Inheritance is often overused, even by experienced developers. See *Exceptional C++* [Sutter00] Item 24 for more information about many other reasons, besides exception safety, why and how you should use delegation instead of inheritance wherever possible. Always minimize coupling. If a class relationship can be expressed in more than one way, use the weakest relationship that's practical. In particular, only use inheritance when delegation alone won't suffice.

Inheritance and Polymorphism

What's object orientation without a little inheritance and polymorphism?

Although it's often overused, inheritance is still an important tool—and that includes multiple inheritance. Multiple inheritance comes into its own especially when you're living in the real world and often find yourself in the situation of trying to combine libraries from different vendors. This section shows how to avoid the Siamese Twin problem when combining inheritance-based libraries from different vendors. It also demonstrates the many legitimate (and some illegitimate) uses of pure virtual functions, how to code alternatives to multiple inheritance, and how to control who gets to make use of your inheritance relationships.

ITEM 24: WHY MULTIPLE INHERITANCE?   DIFFICULTY: 6

Some languages, including the SQL99 standard, continue to struggle with the question of whether to support single or multiple inheritance. This Item invites you to consider the issues.

1. What is multiple inheritance (MI), and what extra possibilities or complications does allowing MI introduce into C++?
2. Is MI ever necessary? If yes, show as many situations as you can and argue why MI should be in a language. If no, argue why single inheritance (SI), possibly combined with Java-style interfaces, is equal or superior, and why MI should not be in a language.

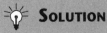 **SOLUTION**

1. **What is multiple inheritance (MI), and what extra possibilities or complications does allowing MI introduce into C++?**

Very briefly, MI means the ability to inherit from more than a single direct base class.

For example:

```
class Derived : public Base1, private Base2
{
  //...
};
```

Allowing MI introduces the possibility that a class may have the same (direct or indirect) base class appear more than once as an ancestor. A simple example of this is the classic diamond-shaped inheritance graph shape shown in Figure 4.

Here B is an indirect base class of D twice, once via C1 and once via C2.

This situation introduces the need for an extra feature in C++: virtual inheritance. The question at issue is: Does the programmer want D to have one B base subobject or two? If the answer is one, then B should be a virtual base class and Figure 4 becomes the Dreaded Diamond of Death. If the answer is two, then B should be a normal (non-virtual) base class.

Finally, the main complication of virtual base classes is that they must be initialized directly by the most-derived class. For more information on this and other aspects of MI, see [Stroustrup00] or [Meyers97] Item 43.

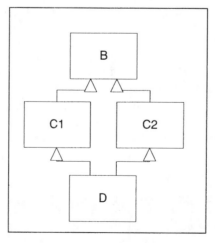

Figure 4: The Dreaded Diamond of Death (if inheritance from B is virtual).

> ## ⤢ Guideline
>
> *Avoid multiple inheritance from more than one non-protocol class (a protocol class means an abstract base class, or ABC, composed entirely of pure virtual functions with no data).*

2. Is MI ever necessary?

Short answer: No feature is strictly "necessary" insofar as any program can be written in assembler (or lower). However, just as most people would rather not code their own virtual function mechanism in plain C, in some cases not having MI requires painful workarounds.

So here we have this wonderful feature called MI. The question is, or at least was, is this a Good Thing?[1]

In short, there are people who think that MI is just a bad idea that should be avoided at all costs. That's not true. Yes, if it's used thoughtlessly, MI can incur unnecessary coupling and complexity. But so does any kind of misused inheritance (see *Exceptional C++* [Sutter00] Item 24), and I think we agree that doesn't make inheritance a Bad Thing. And, yes, any program can be written without resorting to MI, but for that matter, any program can be written without using inheritance at all. In fact, any program can be written in assembler. That doesn't mean it's necessarily a good idea or even something you would feel happy about doing.

If yes, show as many situations as you can and argue why MI should be in a language. If no, argue why single inheritance (SI), possibly combined with Java-style interfaces, is equal or superior, and why MI should not be in a language.

So when is MI appropriate? In short, only when each inheritance, taken individually, is appropriate. *Exceptional C++* Item 24 presented a fairly exhaustive list of when to use inheritance. Most appropriate real-world uses of MI fall into one of three categories.

1. *Combining modules or libraries.* I'm citing this point first for a reason, illustrated again below. Many classes are designed to be base classes—that is, to use them you are intended to inherit from them. The natural consequence is the question:

---

1. In part, the topic for this Item was inspired by events at the SQL standards meeting in June 1998, when multiple inheritance was removed from the ANSI SQL99 draft standard. (Those of you who are interested in databases may see a revised form of MI resurrected in SQL4, if/when we get that far.) This was mainly done because the proposed multiple inheritance specification had technical difficulties, and in order to align with languages like Java that do not support true multiple inheritance. Still, just sitting there and listening to people discussing the merits and demerits of multiple inheritance at such a relatively late date was intriguing. It's something we haven't done much in the C++ world since the formative years, and it made me reminisce aloud about extended newsgroup flame wars from years ago (and some more recent than that) with subject lines like "MI is evil!!!"

What if you want to write a class that extends two libraries, and each library requires you to inherit from one of its classes?

When you're facing this kind of situation, you usually don't have the option of changing the library code to avoid some of the inheritance. You probably purchased the library from a third-party vendor, or maybe it's a module produced by another project team inside your company. Either way, not only can't you change the code, but you may not even have the code! If so, then MI is necessary; there's no other (natural) way to do what you have to do, and using MI is perfectly legitimate.

In practice, I've found that knowing how to use MI to combine vendor libraries is an essential technique that belongs in every C++ programmer's toolchest. Whether you end up using it frequently or not, you should definitely know about it and understand it.

2. *Protocol classes (interface classes).* In C++, MI's best and safest use is to define protocol classes—that is, classes composed of nothing but pure virtual functions. The absence of data members in the base class avoids outright MI's more famous complexities.

Interestingly, different languages/models support this kind of MI through non-inheritance mechanisms. Two examples are Java and COM. Strictly speaking, Java has multiple inheritance, but constrains inheritance of implementation to single inheritance. A Java class can implement multiple "interfaces," where an interface is very similar to a C++ pure abstract base class without data members. COM does not include the concept of inheritance per se (although that's the usual implementation technique for COM objects written in C++), but it likewise has a notion of a composition of interfaces, and COM interfaces resemble a combination of Java interfaces and C++ templates.

3. *Ease of (polymorphic) use.* Using inheritance to let other code use a derived object wherever a base is expected is a powerful concept. In some cases, it can be very useful to let the same derived object be used in the place of several kinds of bases, and that's where MI comes in. For a good example of this, see [Stroustrup00] section 14.2.2, which demonstrates an MI-based design for exception classes in which a most-derived exception class may have a polymorphic Is-A relationship, with multiple direct base classes.

Note that #3 overlaps greatly with #1 and #2. It's frequently useful to do #3 at the same time as one of the others, and for the same reasons.

One more thing to think about: Don't forget that sometimes it's not necessary to just inherit from two different base classes, but to inherit from each one for a different reason. "Polymorphic LSP Is-A public inheritance" isn't the only game in town; there are many other possible reasons to use inheritance. For example, a class may need to inherit privately from base class A to gain access to protected members of class A, but at the same time inherit publicly from base class B to polymorphically implement a virtual function of class B.

ITEM 25: EMULATING MULTIPLE INHERITANCE   DIFFICULTY: 5

If you couldn't use multiple inheritance, how would you emulate it? This exercise will help you to understand firsthand some of the reasons why multiple inheritance works the way it does in C++. In your answer, don't forget to emulate as natural a syntax as possible for the calling code.

Consider the following example:

```
class A
{
public:
  virtual ~A();
  string Name();
private:
  virtual string DoName();
};


class B1 : virtual public A
{
  string DoName();
};


class B2 : virtual public A
{
  string DoName();
};


A::~A() {}
string A::Name()    { return DoName(); }
string A::DoName()  { return "A"; }
string B1::DoName() { return "B1"; }
string B2::DoName() { return "B2"; }

class D : public B1, public B2
{
    string DoName() { return "D";  }
};
```

Demonstrate the best way you can find to "work around" not using multiple inheritance by writing an equivalent (or as near as possible) class D without using MI. How would you get the same effect and usability for D with as little change as possible to syntax in the calling code?

* * * * *

Starter: You can begin by considering the cases in the following test harness.

```cpp
void f1( A&  x ) { cout << "f1:" << x.Name() << endl; }
void f2( B1& x ) { cout << "f2:" << x.Name() << endl; }
void f3( B2& x ) { cout << "f3:" << x.Name() << endl; }

void g1( A   x ) { cout << "g1:" << x.Name() << endl; }
void g2( B1  x ) { cout << "g2:" << x.Name() << endl; }
void g3( B2  x ) { cout << "g3:" << x.Name() << endl; }

int main()
{
  D    d;
  B1* pb1 = &d;    // D* -> B* conversion
  B2* pb2 = &d;
  B1& rb1 = d;     // D& -> B& conversion
  B2& rb2 = d;

  f1( d );         // polymorphism
  f2( d );
  f3( d );

  g1( d );         // slicing
  g2( d );
  g3( d );

                   // dynamic_cast/RTTI
  cout << ( (dynamic_cast<D*>(pb1) != 0) ? "ok " : "bad " );
  cout << ( (dynamic_cast<D*>(pb2) != 0) ? "ok " : "bad " );

  try
  {
    dynamic_cast<D&>(rb1);
    cout << "ok ";
  }
  catch(...)
  {
    cout << "bad ";
  }

  try
  {
    dynamic_cast<D&>(rb2);
    cout << "ok ";
  }
  catch(...)
  {
    cout << "bad ";
  }
}
```

SOLUTION

```
class D : public B1, public B2
{
  string DoName() { return "D";  }
};
```

Demonstrate the best way you can find to "work around" not using multiple inheritance by writing an equivalent (or as near as possible) class D without using MI. How would you get the same effect and usability for D with as little change as possible to syntax in the calling code?

There are a few strategies, each with its weaknesses, but here's one that gets quite close.

```
class D : public B1
{
public:
  class D2 : public B2
  {
  public:
    void   Set ( D* d ) { d_ = d; }
  private:
    string DoName();
    D* d_;
  } d2_;

  D()                      { d2_.Set( this ); }

  D( const D& other ) : B1( other ), d2_( other.d2_ )
                           { d2_.Set( this ); }

  D& operator=( const D& other )
                           {
                             B1::operator=( other );
                             d2_ = other.d2_;
                             return *this;
                           }

  operator B2&()    { return d2_; }

  B2& AsB2()        { return d2_; }

private:
  string DoName()    { return "D"; }
};

string D::D2::DoName(){ return d_->DoName(); }
```

Before reading on, take a moment to consider the code and think about the purpose of each class or function.

Drawbacks

The workaround does a pretty good job of implementing MI, automates most of MI's behavior, and allows all of MI's usability, as long as you rely on coding discipline to fill in the parts that are not completely automated. In particular, here are some drawbacks of this workaround that show which parts of the MI feature are not completely automated.

- Providing `operator B2&()` arguably gives references special (inconsistent) treatment over pointers.
- Calling code has to invoke `D::AsB2()` explicitly to use a `D` as a `B2` (in the test harness, this means changing "`B2* pb2 = &d;`" to "`B2* pb2 = &d.AsB2();`").
- A `dynamic_cast` from `D*` to `B2*` still doesn't work (it's possible to work around this if you're willing to use the preprocessor to redefine `dynamic_cast` calls, but that's an extreme solution).

Interestingly, you may have observed that the `D` object layout in memory is similar to what multiple inheritance would give. That's because we're trying to simulate MI, without all the syntactic sugar and convenience that built-in language support would provide.

You may not need MI often, but when you need it, you *really* need it. This Item is intended to demonstrate that having the required language support for this kind of useful feature is far better than trying to roll your own, even if you can duplicate the functionality exactly through a combination of other features and coding discipline.

ITEM 26: MULTIPLE INHERITANCE AND THE SIAMESE TWIN PROBLEM   DIFFICULTY: 4

Overriding inherited virtual functions is easy, as long as you're not trying to override a virtual function that has the same signature in two base classes. This can happen even when the base classes don't come from different vendors! What's the best way to separate such "Siamese Twin" functions?

Consider the following two classes:

```
class BaseA
{
  virtual int ReadBuf( const char* );
  // ...
};

class BaseB
{
```

```
  virtual int ReadBuf( const char* );
  // ...
};
```

Both BaseA and BaseB are clearly intended to be used as base classes, but they are otherwise unrelated. Their ReadBuf() functions are intended to do different things, and the classes come from different library vendors.

Demonstrate how to write a class Derived, publicly derived from both BaseA and BaseB, which overrides both ReadBuf()s independently to do different things.

 SOLUTION

The purpose of this Item is to show you a minor pitfall that can come up with MI, and how to handle it effectively. Say you're using two vendors' libraries in the same project. Vendor A provides the following base class BaseA.

```
class BaseA
{
public:
  virtual int ReadBuf( const char* );
  // ...
};
```

The idea is that you're supposed to inherit from BaseA, probably overriding some virtual functions, because other parts of vendor A's library are written to expect objects they can use polymorphically as BaseAs. This is a common and normal practice, especially for extensible application frameworks, and there's nothing wrong with it.

Nothing, that is, until you start to use Vendor B's library and discover, to your uneasy amazement:

```
class BaseB
{
public:
  virtual int ReadBuf( const char* );
  // ...
};
```

"Well, that's rather a coincidence," you may think. Not only does vendor B, too, have a base class that you're expected to inherit from, but it happens to have a virtual function with exactly the same signature as one of the virtuals in BaseA. But BaseB's is supposed to do something completely different. And that's the key point.

Both BaseA and BaseB are clearly intended to be used as base classes but they are otherwise unrelated. Their ReadBuf() functions are intended to do different things, and the classes come from different library vendors.

Demonstrate how to write a class Derived, publicly derived from both BaseA and BaseB, which overrides both ReadBuf()s independently to do different things.

The problem becomes clear when you have to write a class that inherits from both BaseA and BaseB, perhaps because you need an object that can be used polymorphically by functions in both vendors' libraries. Here's a naïve attempt at such a function:

```
// Example 26-1: Attempt #1, doesn't work
//
class Derived : public BaseA, public BaseB
{
  // ...

  int ReadBuf( const char* );
      // overrides both BaseA::ReadBuf()
      // and BaseB::ReadBuf()
};
```

Here Derived::ReadBuf() overrides both BaseA::ReadBuf() and BaseB::Read Buf(). To see why that isn't good enough given our criteria, consider the following code:

```
// Example 26-1(a): Counterexample,
// why attempt #1 doesn't work
//
Derived d;
BaseA*  pba = d;
BaseB*  pbb = d;

pba->ReadBuf( "sample buffer" );
    // calls Derived::ReadBuf

pbb->ReadBuf( "sample buffer" );
    // calls Derived::ReadBuf
```

Do you see the problem? ReadBuf() is virtual in both interfaces, and it operates polymorphically just as we expect. But the *same* function, Derived::ReadBuf(), is invoked regardless of which interface is used. Yet BaseA::ReadBuf() and BaseB::ReadBuf() have different semantics and are supposed to do different things, not the same thing. Further, Derived::ReadBuf() has no way to tell whether it's being called through the BaseA interface or the BaseB interface (if either), so we can't put an "if" inside Derived::ReadBuf() to make it do something different depending on how it's called. That's lousy, but we're stuck with it.

"Oh, come on," you may be thinking. "This is an awfully contrived example, isn't it?" Actually, it's not. For example, John Kdllin of Microsoft reports that creating a class derived from both the IOleObject and IConnectionPoint COM interfaces (think of these as abstract base classes composed entirely of public virtual functions) becomes problematic, because (a) both interfaces have a member function declared as virtual HRESULT Unadvise(unsigned long); and (b) typically you have to override each Unadvise() to do different things.

Stop a moment and think about this example. How would you solve this problem? Is there any way we can override the two inherited ReadBuf functions separately so that we can perform different actions in each one, with the right actions getting performed, depending on whether outside code calls through the BaseA or BaseB interface? In short, how can we separate these twins?

How to Separate Siamese Twins

Fortunately, there is a fairly clean solution. The key to the problem is that the two overridable functions have exactly the same name and signature. The key to the solution, therefore, must lie in changing at least one function's signature, and the easiest part of the signature to change is the name.

How do you change a function's name? Through inheritance, of course! What's needed is an intermediate class that derives from the base class, declares a new virtual function, and overrides the inherited version to call the new function. The inheritance hierarchy looks like the one shown in Figure 5.

The code looks like the following:

```
// Example 26-2: Attempt #2, correct
//
class BaseA2 : public BaseA
{
public:
  virtual int BaseAReadBuf( const char* p ) = 0;
private:
  int ReadBuf( const char* p )    // override inherited
  {
    return BaseAReadBuf( p );     // to call new func
  }
};
```

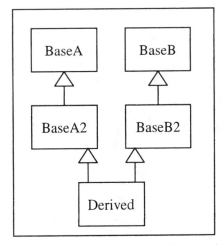

Figure 5: Using intermediate classes to rename inherited virtual functions.

```
class BaseB2 : public BaseB
{
public:
  virtual int BaseBReadBuf( const char* p ) = 0;
private:
  int ReadBuf( const char* p )    // override inherited
  {
    return BaseBReadBuf( p );     // to call new func
  }
};

class Derived : public BaseA2, public BaseB2
{
  /* ... */

public: // or "private:", depending whether other
        // code should be able to call these directly

  int BaseAReadBuf( const char* );
      // overrides BaseA::ReadBuf indirectly
      // via BaseA2::BaseAReadBuf

  int BaseBReadBuf( const char* );
      // overrides BaseB::ReadBuf indirectly
      // via BaseB2::BaseBReadBuf
};
```

BaseA2 and BaseB2 may also need to duplicate constructors of BaseA and BaseB so that Derived can invoke them. But that's it. (Often a simpler way than duplicating the constructors in code is to have BaseA2 and BaseB2 derive virtually so that Derived has direct access to the base constructors.) BaseA2 and BaseB2 are abstract classes, so they don't need to duplicate any other BaseA or BaseB functions or operators, such as assignment operators.

Now everything works as it should.

```
// Example 26-2(a): Why attempt #2 works
//
Derived d;
BaseA*  pba = d;
BaseB*  pbb = d;

pba->ReadBuf( "sample buffer" );
    // calls Derived::BaseAReadBuf

pbb->ReadBuf( "sample buffer" );
    // calls Derived::BaseBReadBuf
```

Further-derived classes need only to know that they must not further override ReadBuf itself. If they do, it will disable the renaming stubs that we installed in the intermediate classes.

ITEM 27: (IM)PURE VIRTUAL FUNCTIONS   **DIFFICULTY: 7**

Does it ever make sense to make a function pure virtual, but still provide a body?

1. What is a pure virtual function? Give an example.
2. Why might you declare a pure virtual function and also write a definition (body)? Give as many possible reasons or situations as you can.

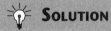 **SOLUTION**

1. What is a pure virtual function? Give an example.

A pure virtual function is a virtual function you want to force concrete derived classes to override. If a class has any non-overridden pure virtuals, it is an "abstract" class, and you can't create objects of that type.

```
// Example 27-1
//
class AbstractClass
{
  // declare a pure virtual function:
  // this class is now abstract
  virtual void f(int) = 0;
};

class StillAbstract : public AbstractClass
{
  // does not override f(int),
  // so this class is still abstract
};

class Concrete : public StillAbstract
{
public:
  // finally overrides f(int),
  // so this class is concrete
  void f(int) { /*...*/ }
};

AbstractClass a;    // error, abstract class
StillAbstract b;    // error, abstract class
Concrete      c;    // ok, concrete class
```

2. **Why might you declare a pure virtual function and also write a definition (body)? Give as many possible reasons or situations as you can.**

Let's consider the three main reasons you might do this. Of these three reasons, #1 is commonplace, #2 and #3 are useful but somewhat more rare, and #4 is a workaround used occasionally by advanced programmers who are working with weaker compilers. (Of course we need a fourth entry in a three-reason list, for the self-evident reason that no trilogy is complete without a fourth item.[2])

1. Pure Virtual Destructor

All base class destructors should be either virtual and public, or nonvirtual and protected. In brief, here's the reason: First, recall that you should always avoid deriving from a concrete class. Assuming that it's given that the base class is therefore not concrete, and therefore doesn't necessarily need a public destructor for the purpose of being instantiated on its own, you're left with one of two situations. Either (a) you want to allow polymorphic deletion through a base pointer, in which case the destructor must be virtual and public; or (b) you don't, in which case the destructor should be nonvirtual and protected, the latter to prevent the unwanted usage. For more, see [Sutter01].

If the class should be abstract (you want to prevent instantiating it) but it doesn't have any other pure virtual functions and it has a public destructor, make the destructor pure virtual (it should be anyway).

```
// Example 27-2(a)
//
// file b.h
//
class B
{
public: /*...other stuff...*/
  virtual ~B() = 0; // pure virtual destructor
};
```

Of course, any derived class's destructor must implicitly call the base class's destructor, so the destructor must still be defined (even if it's empty).

```
// Example 27-2(a), continued
//
// file b.cpp
//
B::~B() { /* possibly empty */ }
```

---

2. "Our main weapon is surprise. Fear and surprise are our two main weapons." (*Monty Python's Flying Circus*)

If this definition were not supplied, you could still derive other classes from B, but they could never be instantiated, which makes them not particularly useful.

 Guideline

Always make base class destructors virtual and public or nonvirtual and protected.

2. Force Conscious Acceptance of Default Behavior

If a derived class doesn't choose to override a normal virtual function, it just inherits the base version's behavior by default. If you want to provide a default behavior but not let derived classes just inherit it "silently" like this, you can make it pure virtual and still provide a default the derived class author has to call deliberately if he wants it.

```
// Example 27-2(b)
//
class B
{
protected:
  virtual bool f() = 0;
};

bool B::f()
{
  return true;   // this is a good default, but
}                // shouldn't be used blindly

class D : public B
{
  bool f()
  {
    return B::f(); // if D wants the default
  }                // behaviour, it has to say so
};
```

In the "gang of four" book *Design Patterns* [Gamma95], the State pattern demonstrates one example of how this technique can be put to good use.

3. Provide Partial Behavior

It's often useful to provide partial behavior to a derived class which the derived class must still complete. The idea is that the derived class executes the base class's implementation as part of its own implementation:

```
// Example 27-2(c)
//
class B
{
  // ...
protected:
  virtual bool f() = 0;
};

bool B::f()
{
  // do something general-purpose
}

class D : public B
{
  bool f()
  {
    // first, use the base class's implementation
    B::f();

    // ... now do more work ...
  }
};
```

Referring again to [Gamma95], the Decorator pattern demonstrates a good use for this technique.

4. Work Around Poor Compiler Diagnostics

There are situations in which you could accidentally end up calling a pure virtual function (indirectly from a base constructor or destructor; see your favorite advanced C++ book for examples). Of course, well-written code normally won't get into these problems, but no one's perfect, and once in a while it happens.

Unfortunately, not all compilers[3] actually tell you when this is the problem. Those that don't can give you spurious unrelated errors that take forever to track down. "Argh," you scream when you finally diagnose the problem some hours later, "why didn't the compiler just *tell* me that's what I did?!" (Answer: Because that's one manifestation of "undefined behavior.")

One way to protect yourself against this wasted debugging time is to provide definitions for the pure virtual functions that should never be called, and put some really evil code into those definitions, which lets you know right away if you call them accidentally.

For example:

---

3. Well, technically it's the runtime environment that catches this sort of thing. I'll say *compiler* anyway, because it's generally the compiler that ought to slip in the code that checks this for you at runtime.

```
// Example 27-2(d)
//
class B
{
public:
  bool f();      // possibly instrumented, calls do_f()
                 // (Non-Virtual Interface pattern)
private:
  virtual bool do_f() = 0;
};

bool B::do_f()   // this should NEVER be called
{
  if( PromptUser( "pure virtual B::f called -- "
                  "abort or ignore?" ) == Abort )
    DieDieDie();
}
```

In the common DieDieDie() function, do whatever is necessary on your system to get into the debugger or dump a stack trace or otherwise get diagnostic information. Here are some common methods that will get you into the debugger on most systems. Pick the one you like best.

```
void DieDieDie()   // a C way to scribble through a null
{                  // pointer... a proven crowd-pleaser
  memset( 0, 1, 1 );
}

void DieDieDie()   // another C-style method
{
  abort();
}

void DieDieDie()   // a C++ way to scribble through a null
                   // data pointer
  *static_cast<char *>(0) = 0;
}

void DieDieDie()   // a C++ way to follow a null function
                   // pointer to code that doesn't exist
  static_cast<void(*)()>(0)();
}

void DieDieDie()   // unwind back to last "catch(...)"
{
  class LocalClass {};
  throw LocalClass();
}

void DieDieDie()   // an alternative for standardistes
{
  throw std::logic_error();
}
```

```
                        // for standardistes having good compilers
      void DieDieDie() throw()
      {
        throw 0;
      }
```

You get the idea. Be creative. There's no shortage of ways to deliberately crash a program, but the idea is to do it in a way that will cause your runtime debugger to place you as close to the point of failure as possible. Scribbling through a null pointer is one of the bets that pays most consistently.

ITEM 28: CONTROLLED POLYMORPHISM   DIFFICULTY: 3

Is-A polymorphism is a very useful tool in OO modeling. But, sometimes, you may want to restrict which code can use certain classes polymorphically. This Item gives an example and shows how to get the intended effect.

Consider the following code:

```
class Base
{
public:
  virtual void VirtFunc();
  // ...
};

class Derived : public Base
{
public:
  void VirtFunc();
  // ...
};

void SomeFunc( const Base& );
```

There are two other functions. The goal is to allow f1() to use Derived objects polymorphically where a Base is expected, yet prevent all other functions (including f2()) from doing so.

```
void f1()
{
  Derived d;
  SomeFunc( d ); // works, OK
}

void f2()
{
```

```
      Derived d;
      SomeFunc( d ); // we want to prevent this
    }
```

Demonstrate how to achieve this effect.

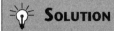 **SOLUTION**

Consider the following code:

```
class Base
{
public:
  virtual void VirtFunc();
  // ...
};

class Derived : public Base
{
public:
  void VirtFunc();
  // ...
};

void SomeFunc( const Base& );
```

The reason why all code can use Derived objects polymorphically where a Base is expected is because Derived inherits publicly from Base (no surprises here).

If, instead, Derived inherited privately from Base, then almost no code could use Deriveds polymorphically *as* Bases. The reason for the *almost* is that code with access to the private parts of Derived can still access the private base classes of Derived and can therefore use Deriveds polymorphically in place of Bases. Normally, only the member functions of Derived have such access. However, we can use C++'s friend feature to extend similar access to other outside code.

Putting the pieces together, we get the following:

There are two other functions. The goal is to allow f1() to use Derived objects polymorphically where a Base is expected, yet prevent all other functions (including f2()) from doing so.

```
void f1()
{
  Derived d;
  SomeFunc( d ); // works, OK
}
```

```
void f2()
{
  Derived d;
  SomeFunc( d ); // we want to prevent this
}
```

Demonstrate how to achieve this effect.

The answer is to write:

```
class Derived : private Base
{
public:
  void VirtFunc();
  // ...
  friend void f1();
};
```

This solves the problem cleanly, although it does give f1() greater access than f1() had in the original version.

Memory and Resource Management

Smart pointers and `std::auto_ptr` are key tools at our disposal for safe and efficient management of memory and other resources, including real-world objects such as disk files and database transaction locks. How can we safely use `auto_ptr` and use common design patterns to adapt it in order to avoid common pitfalls? Can you use `auto_ptr` as a class member, and what must you absolutely be aware of if you do elect to use it that way? Finally, can you avoid the problem by doing better, by writing a special-purpose smart pointer designed to hold a member object at arm's length? Indeed you can. Indeed you can...

ITEM 29: USING auto_ptr   DIFFICULTY: 5

This Item illustrates a common pitfall with using `auto_ptr`. What is the problem, and how can you solve it?

1. Consider the following function, which illustrates a common mistake when using `auto_ptr`:

```
template<typename T>
void f( size_t n ) {
  auto_ptr<T> p1( new T );
  auto_ptr<T> p2( new T[n] );

  // ... more processing ...
}
```

What is wrong with this code? Explain.

2. How would you fix the problem? Consider as many options as possible, including the Adapter pattern, alternatives to the problematic construct, and alternatives to `auto_ptr`.

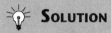 **SOLUTION**

Problem: Arrays and `auto_ptr` Don't Mix

1. Consider the following function, which illustrates a common mistake when using `auto_ptr`:

```
template<typename T>
void f( size_t n ) {
  auto_ptr<T> p1( new T );
  auto_ptr<T> p2( new T[n] );

  // ... more processing ...
}
```

What is wrong with this code? Explain.

Every `delete` must match the form of its `new`. If you use single-object `new`, you must use single-object `delete`; if you use the array form of `new[]`, you must use the array form of `delete[]`. Doing otherwise yields undefined behavior, as illustrated in the following slightly modified code.

```
T* p1 = new T;
// delete[] p1; // error
delete p1;       // ok - this is what auto_ptr does

T* p2 = new T[10];
delete[] p2;     // ok
// delete p2;    // error - this is what auto_ptr does
```

The problem with p2 is that `auto_ptr` is intended to contain only single objects, so it always calls `delete`, not `delete[]`, on the pointer it owns. This means that using plain `delete`, p1 will be cleaned up correctly, but p2 will not.

What will actually happen when you use the wrong form of `delete` depends on your compiler. The best you can expect is a resource leak. A more typical result is memory corruption soon followed by a core dump. To see this effect, try the following complete program on your favorite compiler:

```
#include <iostream>
#include <memory>
#include <string>
using namespace std;
```

```
int c = 0;

class X {
public:
  X() : s( "1234567890" ) { ++c; }
 ~X()                     { --c; }
     string s;
};

template<typename T>
void f( size_t n )
{
  {
    auto_ptr<T> p1( new T );
    auto_ptr<T> p2( new T[n] );
  }
  cout << c << " ";    // report # of X objects
}                      // that currently exist

int main()
{
  while( true )
  {
    f<X>(100);
  }
}
```

This program will usually either crash or else output a running update of the number of leaked X objects. (For extra fun, try running a system-monitoring tool in another window that shows your system's total memory usage. It will help you to appreciate how bad the leak can be if the program doesn't crash right off.)

Aside on a Non-problem: Zero-Length Arrays Are Okay

What if `f()`'s parameter is zero (for example, in the call `f<int>(0)`)? Then the second new turns into `new T[0]`, and programmers often wonder: "Hmm, is this okay? Can we have a zero-length array?"

The answer is yes. Zero-length arrays are perfectly okay, kosher, and fat-free. The result of `new T[0]` is just a pointer to an array with zero elements, and that pointer behaves just like any other result of `new T[n]` including the fact that you may not attempt to access more than n elements of the array. In this case, you may not attempt to access any elements at all because there aren't any.

From 5.3.4 [expr.new], paragraph 7:

> *When the value of the expression in a direct-new-declarator is zero, the allocation function is called to allocate an array with no elements. The pointer returned by the new-expression is non-null. [Note: If the library*

allocation function is called, the pointer returned is distinct from the pointer to any other object.]

"If you can't do anything with zero-length arrays (other than remember their address)," you may wonder, "why should they be allowed?" One important reason is that it makes it easier to write code that does dynamic array allocation. For example, the function f() above would be needlessly more complex if it were forced to check the value of its n parameter before performing the new T[n] call.

Of course, getting back to the main problem, just because zero-length arrays are legal doesn't mean we can get an auto_ptr to own one, any more than we can get an auto_ptr to own an array of any other length. We can't. The array-deletion problem remains.

2. How would you fix the problem? Consider as many options as possible, including the Adapter pattern, alternatives to the problematic construct, and alternatives to auto_ptr.

There are several options (some better, some worse). Here are four:

Option 1: Roll Your Own auto_array

This can be both easier and harder than it sounds.

Option 1 (a): ... By Deriving from auto_ptr (Score: 0 / 10)

Bad idea. For example, you'll have a lot of fun reproducing all the ownership and helper-class semantics. This might be tried only by true gurus, but true gurus would never try it because there are easier ways.

Advantages: Few.
Disadvantages: Too many to count.

Option 1 (b): ... By Cloning auto_ptr Code (Score: 8 / 10)

The idea here is to take the code from your library's implementation of auto_ptr, clone it (renaming it auto_array or something like that), and change the delete statements to delete[] statements.

Advantages:

a) *Easy to implement (once).* We don't need to hand-code our own auto_array, and we keep all the semantics of auto_ptr automatically, which helps avoid surprises for future maintenance programmers who are already familiar with auto_ptr.

b) *No significant space or time overhead.*

Disadvantage:

a) *Hard to maintain.* You'll probably want to be careful to keep your `auto_array` in sync with your library's `auto_ptr` when you upgrade to a new compiler/library version or switch compiler/library vendors.

Option 2: Use the Adapter Pattern (Score: 7 / 10)

This option came out of a discussion I had with C++ World attendee Henrik Nordberg, after one of my talks. Henrik's first reaction to the problem code was to wonder whether it would be easiest to write an adapter to make the standard `auto_ptr` work correctly, instead of rewriting `auto_ptr` or using something else. This idea has some real advantages and deserves analysis despite its few drawbacks.

Here's the idea. Instead of writing

```
auto_ptr<T> p2( new T[n] );
```

we write

```
auto_ptr< ArrDelAdapter<T> >
  p2( new ArrDelAdapter<T>(new T[n]) );
```

where the `ArrDelAdapter` (array deletion adapter) has a constructor that takes a T* and a destructor that calls `delete[]` on that pointer:

```
template<typename T>
class ArrDelAdapter {
public:
  ArrDelAdapter( T* p ) : p_(p) { }
  ~ArrDelAdapter() { delete[] p_; }
  // operators like "->" "T*" and other helpers
private:
  T* p_;
};
```

Since there is only one `ArrDelAdapter<T>` object, the single-object delete statement in `~auto_ptr()` is fine. Because `~ArrDelAdapter<T>` correctly calls `delete[]` on the array, the original problem has been solved.

Sure, this may not be the most elegant and beautiful approach in the world, but at least we didn't have to hand-code our own `auto_array` template!

Advantage:

a) *Easy to implement (initially).* We don't need to write an `auto_array`. In fact, we get to keep all the semantics of `auto_ptr` automatically, which helps avoid surprises for future maintenance programmers who are already familiar with `auto_ptr`.

Disadvantages:

a) *Hard to read.* This solution is rather verbose.

b) *(Possibly) hard to use.* Any code later in f that uses the value of the p2 auto_ptr will need syntactic changes, which will often be made more cumbersome by extra indirections.

c) *Incurs space and time overhead.* This code requires extra space to store the required adapter object for each array. It also requires extra time, because it performs twice as many memory allocations (this can be ameliorated by using an overloaded operator new), and then an extra indirection each time calling code accesses the contained array.

Having said all that, even though other alternatives turn out to be better in this particular case, I was very pleased to see people immediately think of using the Adapter pattern. Adapter is widely applicable and one of the core patterns every programmer should know.

 Guideline

Know about and use design patterns.

Just a final note on Option 2: It's worth pointing out that writing

```
auto_ptr< ArrDelAdapter<T> >
  p2( new ArrDelAdapter<T>(new T[n]) );
```

isn't much different from writing

```
auto_ptr< vector<T> > p2( new vector<T>(n) );
```

Think about that for a moment. For example, ask yourself, "What, if anything, am I gaining by allocating the vector dynamically that I wouldn't have if I just wrote vector p2(n);?" Then see Option 4.

Option 3: Replace auto_ptr with Hand-Coded Exception-Handling Logic (Score: 1 / 10)

Function f() uses auto_ptr for automatic cleanup and probably for exception safety. Instead, we could drop auto_ptr for the p2 array and hand-code our own exception-handling logic.

That is, instead of writing:

```
auto_ptr<T> p2( new T[n] );
//
// ... more processing ...
//
```

we write something like:

```
T* p2( new T[n] );
try {
  //
  // ... more processing
  //
}
delete[] p2;
```

Advantages:

a) *Easy to use.* This solution has little impact on the code in "more processing" that uses p2; probably all that's necessary is to remove .get() wherever it occurs.

b) *No significant space or time overhead.*

Disadvantages:

a) *Hard to implement.* This solution probably involves many more code changes than are suggested by the above. The reason is that while the auto_ptr for p1 will automatically clean up the new T no matter how the function exits, to clean up p2 we now have to write cleanup code along every code path that might exit the function. For example, consider the case in which "more processing" includes more branches, some of which end with "return;".

b) *Brittle.* See (a): Did we put the right cleanup code along all code paths?

c) *Hard to read.* See (a): The extra cleanup logic is likely to obscure the function's normal logic.

Option 4: Use a `vector` Instead of an Array (Score: 9.5 / 10)

Most of the problems we've encountered have been due to the use of C-style arrays. If appropriate, and it's almost always appropriate, it would be better to use a vector instead of a C-style array. After all, a major reason why vector exists in the standard library is to provide a safer and easier-to-use replacement for C-style arrays!

So instead of writing:

```
auto_ptr<T> p2( new T[n] );
```

we write:

```
vector<T> p2( n );
```

Advantages:

a) *Easy to implement (initially).* We still don't need to write an auto_array.

b) *Easy to read.* People who are familiar with the standard containers (and that should be everyone by now!) will immediately understand what's going on.

c) *Less brittle.* Since we're pushing down the details of memory management, our code is (usually) further simplified. We don't need to manage the buffer of T objects—that's the job of the vector<T> object.

d) No significant space or time overhead.

Disadvantages:

a) *Syntactic changes.* Any code later in f that uses the value of the p2 auto_ptr will need syntactic changes, although the changes will be fairly simple and not as drastic as those required by Option 2.

b) *(Sometimes) usability changes.* You can't instantiate any standard container (including a vector) of T objects if those T objects are not copy-constructible and assignable. Most types are both copy-constructible and assignable. But if they are not, this solution won't work.

Note that passing or returning a vector by value is more work than passing or returning an auto_ptr. I consider this objection somewhat of a red herring, however, because it's an unfair comparison. If you want to get the same effect, you simply pass a pointer or reference to the vector.

 Guideline

Prefer using vector instead of built-in (C-style) arrays.

ITEM 30: SMART POINTER MEMBERS, PART 1: A PROBLEM WITH auto_ptr   DIFFICULTY: 5

Most C++ programmers know they have to take special care for classes with pointer members. But what about classes with auto_ptr members? And can we make life safer for ourselves and our users by devising a smart pointer class designed specifically for class membership?

1. Consider the following class:

```
// Example 30-1
//
class X1
{
  // ...
```

```
private:
  Y* y_;
};
```

If an X1 object owns its pointed-at Y object, why can't the author of X1 use the compiler-generated destructor, copy constructor, and copy assignment?

2. What are the advantages and drawbacks of the following approach?

```
// Example 30-2
//
class X2
{
  // ...
private:
  auto_ptr<Y> y_;
};
```

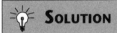 **SOLUTION**

Recap: Problems of Pointer Members

1. Consider the following class:

```
// Example 30-1
//
class X1
{
  // ...
private:
  Y* y_;
};
```

If an X1 object owns its pointed-at Y object, why can't the author of X1 use the compiler-generated destructor, copy constructor, and copy assignment?

If X1 owns its pointed-at Y, the compiler-generated versions will do the wrong thing. First, note that some function (probably an X1 constructor) has to create the owned Y object, and there has to be another function (likely the destructor X1::~X1()) that deletes it:

```
// Example 30-1(a): Ownership semantics.
//
{
  X1 a; // allocates a new Y object and points at it

  // ...
```

```
} // as a goes out of scope and is destroyed, it
  // deletes the pointed-at Y
```

Then use of the default memberwise copy construction will cause multiple X1 objects to point at the same Y object, which will cause strange results as modifying one X1 object changes the state of another, and which will also cause a double `delete` to take place:

```
// Example 30-1(b): Sharing, and double delete.
//
{
  X1 a;    // allocates a new Y object and points at it

  X1 b( a ); // b now points at the same Y object as a

  // ... manipulating a and b modifies
  // the same Y object ...

} // as b goes out of scope and is destroyed, it
  // deletes the pointed-at Y... and so does a, oops
```

Any use of the default memberwise copy assignment will also cause multiple X1 objects to point at the same Y object, which will cause the same state sharing, the same double `delete`, and as an added bonus will also cause leaks when some objects are never deleted at all:

```
// Example 30-1(c): Sharing, double delete, plus leak.
//
{
  X1 a;    // allocates a new Y object and points at it

  X1 b;    // allocates a new Y object and points at it

  b = a; // b now points at the same Y object as a,
         // and no one points at the Y object that
         // was created by b

  // ... manipulating a and b modifies
  // the same Y object ...

} // as b goes out of scope and is destroyed, it
  // deletes the pointed-at Y... and so does a, oops

  // the Y object allocated by b is never deleted
```

In other code, we normally apply the good practice of wrapping bald pointers in manager objects that own them and simplify cleanup. If the Y member was held by such a manager object instead of by a bald pointer, wouldn't that ameliorate the situation? This brings us to the following key questions.

What About auto_ptr Members?

2. **What are the advantages and drawbacks of the following approach?**

```
// Example 30-2
//
class X2
{
  // ...
private:
  auto_ptr<Y> y_;
};
```

This has some benefits, but it doesn't do a whole lot to solve the problem that the automatically generated copy construction and copy assignment functions will do the wrong thing. It just makes them do different wrong things.

First, if X2 has any user-written constructors, making them exception-safe is easier because if an exception is thrown in the constructor, the auto_ptr will perform its cleanup automatically. The writer of X2 is still forced, however, to allocate his own Y object and hold it, however briefly, by a bald pointer before the auto_ptr object assumes ownership.

Next, the automatically generated destructor now does, in fact, do the right thing. As an X2 object goes out of scope and is destroyed, the auto_ptr<Y> destructor automatically performs cleanup by deleting the owned Y object. Even so, there is a subtle caveat here that has already caught me once: If you rely on the automatically generated destructor, then that destructor will be defined in each translation unit that uses X2. That means that the definition of Y must be visible to pretty much anyone who uses an X2. This is not so good if Y is a Pimpl, for example, and the whole point is to hide Y's definition from clients of X2. So you can rely on the automatically generated destructor, but only if the full definition of Y is supplied along with X2 (for example, if x2.h includes y.h):

```
// Example 30-2(a): Y must be defined.
//
{
  X2 a; // allocates a new Y object and points at it

  // ...

} // as a goes out of scope and is destroyed, it
  // deletes the pointed-at Y, and this can only
  // happen if the full definition of Y is available
```

If you don't want to provide the definition of Y, you must write the X2 destructor explicitly, even if it's empty.

Next, the automatically generated copy constructor will no longer have the double-delete problem described in Example 30-1(b). That's the good news. The not-so-good news is that the automatically generated version introduces another problem—

grand theft. The X2 object being constructed rips away the Y belonging to the copied-from X2 object, including all knowledge of the Y object.

```
// Example 30-2(b): Grand theft pointer.
//
{
  X2 a; // allocates a new Y object and points at it

  X2 b( a ); // b rips away a's Y object, leaving a's
             // y_ member with a null auto_ptr

  // if a attempts to use its y_ member, it won't
  // work; if you're lucky, the problem will manifest
  // as an immediate crash, otherwise it will likely
  // manifest as a difficult-to-diagnose intermittent
  // failure
}
```

The only redeeming point about the grand theft, and it isn't much, is that at least the automatically generated X2 copy constructor gives some fair warning that theft-like behavior may be impending.[1] Why? Because its signature will be X2::X2(X2&). Note that it takes its parameter by reference to non-const. That's what auto_ptr's copy constructor does, after all, and so X2's automatically generated one has to follow suit. This is pretty subtle, though, but at least it prevents copying from a const X2.

Finally, the automatically generated copy assignment operator will no longer have either the double-delete problem or the leak problem, both of which were described in Example 30-1(c). That's the good news. Alas, again, there's some not-so-good news. The same grand theft occurs: The assigned-to X2 object rips away the Y belonging to assigned-from X2 object, including all knowledge of the Y object, and in addition it (possibly prematurely) deletes the Y object it originally owned.

```
// Example 30-2(c): More grand theft pointer.
//
{
  X2 a;   // allocates a new Y object and points at it

  X2 b;   // allocates a new Y object and points at it

  b = a; // b deletes its pointed-at Y, rips away
         // a's Y, and leaves a with a null auto_ptr
         // again

  // as in Example 30-2(b), any attempts by a to use its
  // y_ member will be disastrous
}
```

---

1. Alas, the non-constness of the parameter is rather invisible. The function is silently generated by the compiler, and you never actually get to see the signature appear as human-readable code anywhere.

Similarly above, at least the thieving behavior is hinted at, because the automatically generated function will be declared as X2& X2::operator=(X2&), thus advertising (albeit in the fine print, not in a front-page banner headline) that the operand can be modified.

In summary, then, auto_ptr does give some benefits, particularly by automating cleanup for constructors and the destructor. It does not, however, of itself answer the main original problems in this case—that we have to write our own copy construction and copy assignment for X2 or else disable them if copying doesn't make sense for the class. For that, we can do better with something a little more special-purpose.

Variations on a Theme by ValuePtr

The meat of this miniseries of Items involves developing successively refined versions of a ValuePtr template that is more suitable than auto_ptr for the kinds of uses outlined above.

A note on exception specifications: For reasons I won't go into here, exception specifications are not as useful as you might think. On the other hand, it is important to know which exceptions a function might throw, especially if it is known to throw none at all, giving the nothrow guarantee. You don't need exception specifications to document behavior, so I am going to assert the following:

> *For every version of ValuePtr<T> presented in these two Items, all member functions provide the nothrow guarantee except that construction or assignment from a ValuePtr<U> (where U could be T) might emit an exception thrown from a T constructor.*

Now let's get into the meat of it in Item 31.

ITEM 31: SMART POINTER MEMBERS, PART 2: TOWARD A ValuePtr   DIFFICULTY: 6

Can we make life safer for ourselves and our users by devising a smart pointer class designed specifically for class membership?

1. Write a suitable ValuePtr template that is used as shown here:

```
// Example 31-1
//
class X
{
  // ...
private:
  ValuePtr<Y> y_;
};
```

to suit three specific circumstances:

a) Copying and assigning ValuePtrs is not allowed.

b) Copying and assigning ValuePtrs is allowed and has the semantics of creating a copy of the owned Y object using the Y copy constructor.

c) Copying and assigning ValuePtrs is allowed and has the semantics of creating a copy of the owned Y object, which is performed using a virtual Y::Clone() method if present and the Y copy constructor otherwise.

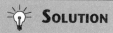 **SOLUTION**

A Simple ValuePtr: **Strict Ownership Only**

1. Write a suitable ValuePtr template that is used as shown here:

```
// Example 31-1
//
class X
{
  // ...
private:
  ValuePtr<Y> y_;
};
```

We are going to consider three cases. In all three, the constructor benefit still applies: Cleanup is automated and there's less work for the writer of X::X() to be exception-safe and avoid leaks from failed constructors.[2] Also, in all three, the destructor restriction still applies: Either the full definition of Y must accompany X, or the X destructor must be explicitly provided, even if it's empty.

to suit three specific circumstances:

a) Copying and assigning ValuePtrs is not allowed.

There's really not much to it:

```
// Example 31-2(a): Simple case: ValuePtr without
// copying or assignment.
//
template<typename T>
```

---

2. It is also possible to have ValuePtr itself perform the construction of the owned Y object, but I will omit that for clarity and because it pretty much just gives ValuePtr<Y> the same Y value semantics, begging the question: Why not just use a plain old Y member?

```
class ValuePtr
{
public:
  explicit ValuePtr( T* p = 0 ) : p_( p ) { }

  ~ValuePtr() { delete p_; }
```

Of course, there has to be some way to access the pointer, so add something like the following, which parallels `std::auto_ptr`:

```
  T& operator*() const { return *p_; }

  T* operator->() const { return p_; }
```

What else might we need? For many smart pointer types, it can make sense to provide additional facilities that parallel `auto_ptr`'s `reset()` and `release()` functions to let users arbitrarily change which object is owned by a `ValuePtr`. It may seem at first as if such facilities would be a good idea because they contribute to `ValuePtr`'s intended purpose and usage as a class member. Consider, for example, Examples 22-2 and 22-3 in Item 22, where the class member holds a Pimpl pointer and it's desirable to write an exception-safe assignment operator. Then you need a way to swap `ValuePtrs` without copying the owned objects. But providing `reset()`- and `release()`-like functions isn't the right way to do it because it allows too much. It would let users do what they need for swapping and exception safety, but it would also open the door for many other (unneeded) options that don't contribute to the purpose of `ValuePtr` and can cause problems if abused.

So what to do? Instead of providing overly general facilities, understand your requirements well enough to provide just the facility you really need:

```
  void Swap( ValuePtr& other ) { swap( p_, other.p_ ); }

private:
  T* p_;

  // no copying
  ValuePtr( const ValuePtr& );
  ValuePtr& operator=( const ValuePtr& );
};
```

We take ownership of the pointer and delete it afterward. We handle the null pointer case, and copying and assignment are specifically disabled in the usual way by declaring them private and not defining them. Construction is explicit as good practice to avoid implicit conversions, which are never needed by `ValuePtr`'s intended audience.

This part was pretty straightforward, but the next steps have some subtleties attached.

Copy Construction and Copy Assignment

b) Copying and assigning ValuePtrs is allowed and has the semantics of creating a copy of the owned Y object using the Y copy constructor.

Here's one way to write it that satisfies the requirements but isn't as general purpose as it could be. It's the same as Example 31-2(a), but with copy construction and copy assignment defined:

```
// Example 31-2(b): ValuePtr with copying and
// assignment, take 1.
//
template<typename T>
class ValuePtr
{
public:
  explicit ValuePtr( T* p = 0 ) : p_( p ) { }

  ~ValuePtr() { delete p_; }

  T& operator*() const { return *p_; }

  T* operator->() const { return p_; }

  void Swap( ValuePtr& other ) { swap( p_, other.p_ ); }

  //--- new code begin ----------------------------
  ValuePtr( const ValuePtr& other )
    : p_( other.p_ ? new T( *other.p_ ) : 0 ) { }
```

Note that it's important to check whether other's pointer is null or not. Because now, however, operator=() is implemented in terms of copy construction, we have to put the check in only one place.

```
  ValuePtr& operator=( const ValuePtr& other )
  {
    ValuePtr temp( other );
    Swap( temp );
    return *this;
  }
  //--- new code end ------------------------------

private:
  T* p_;
};
```

This satisfies the stated requirements because, in the intended usage, there's no case in which we will be copying or assigning from a ValuePtr that manages any type other than T. If that's all we know you'll ever need, that's fine. But whenever we design a class, we should at least consider designing for extensibility if it doesn't cost us much extra work and could make the new facility more useful to users in the future.

At the same time, we need to balance such "design for reusability" with the danger of overengineering—that is, of providing an overly complex solution to a simple problem. This brings us to the next point.

Templated Construction and Templated Assignment

One question to consider is: What is the impact on the Example 31-2(b) code if we want to allow for the possibility of assigning between different types of ValuePtr in the future? That is, we want to be able to copy or assign a ValuePtr<X> to a ValuePtr<Y> if X is convertible to Y.

It turns out that the impact is minimal. Duplicate the copy constructor and the copy assignment operators with templated versions that just add template<typename U> in front and take a parameter of type ValuePtr<U>&, as follows:

```cpp
// Example 31-2(c): ValuePtr with copying and
// assignment, take 2.
//
template<typename T>
class ValuePtr
{
public:
  explicit ValuePtr( T* p = 0 ) : p_( p ) { }

  ~ValuePtr() { delete p_; }

  T& operator*() const { return *p_; }

  T* operator->() const { return p_; }

  void Swap( ValuePtr& other ) { swap( p_, other.p_ ); }

  ValuePtr( const ValuePtr& other )
    : p_( other.p_ ? new T( *other.p_ ) : 0 ) { }

  ValuePtr& operator=( const ValuePtr& other )
  {
    ValuePtr temp( other );
    Swap( temp );
    return *this;
  }

  //--- new code begin ----------------------------
  template<typename U>
  ValuePtr( const ValuePtr<U>& other )
    : p_( other.p_ ? new T( *other.p_ ) : 0 ) { }

  template<typename U>
  ValuePtr& operator=( const ValuePtr<U>& other )
  {
    ValuePtr temp( other );
```

```
    Swap( temp );
    return *this;
  }

private:
  template<typename U> friend class ValuePtr;
  //--- new code end -----------------------------

T* p_;
};
```

Did you notice the trap we avoided? We still need to write the nontemplated forms of copying and assignment in order to suppress the automatically generated versions, because a templated constructor is never a copy constructor and a templated assignment operator is never a copy assignment operator. For more information about this, see *Exceptional C++* [Sutter00] Item 5.

There is still one subtle caveat, but fortunately it's not a big deal. I'd say that it's not even our responsibility as the authors of ValuePtr. The caveat is this: With either the templated or nontemplated copy and assignment functions, the source object, other, could still be holding a pointer to a derived type, in which case we're slicing. For example:

```
class A {};
class B : public A {};
class C : public B {};

ValuePtr<A> a1( new B );
ValuePtr<B> b1( new C );

// calls copy constructor, slices
ValuePtr<A> a2( a1 );

// calls templated constructor, slices
ValuePtr<A> a3( b1 );

// calls copy assignment, slices
a2 = a1;

// calls templated assignment, slices
a3 = b1;
```

I point this out because this is the sort of thing one shouldn't forget to write up in the ValuePtr documentation to warn users, preferably in a "Don't Do That" section. There's not much else we, the authors of ValuePtr, can do in code to stop this kind of abuse.

So which is the right solution to problem 1(b), Example 31-2(b) or Example 31-2(c)? Both are good solutions, and it's really a judgment call based on your own experience at balancing design-for-reuse and overengineering-avoidance. I imagine that minimalist-design advocates would automatically use 2(b) because it's enough to satisfy the minimum requirements. I can also imagine situations in which ValuePtr is in a library written by one group and shared by several distinct teams, and in which 2(c) will end up saving overall development effort through reuse and the prevention of reinvention.

Adding Extensibility Using Traits

But what if Y has a virtual Clone() method? It may seem from Item 30 Example 30-1 that X always creates its own owned Y object, but it might get it from a factory or from a new expression of some derived type. As we've already seen, in such a case the owned Y object might not really be a Y object at all, but of some type derived from Y, and copying it as a Y would slice it at best and render it unusable at worst. The usual technique in this kind of situation is for Y to provide a special virtual Clone() member function that allows complete copies to be made even without knowing the complete type of the object pointed at.

What if someone wants to use a ValuePtr to hold such an object, that can only be copied using a function other than the copy constructor? This is the point of our final question.

   **c) Copying and assigning ValuePtrs is allowed and has the semantics of cre-
       ating a copy of the owned Y object, which is performed using a virtual
       Y::Clone() method if present and the Y copy constructor otherwise.**

In the ValuePtr template, we don't know what our contained T type really is; we don't know whether it has a virtual Clone() function. Therefore, we don't know the right way to copy it. Or do we?

One solution is to apply a technique widely used in the C++ standard library itself, namely traits. (For more about traits, turn to Item 4.) To implement a traits-based approach, let's first change Example 31-2(c) slightly to remove some redundancy. You'll notice that both the templated constructor and the copy constructor have to check the source for nullness. Let's put all that work in a single place and have a single CreateFrom() function that builds a new T object. In a moment, we'll also see another reason to do it this way.

```
// Example 31-2(d): ValuePtr with copying and
// assignment, Example 31-2(c) with a little
// factoring.
//
template<typename T>
class ValuePtr
{
public:
  explicit ValuePtr( T* p = 0 ) : p_( p ) { }

  ~ValuePtr() { delete p_; }
```

```
                        T& operator*() const { return *p_; }

                        T* operator->() const { return p_; }

                        void Swap( ValuePtr& other ) { swap( p_, other.p_ ); }

                        ValuePtr( const ValuePtr& other )
                          : p_( CreateFrom( other.p_ ) ) { } // changed

                        ValuePtr& operator=( const ValuePtr& other )
                        {
                          ValuePtr temp( other );
                          Swap( temp );
                          return *this;
                        }

                        template<typename U>
                        ValuePtr( const ValuePtr<U>& other )
                          : p_( CreateFrom( other.p_ ) ) { } // changed

                        template<typename U>
                        ValuePtr& operator=( const ValuePtr<U>& other )
                        {
                          ValuePtr temp( other );
                          Swap( temp );
                          return *this;
                        }

                 private:
                      //--- new code begin ----------------------------
                      template<typename U>
                      T* CreateFrom( const U* p ) const
                      {
                        return p ? new T( *p ) : 0;
                      }
                      //--- new code end ------------------------------

                        template<typename U> friend class ValuePtr;

                        T* p_;
                 };
```

Now, CreateFrom() gives us a nice hook to encapsulate all knowledge about different ways of copying a T.

Applying Traits

Now we can apply the traits technique using something like the following approach. Note that this is not the only way to apply traits. There are other ways besides traits to deal with different ways of copying a T. I chose to use a single traits class template with a single static Clone() member that calls whatever is needed to do the actual cloning, and that can be thought of as an adapter. This follows the style of char_traits, for example, where basic_string simply delegates the work of defining the character-handling policy to a traits class. (Alternatively, for example, the traits class could provide typedefs and other aids so that the ValuePtr template can figure out what to do, but still have to do it itself. I don't like that because it feels like a needless division of responsibilities. For something this simple, why have one place figure out the right thing to do, but a different place actually do it?)

```
template<typename T>
class ValuePtr
{
  // ...

  template<typename U>
  T* CreateFrom( const U* p ) const
  {
    // the "Do the Right Thing" fix... but how?
    return p ? VPTraits<U>::Clone( p ) : 0;
  }
};
```

We want VPTraits to be a template that does the actual cloning work, where the main template's implementation of Clone() uses U's copy constructor. Two notes: First, since ValuePtr assumes responsibility for the null check, VPTraits::Clone() doesn't have to do it; and second, if T and U are different, this function can compile only if a U* is convertible to a T*, in order to correctly handle polymorphic cases when T is Base and U is Derived.

```
template<typename T>
class VPTraits
{
public:
  static T* Clone( const T* p ) { return new T( *p ); }
};
```

Then VPTraits is specialized as follows for any given Y that does not want to use copy construction. For example, say that some Y has a virtual Y* CloneMe() function, and some Z has a virtual void CopyTo(Z&) function. Then VPTraits<Y> is specialized to let that function do the cloning:

```
// The most work any user has to do, and it only
// needs to be done once, in one place:
//
template<>
class VPTraits<Y>
{
public:
  static Y* Clone( const Y* p )
    { return p->CloneMe(); }
```

```
};

template<>
class VPTraits<Z>
{
public:
  static Z* Clone( const Z* p )
    { Z* z = new Z; p->CopyTo(*z); return z; }
};
```

This is much better because the design is closed for modification but open for extension, and it will work with whatever flavor and signature of CloneMe() is ever invented in the future. Clone() only needs to create the object under the covers in whatever way it deems desirable, and the only visible result is a pointer to the new object—another good argument for strong encapsulation.

To use ValuePtr with a brand new type Y that was invented centuries after ValuePtr was written and its authors turned to dust, the new fourth-millennium user (or author) of Y merely needs to specialize VPTraits once for all time, then use ValuePtr<Y>s all over the place in her code wherever desired. That's pretty easy. And if Y doesn't have a virtual Clone() function, the user (or author) of Y doesn't even need to do that, but can use ValuePtr without any work at all.

A brief coda: Since VPTraits has only a single static function template, why make it a class template instead of just a function template? The main motive is for encapsulation (in particular, better name management) and extensibility. We want to avoid cluttering the global namespace with free functions. The function template could be put at namespace scope in whatever namespace ValuePtr itself is supplied in. But even then, this couples it more tightly to ValuePtr as opposed to use by other code also in that namespace. The Clone() function template may be the only kind of trait we need today, but what if we need new ones tomorrow? If the additional traits are functions, we'd otherwise have to continue cluttering things up with extra free functions. But what if the additional traits are typedefs or even class types? VPTraits gives us a nice place to encapsulate all those things.

ValuePtr **with Traits**

Here is the code for a ValuePtr that incorporates cloning traits, along with all the earlier requirements in Question 3.[3] Note that the only change from Example 31-2(d) is a

---

3. Alternatively, one might also choose to provide a traits object as an additional ValuePtr template parameter Traits that just defaults to VPTraits<T> the same way std::basic_string does it.

    ```
    template<typename T, typename Traits = VPTraits<T> >
    class ValuePtr { /*...*/ };
    ```

    so that it's even possible for users to have different ValuePtr<X> objects in the same program copy in various ways. That additional flexibility doesn't seem to make a lot of sense in this particular case, so I'm not doing it that way—but be aware of what's possible.

one-line change to ValuePtr and one new template with a single simple function. Now that's what I call minimum impact, given all of the flexibility we've just bought.

```
// Example 31-2(e): ValuePtr with copying and
// assignment and full traits-based
// customizability.
//
//--- new code begin -------------------------------
template<typename T>
class VPTraits
{
static T* Clone( const T* p ) { return new T( *p ); }
};
//--- new code end ---------------------------------

  template<typename T>
class ValuePtr
{
public:
  explicit ValuePtr( T* p = 0 ) : p_( p ) { }

  ~ValuePtr() { delete p_; }

  T& operator*() const { return *p_; }

  T* operator->() const { return p_; }

  void Swap( ValuePtr& other ) { swap( p_, other.p_ ); }

  ValuePtr( const ValuePtr& other )
    : p_( CreateFrom( other.p_ ) ) { }

  ValuePtr& operator=( const ValuePtr& other )
  {
    ValuePtr temp( other );
    Swap( temp );
    return *this;
  }

  template<typename U>
  ValuePtr( const ValuePtr<U>& other )
    : p_( CreateFrom( other.p_ ) ) { }

  template<typename U>
  ValuePtr& operator=( const ValuePtr<U>& other )
  {
    ValuePtr temp( other );
    Swap( temp );
    return *this;
  }

private:
  template<typename U>
```

```
  T* CreateFrom( const U* p ) const
  {
//--- new code begin ---------------------------
    return p ? VPTraits<U>::Clone( p ) : 0;
//--- new code end ---------------------------
  }

  template<typename U> friend class ValuePtr;

  T* p_;
};
```

A Usage Example

Here is an example that shows the typical implementation of the major functions (construction, destruction, copying, and assignment) for a class that uses our final version of ValuePtr, ignoring more-detailed issues, such as whether the destructor ought to be present (or inline) because Y is or is not defined.

```
// Example 31-3: Sample usage of ValuePtr.
//
class X
{
public:
  X() : y_( new Y(/*...*/) ) { }

  ~X() { }

  X( const X& other ) : y_( new Y(*(other.y_) ) ) { }

  void Swap( X& other ) { y_.Swap( other.y_ ); }

  X& operator=( const X& other )
  {
    X temp( other );
    Swap( temp );
    return *this;
  }

private:
  ValuePtr<Y> y_;
};
```

Summary

One moral I would like you to take away from this Item is to always be aware of extensibility as you're designing.

 Guideline

By default, prefer to design for reuse.

While avoiding the trap of overengineering, always be aware of a longer-term view. You can always decide to reject it, but always be aware of it, so that you save time and effort in the long run, both for yourself and for all the grateful users who will be happily reusing your code with their own new classes for years to come.

Free Functions and Macros

Other sections in this book have focused on C++'s powerful support for generic programming and object-oriented programming. Still and all, there's something to be said for plain old functions, and even for the macro facilities inherited (so to speak) from the C language.

Have you ever used a language that supported nested functions? If so, you might have wondered whether it's possible, or worthwhile, to try to get the same effect in C++, and you can find the answer in Item 33. What are preprocessor macros good for, even though much of the time they can be downright evil? Turn to Items 34 and 35 for these answers and more.

But first, there's a certain kind of "machine-like" programming structure that's incredibly useful in many application domains and crops up frequently in real-world systems. From a language point of view, this structure can often make it desirable to write functions that return pointers to—themselves! What is this programming structure, and how can we write such odd-looking recursive function declarations? For the answer, turn to Item 32.

ITEM 32: RECURSIVE DECLARATIONS   DIFFICULTY: 6

Can you write a function that returns a pointer to itself? If so, why would you want to?

1. What is a pointer to function? How can it be used?
2. Assume it is possible to write a function that can return a pointer to itself. That function could equally well return a pointer to any function with the same signature as itself. When might this be useful? Explain.
3. Is it possible to write a function f() that returns a pointer to itself? It should be usable in the following natural way:

```
// Example 32-3
//
// FuncPtr is a typedef for a pointer to a
// function with the same signature as f()
//
FuncPtr p = f();        // executes f()
(*p)();                 // executes f()
```

If it is possible, demonstrate how. If it is not possible, explain why.

 SOLUTION

Function Pointers: Recap

1. What is a pointer to function? How can it be used?

Just as a pointer to an object lets you dynamically point at an object of a given type, a pointer to a function lets you dynamically point at a function with a given signature. For example:

```
// Example 32-1
//

// Create a typedef called FPDoubleInt for a function
// signature that takes a double and returns an int.
//
typedef int (*FPDoubleInt)( double );

// Use it.
//
int f( double ) { /* ... */ }
int g( double ) { /* ... */ }
int h( double ) { /* ... */ }

FPDoubleInt fp;
fp = f;
fp( 1.1 );      // calls f()
fp = g;
fp( 2.2 );      // calls g()
fp = h;
fp( 3.14 );     // calls h()
```

When applied well, pointers to functions can allow significant runtime flexibility. For example, the standard C function qsort() takes a pointer to a comparison function with a given signature, which allows calling code to extend qsort()'s behavior by providing a custom comparison function.

A Brief Look at State Machines

2. **Assume it is possible to write a function that can return a pointer to itself. That function could equally well return a pointer to any function with the same signature as itself. When might this be useful? Explain.**

Many situations come to mind, but one common example is when implementing a state machine.

In brief, a state machine is composed of a set of possible states, along with a set of legal transitions between those states. For example, a simple state machine might look something like Figure 6.

When we are in the Start state, if we receive the input a, we transition to state S2; otherwise, if we receive the input be, we transition to state Stop. Any other input is illegal in state Start. In state S2, if we receive the input see, we transition to state Stop; any other input is illegal in state S2. For this state machine, there are only two valid input streams: be and asee.

To implement a state machine, it is sometimes sufficient to make each state a function. All the state functions have the same signature and each one returns a pointer to the next function (state) to be called. For example, here is an oversimplified code fragment that illustrates the idea.

```
// Example 32-2
//
StatePtr Start( const string& input );
StatePtr S2   ( const string& input );
StatePtr Stop ( const string& input );
StatePtr Error( const string& input ); // error state
```

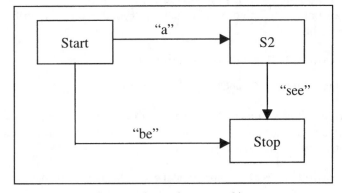

Figure 6: A sample state machine.

```
StatePtr Start( const string& input )
{
  if( input == "a" )
  {
    return S2;
  }
  else if( input == "be" )
  {
    return Stop;
  }
  else
  {
    return Error;
  }
}
```

See your favorite computer science textbook for more information about state machines and their uses.

Of course, the above code doesn't say what StatePtr is, and it's not necessarily obvious how to say what it should be. This leads us nicely into the final question.

How Can a Function Return a Pointer to Itself?

3. Is it possible to write a function f() that returns a pointer to itself? It should be usable in the following natural way:

```
// Example 32-3
//
// FuncPtr is a typedef for a pointer to a
// function with the same signature as f()
//
FuncPtr p = f();      // executes f()
(*p)();               // executes f()
```

If it is possible, demonstrate how. If it is not possible, explain why.

Yes, it's possible, but it's not obvious.

For example, one might first try using a typedef directly, writing code that looks something like this:

```
// Example 32-3(a): Naïve attempt (doesn't work)
//
typedef FuncPtr (*FuncPtr)(); // error
```

Alas, this kind of recursive typedef isn't allowed. Some people, thinking that the type system is just getting in the way, try to do an end run around the type system "nuisance" by casting to and from void*:

```
// Example 32-3(b): A nonstandard and nonportable hack
//
typedef void* (*FuncPtr)();

void* f() { return (void*)f; }  // cast to void*
```

```
FuncPtr p = (FuncPtr)(f());       // cast from void*
p();
```

This isn't a solution because it doesn't satisfy the criteria of the question. Worse, it is dangerous because it deliberately defeats the type system; it is onerous because it forces all users of f() to write casts. Worst of all, Example 32-3(b) is not supported by the standard. Although a void* is guaranteed to be big enough to hold the value of any object pointer, it is not guaranteed to be suitable to hold a function pointer. On some platforms, a function pointer is larger than an object pointer. Even if code like Example 32-3(b) happens to work on the compiler you're using today, it's not portable and may not work on another compiler, or even on the next release of your current compiler.

Of course, one way around this is to cast to and from another function pointer type instead of a simple void*:

```
// Example 32-3(c): Standard and portable,
// but nonetheless still a hack
//
typedef void (*VoidFuncPtr)();
typedef VoidFuncPtr (*FuncPtr)();

VoidFuncPtr f() { return (VoidFuncPtr)f; }
                            // cast to VoidFuncPtr

FuncPtr p = (FuncPtr)f(); // cast from VoidFuncPtr
p();
```

This code is technically legal, but it has all but one of the major disadvantages of Example 32-3(b). It is a dangerous hack because it deliberately defeats the type system. It imposes an unacceptable burden on all users of f() by requiring them to write casts. And, of course, it's still not really a solution at all because it doesn't meet the requirements of the problem.

Can we really do no better?

A Correct and Portable Way

Fortunately, we can get exactly the intended effect required by Question #3 in a completely type-safe and portable way, without relying on nonstandard code or type-unsafe casting. The way to do it is to add a level of indirection in the form of a proxy class that takes, and has an implicit conversion to, the desired pointer type.

```
// Example 32-3(d): A correct solution
//
class FuncPtr_;
typedef FuncPtr_ (*FuncPtr)();
```

```
class FuncPtr_
{
public:
  FuncPtr_( FuncPtr p ) : p_( p ) { }
  operator FuncPtr() { return p_; }
private:
  FuncPtr p_;
};
```

Now we can declare, define, and use f() naturally:

```
FuncPtr_ f() { return f; } // natural return syntax

int main()
{
  FuncPtr p = f();  // natural usage syntax
  p();
}
```

This solution has three main strengths:

1. It solves the problem as required. Better still, it's type-safe and portable.
2. Its machinery is transparent. You get natural syntax for the caller/user, and natural syntax for the function's own "`return myname;`" statement.
3. It probably has zero overhead. On modern compilers, the proxy class, with its storage and functions, should inline and optimize away to nothing.

Coda

Normally, a special-purpose `FuncPtr_` proxy class like this (which contains some old object and doesn't really care much about its type) just cries out to be templatized into a general-purpose `Holder` proxy. Alas, you can't just directly templatize the `FuncPtr_` class above, because then the `typedef` would have to look something like the following,

```
typedef Holder<FuncPtr> (*FuncPtr)();
```

which is self-referential.

ITEM 33: SIMULATING NESTED FUNCTIONS   DIFFICULTY: 5

C++ has nested classes, but not nested functions. When might nested functions be useful, and can they be simulated in C++?

1. What is a nested class? Why can it be useful?
2. What is a local class? Why can it be useful?

3. C++ does not support nested functions. That is, we cannot write something like

```
// Example 33-3
//
int f( int i )
{
  int j = i*2;

  int g( int k )  // not valid C++
  {
    return j+k;
  }

  j += 4;

  return g( 3 );
}
```

Demonstrate how it is possible to achieve the same effect in standard C++, and show how to generalize the solution.

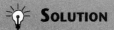 **SOLUTION**

Recap: Nested and Local Classes

C++ provides many useful tools for information hiding and dependency management. As we recap nested classes and local classes, don't fixate too much on the syntax and semantics. Rather, focus on how these features can be used to write solid, maintainable code and express good object designs—designs that prefer weak coupling and strong cohesion.

1. What is a nested class? Why can it be useful?

A nested class is a class enclosed within the scope of another class. For example:

```
// Example 33-1: Nested class
//
class OuterClass
{
/*...public, protected, or private...*/:
  class NestedClass
  {
    // ...
  };

  // ...
};
```

Nested classes are useful for organizing code and controlling access and dependencies. Nested classes obey access rules just as other parts of a class do. So, in Example 33-1, if `NestedClass` is `public`, then any outside code can name it as `Outer Class::NestedClass`. Often, nested classes contain private implementation details, and are therefore made `private`. In Example 33-1, if `NestedClass` is `private`, then only `OuterClass`'s members and friends can use `NestedClass`.

Note that you can't get the same effect with namespaces alone, because namespaces merely group names into distinct areas. Namespaces do not by themselves provide access control, whereas classes do. So, if you want to control access rights to a class, one tool at your disposal is to nest it within another class.

2. What is a local class? Why can it be useful?

A local class is a class defined within the scope of a function—any function, whether a member function or a free function. For example:

```
// Example 33-2: Local class
//
int f()
{
  class LocalClass
  {
    // ...
  };

  // ...
};
```

Like nested classes, local classes can be a useful tool for managing code dependencies. In Example 33-2, only the code within `f()` itself knows about `LocalClass` and is able to use it. This can be useful when `LocalClass` is, say, an internal implementation detail of `f()` that should never be advertised to other code.

You can use a local class in most places where you can use a nonlocal class, but there is a major restriction to keep in mind. A local or unnamed class cannot be used as a template parameter. From the C++ standard [C++98] section 14.3.1/2:

> *A local type, a type with no linkage, an unnamed type or a type compounded from any of these types shall not be used as a template-argument for a template type-parameter. [Example:*

```
template<class T>
class X { /* ... */ };
void f()
{
  struct S { /* ... */ };
  X<S> x3;  // error: local type used as
            //   template-argument
  X<S*> x4; // error: pointer to local type
```

```
                         // used as template-argument
    }
```

--end example]

Both nested classes and local classes are among C++'s many useful tools for information hiding and dependency management.

Nested Functions: Overview

Some languages (but not C++) allow nested functions, which have similarities to nested classes. A nested function is defined inside another function, the "enclosing function," such that:

- The nested function has access to the enclosing function's variables; and
- The nested function is local to the enclosing function—that is, it can't be called from elsewhere unless the enclosing function gives you a pointer to the nested function.

Just as nested classes can be useful because they help control the visibility of a class, nested functions can be useful because they help control the visibility of a function.

C++ does not have nested functions. But can we get the same effect? This brings us to the following key question.

3. C++ does not support nested functions. That is, we cannot write something like

```
// Example 33-3
//
int f( int i )
{
  int j = i*2;

  int g( int k )  // not valid C++
  {
    return j+k;
  }

  j += 4;

  return g( 3 );
}
```

Demonstrate how it is possible to achieve the same effect in standard C++, and show how to generalize the solution.

Yes, it is possible, with only a little code reorganization and a minor limitation. The basic idea is to turn a function into a function object. This discussion, not coincidentally, will also serve to nicely illustrate some of the power of function objects.

Attempts at Simulating Nested Functions in C++

To solve a problem like Question #3, most people start out by trying something like the following:

```
// Example 33-3(a): Naïve "local function object"
// approach (doesn't work)
//
int f( int i )
{
  int j = i*2;

  class g_
  {
  public:
    int operator()( int k )
    {
      return j+k;    // error: j isn't accessible
    }
  } g;

  j += 4;

  return g( 3 );
}
```

In Example 33-3(a), the idea is to wrap the function in a local class and call the function through a function object.

It's a nice idea, but it doesn't work for a simple reason: The local class object doesn't have access to the enclosing function's variables.

"Well," one might say, "why don't we just give the local class pointers or references to all the function's variables?" Indeed, that's usually the next attempt.

```
// Example 33-3(b): Naïve "local function object plus
// references to variables" approach (complex,
// fragile)
//
int f( int i )
{
  int j = i*2;

  class g_
  {
  public:
    g_( int& j ) : j_( j ) { }

    int operator()( int k )
    {
      return j_+k;  // access j via a reference
    }
```

```
private:
  int& j_;
} g( j );

j += 4;

return g( 3 );
}
```

All right, I have to admit that this "works"—but only barely. This solution is fragile, difficult to extend, and can rightly be considered a hack. For example, consider that just to add a new variable requires four changes:

a) Add the variable;

b) Add a corresponding private reference to g_;

c) Add a corresponding constructor parameter to g_; and

d) Add a corresponding initialization to g_::g_().

That's not very maintainable. It also isn't easily extended to multiple local functions. Couldn't we do better?

A Somewhat Improved Solution

We can do better by moving the variables themselves into the local class.

```
// Example 33-3(c): A better solution
//
int f( int i )
{
  class g_
  {
  public:
    int j;

    int operator()( int k )
    {
      return j+k;
    }
  } g;

  g.j = i*2;
  g.j += 4;

  return g( 3 );
}
```

This is a solid step forward. Now g_ doesn't need pointer or reference data members to point at external data; it doesn't need a constructor; and everything is much more natural all around. Note also that the technique is now extensible to any number of local functions, so let's go a little crazy and add some more local functions called x(), y(), and z(), and while we're at it, why not rename g_ itself to be more indicative of what the local class is actually doing?

```
// Example 33-3(d): Nearly there!
//
int f( int i )
{
  // Define a local class that wraps all
  // local data and functions.
  //
  class Local_
  {
  public:
    int j;

    // All local functions go here:
    //
    int g( int k )
    {
      return j+k;
    }
    void x() { /* ... */ }
    void y() { /* ... */ }
    void z() { /* ... */ }
  } local;

  local.j = i*2;
  local.j += 4;

  local.x();
  local.y();
  local.z();

  return local.g( 3 );
}
```

This still has the problem that when you need to initialize j using something other than default initialization, you have to add a clumsy constructor to the local class just to pass through the initialization value. The original question tried to initialize j to the value of i*2. Here, we've had to create j and then assign the value, which isn't exactly the same thing and could be difficult for more-complex types.

A Complete Solution

If you don't need f itself to be a *bona fide* function (for example, if you don't take pointers to it), you can turn the whole thing into a function object and elegantly support non-default initialization into the bargain.

```
// Example 33-3(e): A complete and nicely
// extensible solution
```

```
//
class f
{
  int  retval; // f's "return value"
  int  j;
  int  g( int k ) { return j + k; };
  void x() { /* ... */ }
  void y() { /* ... */ }
  void z() { /* ... */ }

public:
  f( int i )    // original function, now a constructor
    : j( i*2 )
  {
    j += 4;
    x();
    y();
    z();
    retval = g( 3 );
  }
  operator int() const // returning the result
  {
    return retval;
  }
};
```

The code is shown inline for brevity, but all the private members could also be hidden behind a Pimpl, giving the same full separation of interface from implementation we had with the original simple function.

Note that this approach is easily extensible to member functions. For example, suppose that f() is a member function instead of a free function, and we would like to write a nested function g() inside f() as follows:

```
// Example 33-4: This isn't legal C++, but it
// illustrates what we want: a local function
// inside a member function
//
class C
{
  int data_;

public:
  int f( int i )
  {
    // a hypothetical nested function
    int g( int i ) { return data_ + i; }

    return g( data_ + i*2 );
  }
};
```

We can express this by turning f() into a class, as demonstrated in Example 33-3(e), except whereas in Example 33-3(e) the class was at global scope, it is now a nested class and accessed via a passthrough helper function.

```cpp
// Example 33-4(a): The complete and nicely
// extensible solution, now applied to a
// member function
//
class C
{
  int data_;
  friend class C_f;
public:
  int f( int i );
};

class C_f
{
  C*  self;
  int retval;
  int g( int i ) { return self->data_ + i; }

public:
  C_f( C* c, int i ) : self( c )
  {
    retval = g( self->data_ + i*2 );
  }

  operator int() const { return retval; }
};

int C::f( int i ) { return C_f( this, i ); }
```

Summary

This approach illustrated above in Examples 33-3(e) and 33-4(a) simulates most of the features of local functions and is easily extensible to any number of local functions. Its main weakness is that it requires that all variables be defined at the start of the "function" and doesn't (easily) allow us to declare variables closer to point of first use. It's also more tedious to write than a local function would be, and it is clearly a workaround for a language limitation. But, in the end, it's not bad, and it demonstrates some of the power inherent in function objects over plain functions.

The purpose of this Item wasn't just to learn about how nice it might be to have local functions in C++. The purpose was, as always, to set a specific design problem, explore alternative methods for solving it, and weigh the solutions to pick the best-engineered option. Along the way, we also got to experiment with various C++ features and see through use what makes function objects useful.

When designing your programs, strive for simplicity and elegance wherever possible. Some of the intermediate above solutions would arguably "work" but should never be allowed to see the light of day in production code. They are complex, difficult to understand, and therefore difficult and expensive to maintain.

Guideline

Prefer clarity. Avoid complex designs. Eschew obfuscation.

Simpler designs are easier to code and test. Avoid complex solutions, which are almost certain to be fragile and harder to understand and maintain. While being careful to avoid the trap of overengineering, recognize that even if coming up with a judicious simple design takes a little extra time up front, the long-term benefits usually make that time well spent. Putting in a little time now often means saving more time later. And most people would agree that the "more time later" is better spent with the family at the cottage than slaving away over a hot keyboard, trying to find those last few bugs in a complicated rat's nest of code.

ITEM 34: PREPROCESSOR MACROS   DIFFICULTY: 4

Preprocessor macros are part of C++'s heritage from C. This Item considers whether they are still relevant in the modern C++ scheme of things.

With flexible features such as overloading and type-safe templates available, why would a C++ programmer ever write a preprocessor directive like "#define"?

 SOLUTION

C++ features often, but not always, cancel out the need for using #define. For example, "const int c = 42;" is superior to "#define c 42" because it provides type safety, and avoids accidental preprocessor edits, among other reasons.

There are, however, still a few good reasons to write #define.

1. Header Guards

This is the usual trick to prevent multiple header inclusions.

```
#ifndef MYPROG_X_H
#define MYPROG_X_H
```

```
// ... the rest of the header file x.h goes here...
#endif
```

2. Accessing Preprocessor Features

It's often nice to insert things such as line numbers and build times in diagnostic code. An easy way to do this is to use predefined standard macros such as __FILE__, __LINE__, __DATE__, and __TIME__. For the same and other reasons, it's often useful to use the stringizing and token-pasting preprocessor operators (# and ##).

3. Selecting Code at Compile Time (or Build-Specific Code)

This is an important, if overused, category of uses for the preprocessor. Although I am anything but a fan of preprocessor magic, there are things you just can't do as well, or at all, in any other way.

a) Debug Code

Sometimes, you want to build your system with certain "extra" pieces of code (typically, debugging information) and sometimes you don't.

```
void f()
{
#ifdef MY_DEBUG
  cerr << "some trace logging" << endl;
#endif
  // ... the rest of f() goes here...
}
```

The thing about this code, though, is that what we really have is two different programs. When we compile it with MY_DEBUG defined, we get source code that includes output to cerr, and the compiler will check that line's syntax and semantics, too. When we compile it without MY_DEBUG defined, we get a different program that does not include the output to cerr, and the compiler cannot verify the correctness of the excluded code.

Usually it is better to use a conditional expression instead of the #define.

```
void f()
{
  if( MY_DEBUG )
  {
    cerr << "some trace logging" << endl;
  }
```

```
    // ... the rest of f() goes here...
}
```

This way, there's only one program to compile and test, the compiler can validate all the code, and the compiler can easily eliminate the unreachable code if MY_DEBUG isn't true.

b) Platform-Specific Code

Usually, it's best to deal with platform-specific code using a factory pattern, because this approach makes for better code organization and runtime flexibility. Sometimes, however, there are just too few differences to justify a factory, and the preprocessor can be a useful way to switch optional code.

c) Variant Data Representations

A common example is that a module may define a list of error codes, which outside users should see as a simple enum with comments, but which inside the module should be stored in a map for easy lookup. That is:

```
// For outsiders
//
enum Error
{
  ERR_OK = 0,              // No error
  ERR_INVALID_PARAM = 1, // <description>
  ...
};

// For the module's internal use
//
map<Error,const char*> lookup;
lookup.insert( make_pair( ERR_OK,
                          (const char*)"No error" ) );
lookup.insert( make_pair( ERR_INVALID_PARAM,
                          (const char*)"<description>" ) );
...
```

We'd like to have both representations, without defining the actual information (code/message pairs) twice. With macro magic, we can simply write a list of errors as follows, creating the appropriate structure at compile time:

```
ERR_ENTRY( ERR_OK,            0, "No error" ),
ERR_ENTRY( ERR_INVALID_PARAM, 1, "<description>" ),
...
```

The implementations of ERR_ENTRY and related macros is left to the reader.

These are three common examples, but there are many more. Suffice it to say that although the C preprocessor should be avoided in many places, it still has its share of useful features that can, when used judiciously, make writing C++ code easier and safer.

 Guideline

Avoid preprocessor macros:
- *Except #include guards*
- *Except conditional compilation for portability or debugging in .cpp files (not in .h files!)*
- *Except #pragmas used to disable known-to-be-innocuous warnings, but such #pragmas must always be inside a "conditional compilation for portability" guard to prevent warnings from compilers that do not understand them*

To see what the inventor of the C++ language thinks of the preprocessor, check out section 18 of [Stroustrup94].

ITEM 35: #DEFINITION   DIFFICULTY: 4

What can and can't macros do? Not all compilers agree.

1. Demonstrate how to write a simple max() preprocessor macro that takes two arguments and evaluates to the one that is greater, using normal < comparison. What are the usual pitfalls in writing such a macro?
2. What can a preprocessor macro not create? Why not?

 SOLUTION

Common Macro Pitfalls

1. Demonstrate how to write a simple max() preprocessor macro that takes two arguments and evaluates to the one that is greater, using normal < comparison. What are the usual pitfalls in writing such a macro?

There are four major pitfalls, in addition to several further drawbacks. Focusing on the pitfalls first, here are common ways to go wrong when writing a macro.

1. Don't forget to put parentheses around arguments.

```
// Example 35-1(a): Paren pitfall #1: arguments
//
#define max(a,b) a < b ? b : a
```

The problem here is that the uses of the parameters a and b are not fully parenthesized. Macros only do straight textual substitution, so this can cause some unexpected results. For example:

```
max( i += 3, j )
```

expands to

```
i += 3 < j ? j : i += 3
```

which, because of operator precedence and language rules, actually means

```
i += ((3 < j) ? j : i += 3)
```

This could cause some long debugging sessions. There is also a problem related to sequence points and attempting to modify i twice between sequence points; more on this in a moment.

2. Don't forget to put parentheses around the whole expansion.

Fixing the first problem, we still fall prey to another subtlety.

```
// Example 35-1(b): Paren pitfall #2: expansion
//
#define max(a,b) (a) < (b) ? (b) : (a)
```

The problem now is that the entire expansion is not correctly parenthesized. For example:

```
k = max( i, j ) + 42;
```

expands to

```
k = (i) < (j) ? (j) : (i) + 42;
```

which, because of operator precedence, actually means

```
k = (((i) < (j)) ? (j) : ((i) + 42));
```

If i >= j, k is assigned the value of i+42, as intended. But if i < j, k is assigned the value of j.

We can fix problem #2 by putting parentheses around the entire macro expansion, but this leaves us with yet another problem:

3. Watch for multiple argument evaluation.

Consider what happens if one or both of the expressions has side effects:

```
// Example 35-1(c): Multiple argument evaluation
//
#define max(a,b) ((a) < (b) ? (b) : (a))

max( ++i, j )
```

If the result of ++i >= j, i gets incremented twice, which is probably not what the programmer intended:
```
((++i) < (j) ? (j) : (++i))
```

Similarly, consider

```
max( f(), pi )
```

which expands to

```
((f()) < (pi) ? (pi) : (f()))
```

If the result of f() >= pi, f() gets executed twice, which is almost certainly inefficient and often wrong.

Although we could work around the first two problems, this one is a corker. There is no solution as long as max is a macro.

4. Name tromping.

Finally, macros don't care about scope. (They don't care about much of anything; see [GotW] #63.[1]) They just perform textual substitution, no matter where the text is. This means that if we use macros at all, we have to be careful about what we name them. In particular, the biggest problem with the max macro is that it is highly likely to interfere with the standard max() function template:

```
// Example 35-1(d): Name tromping
//
#define max(a,b) ((a) < (b) ? (b) : (a))

#include <algorithm> // oops!
```

The problem is that inside header <algorithm>, there will be something like the following:

```
template<typename T> const T&
max(const T& a, const T& b);
```

Alas, the macro "helpfully" turns that into an uncompilable mess:

---

1. Available online at *http://www.gotw.ca/gotw/063.htm.*

```
template<typename T> const T&
((const T& a) < (const T& b) ? (const T& b) : (const T& a));
```

If you think that's easy to avoid by putting your macro definition after all #included header files (which really is a good idea in any case), just imagine what the macro does to all your other code that happens to have variables or other things that just happen to be named max.

If you have to write a macro, try to give it an unusual and hard-to-spell name that will be less likely to tromp on other names.

Other Macro Drawbacks

There are a few other major things a macro can't do:

5. Macros can't recurse.

We can write a recursive function, but it's impossible to write a recursive macro. As the C++ standard [C++98] says, in 16.3.4/2:

> If the name of the macro being replaced is found during this scan of the replacement list (not including the rest of the source file's pre-processing tokens), it is not replaced. Further, if any nested replacements encounter the name of the macro being replaced, it is not replaced. These nonreplaced macro name preprocessing tokens are no longer available for further replacement even if they are later (re)examined in contexts in which that macro name preprocessing token would otherwise have been replaced.

6. Macros don't have addresses.

It's possible to form a pointer to any free or member function (for example, to use it as a predicate), but it's not possible to form a pointer to a macro, because a macro has no address. Why not should be obvious—macros aren't code. A macro doesn't have any existence of its own, because it is only a glorified (and not particularly glorious) text substitution rule.

7. Macros are debugger-unfriendly.

In addition to the fact that macros change the underlying code before the compiler gets a chance to see it—and therefore can wreak havoc with variable names and other names—a macro can't be stepped into during debugging.

Have you heard the one about the scientists who started experimenting on lawyers instead of on laboratory macros? It was because…

There Are Some Things Even a Macro Won't Do

There are valid reasons to use macros (for details, turn to Item 34), but there are limits. This brings us to the final question.

2. What can a preprocessor macro not create? Why not?

In the standard, clause 2.1 defines the phases of translation. Preprocessing directives and macro expansions take place in phase 4. Thus, on a compliant compiler, it is not possible for a macro to create any of the following:

- a trigraph (trigraphs are replaced in phase 1);
- a universal character name (\uXXXX, replaced in phase 1);
- an end-of-line line-splicing backslash (replaced in phase 2);
- a comment (replaced in phase 3);
- another macro or preprocessing directive (expanded and executed in phase 4); or
- changes to a character literal (for example, `'x'`) or string literal (for example, `"hello, world"`) via macro names inside the strings.

For this last point, as noted in 16.3/8 footnote 7:

> *Since, by macro-replacement time, all character literals and string literals are preprocessing tokens, not sequences possibly containing identifier-like subsequences (see 2.1.1.2, translation phases), they are never scanned for macro names or parameters.*

A published article[2] once claimed that it's possible for a macro to create a comment as follows:

```
#define COMMENT SLASH(/)
#define SLASH(s) /##s
```

This is nonstandard and not portable, but it's an understandable mistake because it actually works on some popular compilers. Why does it work? Because those compilers don't implement the phases of translation correctly.

---

2.   M. Timperley. "A C/C++ Comment Macro" (*C/C++ Users Journal*, 19(1), January 2001).

Miscellaneous Topics

Some topics are important but don't lend themselves to easy pigeonholing. Our final five Items focus on four language features: initialization; forward declarations; typedef; and a concluding pair on namespaces. Items 39 and 40, in particular, finish off with answers to what is one of the most frequently asked questions about modern C++: When and how should you use namespaces, anyway? Enjoy.

ITEM 36: INITIALIZATION   DIFFICULTY: 3

What's the difference between direct initialization and copy initialization, and when are they used?

---

1. What is the difference between direct initialization and copy initialization?

2. Which of the following cases uses direct initialization, and which uses copy initialization?

```
class T : public S
{
public:
  T() : S(1),          // base initialization
        x(2) {}        // member initialization
  X x;
};

T f( T t )             // passing a function argument
{
  return t;            // returning a value
}

S s;
T t;
```

```
S& r = t;

reinterpret_cast<S&>(t);        // performing a reinterpret_cast
static_cast<S>(t);              // performing a static_cast
dynamic_cast<T&>(r);            // performing a dynamic_cast
const_cast<const T&>(t);        // performing a const_cast

try
{
   throw T();                   // throwing an exception
}
catch( T t )                    // handling an exception
{
}

f( T(s) );                      // functional-notation type conversion
S a[3] = { 1, 2, 3 };           // brace-enclosed initializers
S* p = new S(4);                // new expression
```

☀ SOLUTION

1. What is the difference between direct initialization and copy initialization?

Direct initialization means the object is initialized using a single (possibly conversion) constructor, and is equivalent to the form "T t(u);":

```
U u;
T t1(u); // calls T::T( U& ) or similar
```

Copy initialization means the object is initialized using the copy constructor, after first calling a user-defined conversion if necessary, and is equivalent to the form "T t = u;":

```
T t2 = t1;  // same type: calls T::T( T& ) or similar
T t3 = u;   // different type: calls T::T( T(u) )
            // or T::T( u.operator T() ) or similar
```

Aside: The reason for the "or similar" equivocation is that the copy and conversion constructors could take something slightly different from a plain reference (the reference could be const or volatile, or both), and the user-defined conversion constructor or operator could, in addition, take or return an object rather than a reference. Also, the copy and conversion constructors could have additional default arguments.

Note that in the last case ("T t3 = u;") the compiler could call both the user-defined conversion (to create a temporary object) and the T copy constructor (to construct t3 from the temporary), or it could choose to elide the temporary and construct t3 directly from u (which would end up being equivalent to "T t3(u);"). Either way, the unoptimized code must still be legal. In particular, the copy constructor must still be accessible, even if the call to it is optimized away.

In the C++ standard, the compiler's latitude to elide temporary objects has been restricted compared with the latitude compilers enjoyed in pre-standard times. Elision is still allowed, however, for this optimization and for the return value optimization. For more details, see *Exceptional C++* [Sutter00] Item 42 about the basics, and *Exceptional C++* Item 46 covering the change in the final standard.

Guideline

Prefer using the form "T t(u)" over "T t = u" for variable initialization.

---

2. **Which of the following cases uses direct initialization, and which uses copy initialization?**

In the standard, the thrilling section 8.5 covers most of these. There were also three tricks that don't involve initialization at all. Did you catch them?

```
class T : public S
{
public:
  T() : S(1),            // base initialization
        x(2) {}          // member initialization
  X x;
};
```

Base and member initialization both use direct initialization.

```
T f( T t )               // passing a function argument
{
  return t;              // returning a value
}
```

Passing and returning values both use copy initialization.

```
S s;
T t;
S& r = t;

reinterpret_cast<S&>(t);    // performing a reinterpret_cast
dynamic_cast<T&>(r);        // performing a dynamic_cast
const_cast<const T&>(t);    // performing a const_cast
```

Trick: No initialization of a new object is involved in these cases. Only references are created.

```
static_cast<S>(t);          // performing a static_cast
```

A static_cast uses direct initialization.

```
try
{
  throw T();              // throwing an exception
}
catch( T t )             // handling an exception
{
}
```

Throwing and catching an exception object both use copy initialization.

Note that in this particular code, there are two copies, for a total of three T objects. A copy of the thrown object is made at the throw site. And in this case, a second copy is made because the handler catches the thrown object by value.

In general, though, prefer to catch exceptions by reference, not by value, to avoid making extra copies and to eliminate potential object slicing.[1]

```
f( T(s) );               // functional-notation type conversion
```

This function-style cast uses direct initialization.

```
S a[3] = { 1, 2, 3 };   // brace-enclosed initializers
```

Brace-enclosed initializers use copy initialization.

```
S* p = new S(4);        // new expression
```

Finally, new expressions use direct initialization.

ITEM 37: FORWARD DECLARATIONS   DIFFICULTY: 3

Forward declarations are a great way to eliminate needless compile-time dependencies. But here's an example of a forward-declaration snare. How would you avoid it?

1. Forward declarations are very useful tools. In this case, they don't work as the programmer expected. Why are the marked lines errors?

```
// file f.h
//
class ostream;  // error
class string;   // error
string f( const ostream& );
```

---

1. See also Item 13 in [Meyers96].

2. Without including any other files, write the correct forward declarations for `ostream` and `string` above.

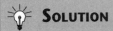 **SOLUTION**

1. Forward declarations are very useful tools. In this case, they don't work as the programmer expected. Why are the marked lines errors?

```
// file f.h
//
class ostream;   // error
class string;    // error
string f( const ostream& );
```

Alas, you cannot forward-declare `ostream` and `string` this way because they are not classes. Both are `typedef`s of templates.

(True, you used to be able to forward-declare `ostream` and `string` this way in pre-standard C++, but that was many years ago. It is no longer possible in the standard language.)

2. Without including any other files, write the correct forward declarations for `ostream` and `string` above.

Short answer: This is not possible. In fact, it turns out there exists no standard and portable way to forward-declare `ostream` without including another file, and there is no standard and portable way to forward-declare `string` at all.

The reason we can't just forward-declare either of these ourselves is that the standard is explicit that we cannot write our own declarations to `namespace std`, which is where `ostream` and `string` live:

> *It is undefined for a C++ program to add declarations or definitions to* `namespace std` *or namespaces within* `namespace std` *unless otherwise specified.*

Among other things, this rule is intended to let vendors provide implementations of the standard library that have more template parameters for library templates than the standard requires (suitably defaulted, of course, to remain compatible). Even if we were allowed to forward-declare standard library templates and classes, we couldn't do it portably, because vendors are allowed to extend those declarations differently from implementation to implementation.

The best you can do (which is not a solution to the problem "without including any other files") is the following:

```
#include <iosfwd>
#include <string>
```

The iosfwd header does contain bona fide forward declarations. The string header does not. This is all you can do and still be portable. Fortunately, forward-declaring string and ostream isn't too much of an issue in practice, because they're generally small and widely used. The same is true for most standard headers. However, beware the pitfalls, and don't be tempted to start forward-declaring templates, or anything else, that belongs to namespace std. That's a high and solemn privilege reserved for the compiler and library writers, and them alone.

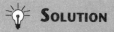 **Guideline**

Never #include a header when a forward declaration will suffice. Prefer to #include only <iosfwd> when the complete definition of a stream is not needed.

See also *Exceptional C++* [Sutter00] Item 26.

ITEM 38: Typedef   DIFFICULTY: 3

Why use typedef? Besides the many traditional reasons, we'll consider typedef techniques that make using the C++ standard library safer and easier.

1. Why use typedef? Name as many situations/reasons as you can.
2. Why is typedef such a good idea in code that uses standard (STL) containers?

SOLUTION

Typedef: **Controlling What's in a Name**

To recap, writing typedef allows you to assign another equivalent name for a type. For example,

```
typedef vector< vector<int> > IntMatrix;
```

lets you write the simpler IntMatrix in place of the more verbose vector< vector<int> >.

1. Why use typedef? Name as many situations/reasons as you can.

Here are several "abilities."

Typeability

Shorter names are easier to type.

Readability

Typedefs can make code, especially long template type names, much more readable. For a simple example, a public newsgroup posting asked what the following code meant:

```
int ( *t(int) )( int* );
```

If you're used to reading C declarations just like you'd read a Victorian English novel (that is, dense and verbose prose that at times feels like slogging through ankle-deep sucking muck), you know the answer and you're fine. If you're not, typedefs really help, even with as meaningless a typedef name as Func:

```
typedef int (*Func)( int* );

Func t( int );
```

Now it's clearer that this is a function declaration, for a function named t that takes an int and returns a pointer to a function that takes an int* and returns an int. (Say that three times fast.) In this case, the typedef is easier to read than the English.

Typedefs can also add semantic meaning. For example, "PhoneBook" is much easier to understand than "map< string, string>," where the latter has little semantic content and could mean nearly anything.

Communication

Typedefs can help to communicate intent. For example, instead of littering the program with lots of unadorned ints, it can be clearer to give the types names, even though at heart they still are just ints. Compare this:

```
int x;
int y;
y = x * 3;   // might be okay -- who knows?
```

with this:

```
typedef int Inches;
typedef int Dollars;

Inches  x;
Dollars y;
y = x * 3;   // hmmm...?
```

Which would you prefer to read if you were the maintenance programmer?

Portability

If you use `typedef`'d names for platform-specific or otherwise nonportable names, you'll find it easier to move to new platforms. After all, it's easier to write this:

```
#if defined USING_COMPILER_A
  typedef __int32 Int32;
  typedef __int64 Int64;
#elif defined USING_COMPILER_B
  typedef int       Int32;
  typedef long long Int64;
#endif
```

than search-and-replace for one of the system-specific names throughout your code. The `typedef` names help to insulate your code from simple platform dependencies. (For reasons why you might not want to use `#define` for this purpose, however, turn to Item 35.)

2. Why is `typedef` such a good idea in code that uses standard (STL) containers?

Flexibility

Changing a `typedef` name in one place is easier than changing all its uses throughout the code. For example, consider the following code:

```
void f( vector<Customer>& custs )
{
  vector<Customer>::iterator i = custs.begin();
  ...
}
```

What if, a few months later, we find out that `vector` isn't the right container after all? If we're storing huge quantities of `Customer` objects, the fact that `vector`'s storage is contiguous[2] may be a disadvantage and we might like to switch to `deque` instead. Or if we find ourselves frequently inserting/removing elements from the middle, we might like to switch to `list` instead.

In the above code, we'd have to make that change everywhere the type name "`vector<Customer>`" appears. How much easier it would be if we had only written:

```
typedef vector<Customer> Customers;
typedef Customers::iterator CustIter;

...

void f( Customers& custs )
{
```

---

2. See Item 7.

```
        CustIter i = custs.begin();
        ...
    }
```

and only needed to change the `typedef` to `list<Customer>` or `deque<Customer>`! Of course, it is not always this easy—for example, our code might be relying on the `Customers::iterator` being a random-access iterator, which a `list<Customer>::iterator` is not. But the `typedef` still insulates us from a lot of tedious changes that would be necessary otherwise.

Traitability

The traits idiom is a powerful way to associate information with a type, and if you want to customize standard containers or algorithms, you'll often need to provide traits. See the coverage of traits in the Generic Programming section of this book, and consider also the case-insensitive `string` example from *Exceptional C++* [Sutter00] Items 2 and 3, where we defined our own `char_traits` replacement.

Summary

Most uses of `typedef` fall into one of these categories. In general, `typedef` makes code easier to write, easier to read, and easier to change through the proverbial "additional level of indirection"—in this case, an indirection in name only is still as sweet.

ITEM 39: NAMESPACES, PART 1: USING-DECLARATIONS AND USING-DIRECTIVES   DIFFICULTY: 2

Standard C++ includes support for namespaces and name visibility control with using-declarations and using-directives. This Item provides a quick recap, laying the groundwork for the next Item's practical application.

What are using-declarations and using-directives, and how are they used? Give examples. Which is order-dependent?

 SOLUTION

Although C++ changed greatly during standardization, few of the changes the committee made are likely to break existing code. There is one change, however, that will cause nearly all earlier C++ code to fail to compile—the addition of namespaces and, particularly, the fact that the whole C++ standard library now lives in namespace std.

If you are a C++ programmer and this hasn't troubled you yet, it probably will soon, because the newest releases of most compilers have conformed to this change. As you start upgrading to the latest release of your compiler, or stop using legacy (and now nonstandard) pre-namespace headers, your code will be forced to adapt.

What are using-declarations and using-directives, and how are they used? Give examples. Which is order-dependent?

Using-Declarations

A *using-declaration* creates a local synonym for a name actually declared in another namespace. For the purposes of overloading and name resolution, a using-declaration works just like any declaration.

```
// Example 39-1(a)
//
namespace A
{
  int f( int );
  int i;
}

using A::f;

int f( int );

int main()
{
  f( 1 );     // ambiguous: A::f() or ::f()?

  int i;
  using A::i; // error, double declaration (just as
              //  writing "int i;" again would be)
}
```

A using-declaration brings in only names whose declarations have already been seen. For example:

```
// Example 39-1(b)
//
namespace A
{
  class X {};
  int Y();
  int f( double );
}
```

```
using A::X;
using A::Y; // only function A::Y(), not class A::Y
using A::f; // only A::f(double), not A::f(int)

namespace A
{
  class Y {};
  int f( int );
}

int main()
{
  X x;      // OK, X is a synonym for A::X

  Y y;      // error, A::Y not visible because the
            // using-declaration preceded the
            // actual declaration that's wanted

  f( 1 );   // oops: this uses a silent implicit
            // conversion and calls A::f(double),
            // NOT A::f(int), because only the
            // first A::f() declaration had been
            // seen at the point of the using-
            // declaration for the name A::f
}
```

This feature makes using-declarations order-dependent, particularly when using names from a namespace split across a group of header files. The order of header inclusion, specifically which headers are included before and after the using-declaration, affects which names the using-declaration brings into scope. Of course, namespace std just happens to fit the description "a namespace split across a group of header files." More on this in the next Item.

Using-Directives

A *using-directive* allows all names in another namespace to be used in the scope of the using-directive. Unlike a using-declaration, a using-directive brings in names declared both before *and after* the using-directive. Of course, the name's declaration still has to be seen before the name can be used. For example:

```
// Example 39-1(c)
//
namespace A
{
  class X {};
  int f( double );
}
```

```
void f()
{
  X x;       // OK, X is a synonym for A::X
  Y y;       // error, no Y has been seen yet
  f( 1 );    // OK, calls A::f(double) with parameter promotion
}

using namespace A;

namespace A
{
  class Y {};
  int f( int );
}

int main()
{
  X x;       // OK, X is a synonym for A::X
  Y y;       // OK, Y is a synonym for A::Y
  f( 1 );    // OK, calls A::f(int)
}
```

Item 40: Namespaces, Part 2: Migrating to Namespaces

Difficulty: 4

What's the best way to use C++'s powerful namespace management facilities while avoiding traps and pitfalls? Further, what's the most effective way to initially migrate your existing C++ code to a namespace-aware compiler and library?

You are working on a MLOC (million-lines-of-code) project with more than 1,000 `.h` and `.cpp` files. The project team is just upgrading to the latest version of your compiler, which finally both supports namespaces and puts all the standard library features into namespace `std` (or your compiler already had namespace support, but until now your team has been using legacy pre-namespace headers such as `<vector.h>`). Unfortunately, this conformance boon (or header migration) has the side effect of breaking your current build. As always, there is never enough time allocated to do a detailed job. You would like to analyze every source file and write exactly the needed using-declarations in each one, but that's infeasible at this time.

What is the most effective way to deal with this problem and safely migrate your code base to the new (and more standard) environment? Discuss alternatives, and prefer the quickest approach that gets the job done, without compromising future safety and usability. How can you best defer unnecessary (for now) migration work to the future, without increasing the overall migration workload later?

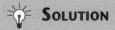 **SOLUTION**

Migrating to Namespaces, Safely and Effectively

The situation described in this question is typical for projects that are just moving to compilers with added support for namespaces, or projects that are just moving away from legacy non-namespace headers. The main problem that needs a solution is that, now, the standard library is in namespace std and so unqualified uses of std:: names in the project code will fail to compile.

For example, code that used to work, such as the following:

```
// Example 40-1: This used to work
//
#include <iostream.h>  // "legacy" pre-standard header

int main()
{
  cout << "hello, world" << endl;
}
```

now requires that you either specifically say which names are in std:

```
// Example 40-2(a): Option A, specify everything
//
#include <iostream>

int main()
{
  std::cout << "hello, world" << std::endl;
}
```

or write using-declarations to bring the necessary std names into scope:

```
// Example 40-2(b): Option B, write using-declarations
//
#include <iostream>
using std::cout;
using std::endl;

int main()
{
  cout << "hello, world" << endl;
}
```

or write a using-directive to simply drag all the std names into scope wholesale:

```
// Example 40-2(c): Option C, write using-directives
//
#include <iostream>

int main()
{
  using namespace std; // or this can go at file scope
  cout << "hello, world" << endl;
}
```

or some combination of the above.

So what's the right way to use namespaces in the long run? And what's the best way to move a large body of existing code to the new rules quickly today, deferring unnecessary (for now) migration work to the future, without increasing the overall migration workload later? The rest of this Item answers these questions.

Guidelines for a Good Long-Term Solution

First, what's the right way to use namespaces in the long run? It's important to decide this first, because knowing the long-term answer will help us determine what to aim for when we craft our best short-term migration strategy.

In short, a good long-term solution for namespace usage should follow at least these rules:

Namespace Rule #1: Never write using-directives in header files.

The reason for Rule #1 is that using-directives causes wanton namespace pollution by bringing in potentially huge numbers of names, many (usually the vast majority) of which are unnecessary. The presence of the unnecessary names greatly increases the possibility of unintended name conflicts—not just in the header itself, but in every module that #includes the header. I find it helpful to think of a using-directive in a header file as a marauding army of crazed barbarians that sows indiscriminate destruction wherever it passes; something that by its mere presence can cause "unintended conflicts," even when you think you're allied with it.

Namespace Rule #2: Never write namespace using-declarations in header files.

(Note the qualifier "*namespace* using-declarations." Of course, you should feel free to write class member using-declarations to bring in base class names as needed.)

This one might surprise you, because Rule #2 goes much further than most popular advice. Most authors recommend that using-declarations never appear *at file scope* in shared header files. That's good advice, as far as it goes, because at file scope a using-declaration causes the same kind of namespace pollution as a using-directive, only less of it.

In my opinion the above "popular advice" doesn't go far enough. You should never write using-declarations in header files at all, not even in a namespace scope. The meaning of the using-declaration may change, depending on what other headers happen to be #included before it in any given module. This kind of unpredictability should never be permitted, for not only is it bad, but it can make your program illegal. Consider just this one possible case: If the header file has the inline code definition for a function f() (for example, say f() is a template, or is part of a template), and some code line within f() changes meaning depending on #includes, then the whole program is illegal because it violates the One Definition Rule (ODR). The ODR requires that the definition of any given entity, here f(), must be identical in every translation unit where it's used. Because it's not, we're banished to Undefined Behavior Land. Even when ODR violations aren't involved, though, unpredictability is still bad, and I'll illustrate this problem again later in Example 40-3(c).

Namespace Rule #3: In implementation files, never write a using-declaration or a using-directive before an #include directive.

All using-declarations and using-directives must come *after* all #include directives. Otherwise, there's a chance the using could change the semantics of the #included header by introducing unexpected names.

Other than that, in your implementation files you can go ahead and use whatever combination of using-declarations and/or using-directives make sense, at file scope and/or function scope, without feeling guilty. Your local decision will be driven by what's convenient for you in that particular file, and won't have potential side effects for other implementation files. Using-declarations and using-directives exist for your convenience, not you for theirs. Do what makes sense (if you have no name collisions, why *not* just use all names?), as long as it affects only your own translation unit and not anybody else's headers or translation units.

"Kinda Sorta" Namespace Rule #4: Use C headers with the new style #include <cheader> instead of the old style #include <header.h>.

This one really isn't as big a deal in practice, but I mention it for theoretical completeness and to keep the standardistes' safety patrol off my back. For backward compatibility with C, C++ still supports all the standard C header names (for example, stdio.h), and when you #include those original versions the associated C library functions are visible in the global namespace as before. But in the same breath, C++ also says that the old header names are deprecated, which puts the world on notice that they may be removed in a future version of the C++ standard. Thus standard C++ strongly encourages programmers to prefer using the new versions of the C headers that start with "c" and drop the ".h" extension (for example, cstdio). When you #include the C headers using the new names, you get the same C library functions, but now they live in namespace std.

So why do I say it's not really a big deal? First, because even though the "name.h" names are officially deprecated, you can bet your coffee money they will never really disappear. Speaking quite frankly, and just between us and these four walls, even if the committee did remove them at some future date, the standard library vendors would still ship the old headers forever as extensions. Why? Because many of you, their customers, have way too much production code out there that uses them. And, of course, the C++ standards committee is aware of this because it's inhabited in part by those same vendors. 'Nuff said. Second, you may have reason to prefer the "name.h" headers because some other standards, such as Posix, require adding new names to the "name.h" headers. If you're using such extensions, it's theoretically safer for you to use the "name.h" style, even though library vendors are likely to provide those same names in the "cname" headers, too, as a common extension for your convenience and for consistency, even though no standard officially requires it.

Long-Term Approaches: A Motivating Example

To illustrate the foregoing rules, consider the following example module and two good long-term approaches for migrating the module to namespaces.

```
// Example 40-3(a): Original namespace-free code
//

//--- file x.h ---
//
#include "y.h"  // defines Y
#include <deque.h>
#include <iosfwd.h>

ostream& operator<<( ostream&, const Y& );
Y operator+( const Y&, int );
int f( const deque<int>& );

//--- file x.cpp ---
//
#include "x.h"
#include "z.h"  // defines Z
#include <ostream.h>

ostream& operator<<( ostream& o, const Y& y )
{
  // ... uses Z in the implementation ...
  return o;
}

Y operator+( const Y& y, int i )
```

```
{
  // ... uses another operator+() in the implementation...
  return result;
}

int f( const deque<int>& d )
{
  // ...
}
```

How can we best migrate the preceding code to a compiler that respects namespaces and a library that puts the standard names in namespace `std`? Before reading on, please stop for a moment and think about the alternatives you might consider. Which ones are good? Which ones aren't? Why?

Have you made a decision? All right, then. There are several ways you might approach this, and I'll describe two common strategies—only one of which is good form.

A Good Long-Term Solution

A good long-term solution is to explicitly qualify every standard name wherever it is mentioned in a header (.h) file, and to write just the using-declarations that are needed inside each source (.cpp) file for convenience, because those names are likely to be widely used in the source file.

```
// Example 40-3(b): A good long-term solution
//

//--- file x.h ---
//
#include "y.h"  // defines Y
#include <deque>
#include <iosfwd>

std::ostream& operator<<( std::ostream&, const Y& );
Y operator+( const Y&, int i );
int f( const std::deque<int>& );

//--- file x.cpp ---
//
#include "x.h"
#include "z.h"  // defines Z
#include <ostream>
using std::deque;    // "using" appears AFTER all #includes
using std::ostream;
using std::operator+;
// or, "using namespace std;" if that suits you
```

```
ostream& operator<<( ostream& o, const Y& y )
{
  // ... uses Z in the implementation ...
  return o;
}

Y operator+( const Y& y, int i )
{
  // ... uses another operator+() in the implementation...
  return result;
}

int f( const deque<int>& d )
{
  // ...
}
```

Note that the using-declarations inside x.cpp had better come after all #include directives, otherwise they may introduce name conflicts into other header files depending on the order in which they're #included. In particular, uses of x.h's operator+() might end up being ambiguous depending on what other operator+() functions are visible, which depends on which standard headers happen to be included before or after the using declaration.

I sometimes encounter people who, even in their .cpp files, like to eschew "using" entirely and explicitly qualify every standard name. I don't recommend doing this, because it's a lot of extra work that normally doesn't deliver any real advantage.

A Not-So-Good Long-Term Solution

In contrast, one often-proposed solution is actually dangerous. This bad long-term "solution" proposes to put all the project's code into its own namespace (which is not objectionable in itself, but isn't as useful as one might think) and write the using-declarations or using-directives in the headers (which unintentionally opens a gaping door for potential problems). The reason some people have proposed this method is that it requires less typing than some other namespace-migration methods:

```
// Example 40-3(c): Bad long-term solution
// (or, Why to never write using-declarations
// in headers, even within a namespace)
//

//--- file x.h ---
//
#include "y.h"  // defines MyProject::Y and adds
                //  using-declarations/directives
                //   in namespace MyProject
#include <deque>
#include <iosfwd>
```

```
namespace MyProject
{
  using std::deque;
  using std::ostream;
  // or, "using namespace std;"

  ostream& operator<<( ostream&, const Y& );
  Y operator+( const Y&, int );
  int f( const deque<int>& );
}

//--- file x.cpp ---
//
#include "x.h"
#include "z.h"   // defines MyProject::Z and adds
                 //   using-declarations/directives
                 //   in namespace MyProject
  // error: potential future name ambiguities in
  //        z.h's declarations, depending on what
  //        using-declarations exist in headers
  //        that happen to be #included before z.h
  //        in any given module (in this case,
  //        x.h or y.h may cause potential changes
  //        in meaning)
#include <ostream>

namespace MyProject
{
  using std::operator+;

  ostream& operator<<( ostream& o, const Y& y )
  {
    // ... uses Z in the implementation ...
    return o;
  }

  Y operator+( const Y& y, int i )
  {
    // ... uses another operator+() in the implementation...
    return result;
  }

  int f( const deque<int>& d )
  {
    // ...
  }
}
```

Note the highlighted error. The reason, as stated, is that the meaning of a using-declaration in a header can change—even when the using-declaration is inside a namespace, not at file scope—depending on what else a client module may happen to #include before it. For example, the statement using std::operator<<; can mean very different things, as can using std::operator+;, depending on what headers have been included so far (never mind that the answer will also vary from one standard library implementation to another). Clearly, it's always bad form to write any kind of code that can silently change meaning depending on the order in which headers are `#included`.

An Effective Short-Term Solution

The reason I've spent time explaining the desirable long-term solution, and discrediting some bad approaches, is that knowing what we want to achieve eventually will help us to pick a simpler short-term solution that won't compromise our long-term solution. So now we're ready to tackle the short-term question: What is the most effective way to migrate your existing code base to deal with namespace `std`?

Speaking pragmatically, the "upgrade to the new compiler version" task is just one of a list of things to be done in our product's release cycle. Upgrading the compiler and migrating to namespaces probably isn't the most urgent item on the task list, and you have lots of other things to do and product features to add. More likely than not, you're under project deadline pressure to boot, so you should prefer the quickest namespace migration approach that gets the job done without compromising future safety and usability. How can you best defer unnecessary (for now) migration work to the future, without increasing the overall migration workload later? First, consider migrating the header files.

Migration Step #1: In every header file, add "`std::`" qualifiers wherever needed.

"Is adding `std::` everywhere really necessary?" you might ask. "Couldn't you just add using-declarations or using-directives in the headers?" Well, adding using-declarations or using-directives would indeed be the least work, but it's work that would have to be undone when you implement the correct long-term solution. Namespace Rules #1 and #2 presented earlier in this Item already reject such an approach, and we've already seen what I hope you'll agree are compelling reasons not to go down that road. Given that we mustn't add using-declarations or using-directives in headers, our only alternative for headers is to add "`std::`" in the right places.

You can do the bulk of the work quickly using automated text substitution—for example using a tool to change "`string`" to "`std::string`" (and so forth for common names like `vector` and `list`) in all "`*.h*`" files. Be careful that you don't accidentally substitute common names that also appear in other namespaces you're using, such as if you're using a third-party tool that has its own nonstandard `string`. Such names will have to be resolved manually.

Migration Step #2: Create a new header file called `myproject_last.h` *that contains the directive* `using namespace std;`. *In every implementation file,* `#include myproject_last.h` *after all other* `#includes`.

Things are a little better with implementation files. We can get away with simply writing a using-directive in each implementation file, as long as the using-directive appears after all #include statements. This doesn't violate the spirit of Rule #1 because this header is special. It's not a normal header that declares something for later use, but a mechanism for injecting code into implementation files at a particular well-controlled point.

Doing it this way has a small advantage over just pasting "using namespace std;" into all your implementation files. On many projects, it's common to have such a header, and so you may have something like myproject_last.h already. If so, you only have to write one line and you're done. If you don't already have such a header, you'll probably find having one to be convenient later on. In any case, whether you paste the line "using namespace std;" or the line "#include "myproject_last.h"" into every file represents the same total amount of work.

Finally, what about the new <cheader> header style? Fortunately, that's optional, so it doesn't need to be done during the initial migration pass (or ever, really).

Here's the result of applying our two-step migration strategy to Example 40-3(a):

```
// Example 40-3(d): Good short-term solution,
// applying our two-step migration
//

//--- file x.h ---
//
#include "y.h"  // defines Y
#include <deque>
#include <iosfwd>

std::ostream& operator<<( std::ostream&, const Y& );
  Y operator+( const Y& y, int i );
int f( const std::deque<int>& );

//--- file x.cpp ---
//
#include "x.h"
#include "z.h"  // defines Z
#include <ostream>
#include "myproject_last.h"
            // AFTER all other #includes
```

```
ostream& operator<<( ostream& o, const Y& y )
{
  // ... uses Z in the implementation ...
  return o;
}

Y operator+( const Y& y, int i )
{
  // ... uses another operator+() in the implementation...
  return result;
}

int f( const deque<int>& d )
{
  // ...
}

//--- common file myproject_last.h ---
//
using namespace std;
```

This does not compromise the long-term solution in that it doesn't do anything that will need to be "undone" for the long-term solution. At the same time, it's simpler and requires fewer code changes than the full long-term solution would. In fact, this approach represents the minimum amount of work we can get away with that will make our code work on a namespace-aware compiler but that won't make us have to go back and undo any of the work later.

Conclusion: Migrating to the Long-Term Solution

Finally, at some happy and quite possibly imaginary point in the future, when you are momentarily free of pressing project deadlines, you can perform a simple migration to the full long-term solution illustrated in Example 40-3(b). Simply follow these steps.

1. In myproject_last.h, comment out the using-directive.
2. Rebuild your project. See what breaks the compile. In each implementation file, add the correct using-declarations and/or using-directives, either at file scope (after all #includes) or within each function. Season to taste.
3. Optionally, in each header or implementation file, change lines that #include C headers to the new <cheader> style. For example, change #include <stdio.h> to #include <cstdio>. This can usually be done quickly using automated text substitution tools. It can be done even more quickly by skipping this step entirely.

If you follow this advice, then even with looming project deadlines, you'll be able to quickly and effectively migrate to a namespace-aware compiler and library, all without compromising your long-term solution.

Afterword

I hope you've enjoyed not just the puzzles and problems in this book and its predecessor *Exceptional C++*, but also the solutions and techniques that have been presented. Most of these solutions and techniques have been carefully designed to be directly applicable and useful to your production coding today. I hope you've found even just a few things here that have been immediately useful in your daily work. If you have, it's been a success.

As before, I should add that there's more where this came from. Today, on the Internet, new *Guru of the Week* issues are being published and discussed and debated on the newsgroup *comp.lang.c++.moderated*, and are archived at the official Web site at *www.Gotw.ca*. These topics and much more will in time be incorporated into the third and concluding volume of the *Exceptional C++* books, *Exceptional C++ Style*. Here's a small sampling of the material you can expect to see in the next book.

- More and new information on popular themes you've already seen in the first two books, including generic programming and template techniques; solid class design using encapsulation, along with ways of enforcing rules for derived classes; efficiency and optimization; effective use of the standard library, with analysis of how much memory and resources the various standard containers use in practice (not just theory) on today's popular platforms; and the *de rigueur* exception safety issues and techniques. These take the next step beyond Items like 1 through 8, 12 through 23, and 26 through 28 in this book.
- Practical information on real-world issues, such as writing code for debuggability, efficient data formats, and compression issues.
- Pragmatic discussions of how memory management issues can vary and potentially affect your code differently on various real-world platforms, even if you're using fully standard-conforming compilers on all those platforms.

- But, most important of all: A set of real-world case studies, dissecting actual production code and code that's been published in print, in order to demonstrate the exceptional style guidelines recommended throughout the *Exceptional C++* books.

Thanks again to all who have expressed interest and support for *Exceptional C++* and this book. I hope you've found this material to be useful in your daily work, as you keep on writing faster, cleaner, and safer C++ programs.

Appendix A: Optimizations That Aren't (in a Multithreaded World)

This appendix ties in closely with the results shown in Items 13 to 16, and Appendix B.

Introduction

Are you working on a multithreaded program today? Chances are you are, or work in a group in which others are. Multithreading is getting more popular because it can make our programs more responsive, more efficient, and more scalable on multiprocessor machines. But even if you only write single-threaded programs, keep reading. If you work in a company (or share libraries) with other projects that are multithreaded, you're probably using multithread-safe builds or versions of some shared libraries, and what I'm going to talk about probably affects you today.

Do you care about performance and optimization? Again, chances are you do. No matter how fast our hardware gets, performance is important. Optimization and multithreading are frequently related, as we use multiple threads to achieve higher performance by letting operations that wait for different resources run in parallel.

What's the Fuss About?

The point of this appendix is that some widely used library optimizations are effective in single-threaded mode, but can actually degrade performance if the library is built for possible multithreaded use. I'm talking about common and popular optimizations that you may be using already, even if you don't know it, because they're present deep inside many popular vendors' libraries.

Here's more bad news: The performance impact is often severe, far heavier than it needs to be, even in some of today's most popular commercial libraries. Why?

Because there's often more than one way to make code thread-safe, and some library writers pick methods that work all the time but aren't the most efficient for their particular situation. Certain popular libraries still use general-purpose constructs, such as mutexes, when more efficient alternatives would do. It makes a big difference.

And here's the worst news of all: Earlier, I wrote, "if the library is built for *possible* multithreaded use." This means the degradation can affect you *even if your program happens to be single-threaded.*

In this discussion, we'll consider again one type of optimization that is often a false optimization, but is commonly found in commercial libraries. I'll also show an easy way to detect the performance hit, if any, so you can check whether you're affected by similar hidden pitfalls in the libraries you're using now. If you are affected, you'll also have the information you need to report the situation to your library vendor, so they can correct the problem.

I'm going to illustrate the general problem with a specific example—the Optimized::String class developed in Items 15 and 16, which uses the copy-on-write (COW) optimization. But please note:

- *COW isn't the only culprit.* Everything I'll discuss applies to any transparent-optimization in which two or more objects can share information or state behind the scenes, where calling code can't see. This includes, but is not limited to, shared-implementation or lazy-copy optimizations such as COW.
- *Strings aren't the only culprit.* Optimizations like these can and have been used for many expensive-to-copy data structures, including collections and containers.

Note that although our code happens to be written in C++, this discussion applies to code written in any language. One reason I'm writing about this topic is that standard C++ strings have acquired an undeserved "slow and inefficient" reputation in some circles. True, there certainly are needlessly inefficient implementations of C++'s string facility out there on the market today. But I want to emphasize the "needlessly" part, point out that there are high-quality implementations too, and show you how to tell them apart so that you can avoid the former.

Recap: Plain Old Original:: String (Item 13)

First, let's consider code examples that use a "plain old string" such as Item 13's Original::String that doesn't perform any copy-on-write (or other shared-information) optimizations under the covers. Whenever you copy or assign this kind of string, it immediately does a deep copy, so as soon as the copy or assignment operation is complete, you really do have two separate and independent string objects that aren't invisibly connected.

Given a plain old string, what does calling code have to do in order to use it safely in single- and multithreaded programs?

Using a Plain Old String: Single-Threaded

Say we want our program to keep track of the last error message we encountered and automatically decorate it with the time the message was generated. We might implement it using a global string value with helper functions to get and set the state:

```
// Example A-1: A simple error recording subsystem
//
String err;
int count = 0;

String GetError()
{
  return err;
}

String SetError( const String& msg )
{
  err = AsString( ++count ) + ": ";
  err += msg;
  err += " (" + TimeAsString() + ")";
  return err;
}
```

As long as our program is single-threaded, we never have to worry about Get-Error() or SetError() being called at the same time on different threads, so all is well. For example, given:

```
String newerr = SetError( "A" );
newerr += " (set by A)";
cout << newerr << endl;

// ...later...
//
newerr = SetError( "B" );
newerr += " (set by B)";
cout << newerr << endl;
```

the output would be something like:

```
1: A (12:01:09.65) (set by A)
2: B (12:01:09.125) (set by B)
```

Using a Plain Old String: Multithreaded

Even if you're already familiar with thread-safety issues and know why and how to share resources between threads safely by serializing access using mutexes, skim this section anyway. It forms the basis for the more-detailed examples later on.

In a nutshell, things are a bit different if our program is multithreaded. Functions like GetError() and SetError() might well be called at the same time on different threads. In that case, calls to these functions could be interlaced, and they will no longer work properly as originally written above. For example, consider what might happen if the following two pieces of code could be executed at the same time:

```
// thread A
String newerr = SetError( "A" );
newerr += " (set by A)";
cout << newerr << endl;

// thread B
String newerr = SetError( "B" );
newerr += " (set by B)";
cout << newerr << endl;
```

There are many ways in which this can go wrong. Here's one: Say thread A is running and, inside the SetError("A") call, gets as far as setting err to "1: " before the operating system decides to preempt it and switch to thread B. Thread B executes completely; then thread A is reactivated and runs to completion. The output would be

```
2: B (12:01:09.125) (set by B)
2: B (12:01:09.125)A (12:01:09.195) (set by A)
```

It's easy to invent situations that produce even stranger output,[1] but in reality you'd be lucky to get anything this sensible. Because a thread's execution can be preempted anywhere, including right in the middle of a String operation, such as String::operator+=() itself, you're far more likely to see just intermittent crashes, as String member functions on different threads attempt to update the same String object at the same time. (If you don't see this problem right away, try writing those String member functions and see what happens if their execution gets interleaved.)

The way to correct this is to make sure that only one thread can be working with the shared resources at a time. We prevent the functions from getting interlaced by "serializing" them with a mutex or similar device. But who should be responsible for doing the serialization? There are two levels at which we could do it. The main trade-off is that the lower the level at which the work is done, the more locking needs to be done, often needlessly. That's because the lower levels don't know whether acquiring a lock is necessary for a given operation, so they have to do it every time, just in case. Excessive locking is a major concern because acquiring a mutex lock is typically an expensive operation on most systems, approaching or surpassing the cost of a general-purpose dynamic memory allocation.

1. *[WRONG] Do locking within String member functions.* This way, the String class itself assumes responsibility for the thread safety of all its objects. This is a bad choice for

---

1. Just interrupting a thread between its SetError() call and the following cout statement could affect the ordering of the output (though not the contents). Exercise for the reader: What are the thread-safety issues relating to cout itself, both within the standard iostreams subsystem and within the calling code? Consider first the ordering of partial output.

two (probably obvious) reasons. First, it doesn't solve the problem because it's at the wrong granularity. Option 1 only ensures that `String` objects won't get corrupted. (That is, they're still valid `String` objects as far as `String` is concerned.) But it can't do anything about the `SetError()` function's interleaving. (The `String` objects can still end up holding unexpected values exactly as just illustrated, which means they're not valid error messages as far as the Error module is concerned.) Second, it can seriously degrade performance because the locking would be done far more frequently than necessary—at least once for every mutating `String` operation, and possibly even for nonmutating operations!

2. *[RIGHT] Do locking in the code that owns/manipulates a `String` object.* This is always the correct choice. Not only is locking done only when it's really needed, but it's done at the right granularity. We lock "an operation" where an operation is, not a low-level `String` member function, but a high-level Error module message-formatting function. Further, the extra code to do the serialization of the error string is isolated in the Error module.

3. *[PROBLEMATIC] Do both.* In the example, so far, Option 2 alone is sufficient. Option 1 is so obviously a bad choice that you might be wondering why I even mention it. The reason is simple: Later in this discussion, we'll see why copy-on-write "optimizations" force us to make that performance-degrading choice and do all locking inside the class. But because (as noted) Option 1 by itself doesn't really solve the whole problem, we can end up having to do Option 1, not instead of, but *in addition to* Option 2. As you might expect, that's just plain bad news.

In our example, implementing Option 2 means that the Error subsystem should take responsibility for serializing access to the `String` object that it owns. Here's a typical way to do it:

```
// Example A-2: A thread-safe error recording subsystem
//
String err;
int count = 0;
Mutex m;  // to protect the err and count values

String GetError()
{
  Lock<Mutex> l(m); //--enter mutual exclusion block------
  String ret = err;
  l.Unlock();        //--exit mutual exclusion block-------
  return ret;
}

string SetError( const String& msg )
{
  Lock<Mutex> l(m); //--enter mutual exclusion block------
  err = AsString( ++count ) + ": ";
  err += msg;
  err += " (" + TimeAsString() + ")";
  String ret = err;
  l.Unlock();        //--exit mutual exclusion block-------
  return ret;
}
```

All is well, because each function body is now atomic as far as `err` and `count` are concerned and no interlacing will occur. `SetError()` calls are automatically serialized so that their bodies do not overlap at all.

For more details about threads, critical sections, mutexes, semaphores, race conditions, the Dining Philosophers Problem, and lots of interesting related topics, see any good text on operating systems or multithreaded programming. From here on, I'll assume you know the basics.

A Helper Lock Manager

Assume that Example A-2 and similar code shown here makes use of a helper lock manager class. The helper ensures that a lock is acquired promptly, and that it's subsequently released exactly once. Wrapping this knowledge in a manager class lets us make code like Example A-2 more exception-safe by avoiding embarrassments such as leaving acquired-and-never-to-be-released locks hanging around if a `String` operation happens to throw an exception.

The `Lock` helper looks something like this:

```
template<typename T>
class Lock
{
public:
  Lock( T& t )
    : t_(t)
    , locked_(true)
  {
    t_.Lock();
  }

  ~Lock()
  {
    Unlock();
  }

  void Unlock()
  {
    if( locked_ )
    {
      t_.Unlock();
      locked_ = false;
    }
  }

private:
  T&   t_;
  bool locked_;
};
```

Now Throw in an "Optimization": Copy-On-Write (COW)

COW, a form of lazy copy that uses reference-counted string representations, is probably the most well-known string optimization. Items 14 to 16 introduce and describe this optimization.

COW doesn't apply only to strings, but the motivation is straightforward. Copying or assigning a plain old string usually involves a general-purpose dynamic memory allocation, which is typically an expensive operation (compared to, say, a function call), so copying a string must become an expensive operation. At the same time, calling code often might make copies of string objects, but then never actually modify the copies. For example, calling code can make a copy of a string object, perform some read-only operations such as printing it out or calculating its length, and then destroy the copy. When that happens, it seems wasteful to have done the work to create a distinct copy only to find out later that it wasn't really needed after all.

So what's different about a COW string, such as the `Optimized::String` described in Items 14 to 16, is that its copy constructor initially performs only a shallow copy and defers the deep copy for as long as possible. Read-only operations on either (source or target) string won't care, after all. Only when a possibly mutating operation is attempted on one of the strings will the string finally be forced to make a deep copy.[2]

Is COW worth it? In a single-threaded program, sometimes. Whether it's really an optimization depends heavily on how string objects are used. See Rob Murray's discussion and empirical measurements in [Murray93] for more information about COW in the real (but single-threaded) world.

The real fun starts when you move to a (possibly) multithreaded environment. As it turns out, using COW can exact an unexpected performance penalty if thread safety is important, and a severe one in some popular (but unnecessarily inefficient) commercial implementations.

Using a COW String: Multithreaded

Now let's return to our friend, the Error subsystem. Here's the problematic calling code again:

```
// thread A
String newerr = SetError( "A" );
newerr += " (set by A)";
cout << newerr << endl;

// thread B
String newerr = SetError( "B" );
```

---

2. COW can also be extended to share substrings, not just entire strings. (See [Niec00].)

```
newerr += " (set by B)";
cout << newerr << endl;
```

As before, the issue is that there has to be some serialization (using, for example, a mutex lock) in order to avoid corrupting the Error module's internal strings and produce reasonable output. But who should be responsible for doing the serialization? Consider the two levels again:

1. **Do locking within `Optimized::String` member functions.** As before, there are two problems with this. It's at the wrong granularity to solve the `SetError()` function's interleaving, and it can seriously degrade performance because the locking would be done at least once for every mutating (and possibly even nonmutating) `String` operation. What's different from before, however, is that this time, Option 1 is necessary anyway (see below).

2. **Do locking in the code that owns/manipulates an `Optimized::String` object.** Again, this is necessary; otherwise we haven't solved the `SetError()` interleaving problem.

Alas, now neither of the preceding does the job by itself. We need something heavyweight:

3. **[NECESSARY] Do both.** This time the story isn't so good: Option 2 is necessary, but *we have to do Option 1 too because the code that owns/manipulates a copy-on-write `Optimized::String` can't.* Calling code alone can never lock the right strings in the right way, because it has no way of knowing which visible string objects might be sharing a representation at any given time. Look again at the thread-safe Error subsystem code from Example A-2. The locking it does is still necessary but is now insufficient, because even though we serialize all access to the internal `err` error string object, the calling code's threads are taking and manipulating copies of that object, which copies might share representation.

   For example, thread A could be safely serialized inside its `SetError()` call, manipulating the Error module's `err` string, at the same time thread B (already past its safely serialized `SetError()`) is appending to its `newerr` string. Note that B's `newerr` string began life as a copy of the `err` string.[3] There's nothing obvious linking the internal `err` string and B's external `newerr` string. In fact, the Error subsystem has no way of knowing that any `newerr` strings even exist, and vice versa. But if the two strings happen to be sharing representation, which is not only possible, but likely, in this example, two threads could both be attempting to execute `String` member functions on the same string representation *even though everything outside `String` itself is safely serialized.*[4]

---

3. Or, equivalently, a copy of a copy of the `err` string if the compiler didn't perform the return value optimization.

4. Certain popular commercial libraries shipping today have variants of precisely this COW bug, where modifying one visible string also incorrectly modifies a different visible string because the libraries fail to perform the deep copy soon enough.

That's why it's not enough for the Error subsystem to perform its usual duty of care. For COW strings, the `Optimized::String` objects must, in addition, always protect themselves. This forces the string class to incur some overhead. But the overhead can be disastrously expensive if the implementation incurs needless inefficiencies.

How severe is the problem? One developer recently reported that he has a single-threaded test program that exercises his (popular) vendor's COW-based library features. The program executes in 18 to 20 seconds when the library is compiled for multithreaded use, and in 0.25 seconds when it's compiled for single-threaded use. (The difference is greater than the numbers imply, because both times include program startup.) It's important to note here that this developer's test program was only *single*-threaded, not multithreaded. But because the library had been compiled for possible multithreaded use, the problem affected him anyway. If 20 programs share a library, and only one program is multithreaded, the library must be built for multithreaded use—and any problem will affect all 20 programs.

Mild versus Severe Inefficiencies

So a thread-safe COW implementation always has to incur serialization overhead, but there's still a vast difference between "necessary" and "indefensible" overhead.

To cut a (very) long story short, it turns out that a thread-safe COW implementation can be written in such a way that the only data to which access needs to be serialized is the reference count itself. (For an exhaustive explanation of this and other aspects of COW and alternative thread-safe implementations, see Items 14 to 16. Item 16 includes a test harness with sample well-optimized source code for no fewer than seven implementations of a limited `String` class—five COW implementations and two non-COW implementations. This discussion summarizes and expands on some of the results.)

So here's the thing: Because the only shared data that needs serialization is the reference count—typically, a single integer—then you can be a lot more efficient than merely using a heavyweight general-purpose thread safety solution. Instead of using a mutex, which is unavoidable when you have to serialize access to larger structures, you can get away with using the following atomic integer operations if they are available on your system: atomic increment, atomic decrement-and-test, and atomic comparison. These atomic integer operations still incur overhead because they're necessarily slower than plain integer operations, but they're still much faster than a more sophisticated construct such as a mutex. They can often be implemented in a single native assembler instruction or in a short series of instructions.

To get a feel for the difference, consider alternative implementations for one member function of a C++-based `String` class, the non-`const` version of `operator[]()`, which returns a reference to a character at a given offset in the string.[5] For a plain

---

5. COW advocates may complain that the difference between COW and non-COW is most noticeable with possibly-mutating functions such as the non-`const` version of `operator[]`. That's true, but this is the easiest function for showing a quick and clear example of the implementation differences between non-COW and various flavors of COW.

(non-COW) implementation, it would look something like this, where `buf_` is a pointer to the `String` object's internal buffer, where it stores its representation:

```
// Plain non-COW operator[] (non-const version).
//
char& String::operator[]( size_t n )
{
  return buf_[n];
}
```

A COW implementation looks pretty much the same, except that it must first ensure that the representation is unshared (in `operator[]()`'s case, there are also reasons why the function should return a reference to non-`const` and why the representation should be marked unshareable, but that's not directly relevant here so I'll omit it; for more of those details, turn to Item 16):

```
// COW operator[] (non-const version).
//
const char& String::operator[]( size_t n )
{
  EnsureUnique();
  return data_->buf[n];
}
```

The key to all this is what has to be done inside `EnsureUnique()` for the different flavors of COW. Here are simplified implementations, which ignore "unshareable" flags and other more-sophisticated operations. Here `data_` points to the internal (and possibly shared) representation, which includes the reference count (`refs`):

```
// Thread-unsafe COW: no locks.
//
void String::EnsureUnique() const
{
  if( data_->refs > 1 )
  {
    StringBuf* newdata = new StringBuf( *data_ );
    --data_->refs;   // now all the real work is
    data_ = newdata; //  done, so take ownership
  }
}

// Thread-safe COW: atomic integer operations.
//
// Uses atomic integer calls to serialize access
// to data_->refs. Note that the IntAtomic* calls
// are not necessarily function calls, but can be
// as efficient as a native assembler instruction.
// They still introduce overhead, however, because
// EnsureUnique must be called by every possibly-
// mutating String function, and the IntAtomic*
// operations are slower than normal integer
```

```
// operations.
//
void String::EnsureUnique() const
{
  if( IntAtomicCompare( data_->refs, 1 ) > 0 )
  {
    StringBuf* newdata = new StringBuf( *data_ );
    if( IntAtomicDecrement( data_->refs ) < 1 )
    {
      delete newdata;  // just in case two threads
      data_->refs = 1; //  are trying this at once
    }
    else
    {                          // now all the real work is
      data_ = newdata; //  done, so take ownership
    }
  }
}


// Thread-safe COW: mutexes.
//
// Each data_ buffer contains a mutex object for
// serializing access to data_->refs.
//
// This method is needlessly inefficient, but it is
// used in some popular commercial string libraries.
// EnsureUnique still is called by every possibly-
// mutating String function, but the overhead is
// worse than with IntAtomic* functions.
//
void String::EnsureUnique() const
{
  Lock<Mutex> l(data_->m); //---------
  if( data_->refs > 1 )
  {
    StringBuf* newdata = new StringBuf( *data_ );
    --data_->refs;
    data_ = newdata;
  }
  l.Unlock(); //-------------------------------
}
```

COW will always add overhead, especially if it's to be made thread-safe. But this should show why there is no reason to use something as indefensibly inefficient as a mutex when atomic integer operations alone will do.

Some Actual Numbers

The difference between "necessary" and "indefensible" overhead can be profound. Here's an example from Item 16's and Appendix B's test results (the entire test harness source code can be downloaded via a link on this book's Web page at *http://www.gotw.ca/publications/mxc++.htm*, if you'd like to try it on your system). The test I'm showing here makes copies of 50-char strings in a tight loop. One-third of the copies are never modified (the classic case for COW optimization, in which the deep copy is entirely avoided); the rest of the copied strings are modified exactly once each. I'm showing the results for six flavors of the String class:

1. "Plain" is a plain non-COW string.
2. "Plain_FastAlloc" is the same as Plain, but uses an optimized memory allocator instead of the default operator new() allocator (note, however, that the latter was very good in its own right on the compiler platform I tested with).
3. "COW_Unsafe" is an efficient but thread-unsafe COW string.
4. "COW_AtomicInt" is an efficient thread-safe COW string that uses atomic integer operations for serializing access to the reference count.
5. "COW_CritSec" is the same as AtomicInt, but uses Win32 critical section locks instead of atomic integer operations.
6. "COW_Mutex" is the same as AtomicInt, but uses Win32 mutex locks instead of atomic integer operations.

Here are illustrative results on one compiler and Windows platform I happened to have handy. Recognize that results will vary on other compilers and platforms; see Appendix B for additional result numbers, and for links to source code that you can compile and try out on your own system.

String Implementation Strategy	Elapsed Time (smaller numbers are better)
Plain	1530ms
Plain_FastAlloc	390ms
COW_Unsafe	1380ms
COW_AtomicInt	1750ms
COW_AtomicInt2	1490ms
COW_CritSec	7800ms
COW_Mutex	23010ms

This is just one scenario, of course. It may or may not be typical of the way your program uses strings. My main purpose in sketching these results is to illustrate the following:

- Thread-safe COW is necessarily less efficient than thread-unsafe COW. In this test case, the thread-safety overhead made the difference between COW's being an optimization and its being a pessimization.
- Poorly implemented thread-safe COW (specifically COW_CritSec, which is implemented the same way as a certain popular string library) incurs a severe performance penalty. Note: If your platform lacks atomic integer operations, you have no

choice but to use a more heavyweight solution. Then COW becomes a severe pessimization for nearly all cases.

- It's not wrong to want to optimize, but a far better (and simpler) optimization is to optimize the memory allocation, not the deep copying. Note also that optimizing the allocator has no thread safety implications. Moral: Don't guess. Measure. Only optimize after measuring where your bottlenecks really are. (Of course, you could always choose to perform both optimizations. But development time is never infinite. Which one gives you more bang for the buck here?)
- Again, this test harness was single-threaded. You pay for the overhead whenever you use a library built for possible multithreaded use, whether you need it or not.

As discussed in Item 16, there are other interesting results. One is that when testing with larger strings on compilers with reasonably efficient default allocators, COW's advantage is not so much that it avoids the cost of the memory allocations, but that it avoids the cost of copying the characters in the string—a result you might find surprising.

A Real-World Example: C++'s `basic_string`

You may be wondering whether these false optimizations really affect you. The chances are pretty good they do. As a common example, if you use an OO language with a string class, you might well be affected.

Historically, COW has long been a popular optimization in many libraries for all sorts of data structures, including strings. Because of this history, the standard C++ `basic_string` template was deliberately specified in such a way that vendors would have the option of producing a conforming implementation that used COW. Perhaps unsurprisingly, all early implementations that I'm familiar with did so, even though COW incurs some of its own overhead,[6] is harder to code, and is a frequent source of subtle bugs and interactions.[7]

A few years ago, our team brought in a certain vendor's implementation of the standard C++ library and tested it in a single-threaded environment. We then rebuilt the library with the multithreaded switch set, only to discover that many of our programs ran several times more slowly than before. "What could be the problem?" we wondered, scratching our heads. "It looked okay in the test harness. We just made some changes in our own code too; could it be that? Are we blocking on some high-level mutexes more than we thought? Did we introduce an inefficiency somewhere?"

A little investigative work with a profiler isolated the problem, but only deepened the mystery. Our program was spending most of its execution time just acquiring and

---

6. Such as flags for ownership and reference counts.
7. Getting the COW code right is more complex than you might think. The most experienced library writers I know have told me repeatedly that they've found their COW code to be a frequent source of bugs. These are people with decades of experience crafting quality libraries, not first-timers.

releasing locks, far more so than could be reasonably expected from the locking performed by our own code. So where was all the locking coming from?

Curious, we investigated further and finally unearthed the problem. A few minutes of digging through the library's source showed that this vendor, like many others, had used the COW optimization in its implementation of basic_string. Naturally, we were using standard C++ strings widely instead of C-style char*'s, and nearly every string operation was causing a lock to be acquired and released.

We took a few minutes to whip up a ten-line sample program that did some reasonable string manipulation in a timed loop. It ran 34 times slower under the multithreaded build of that library than it did under the single-threaded build. We reported the problem, but as far as I know, that library still uses COW today—and an unnecessarily inefficient implementation of COW at that. The vendor's name doesn't matter, because until recently all the most popular implementations of basic_string on Windows and other platforms used COW. Not all COW-based implementations are this inefficient, but some are.

The good news is that, as I write this in 2001, I can finally report that our industry as a whole seems to be shifting away from COW implementations of basic_string. Increasingly, newer versions of compilers are shipping C++ standard libraries that include only non-copy-on-write strings. This is good news, and it's mainly because we as programmers are increasingly writing multithreaded applications and noticing the problems, and writing articles about those problems, and the vendors have noticed. It is in the vendors' interests to give us fast tools, where "fast" means "fast in the way we are using them," and today that has come to mean "fast in multithreaded environments."

The bad news is that, alas, not all vendors have yet moved to non-COW strings. Your natural next question should therefore be:

"Am I Affected?"

If you're using libraries built for possible multithreaded use and performance matters to you, you can and should do the same thing we did. Run profiles of your code to determine the data structures you use most. Do this by member function hit count, not necessarily by time spent in the function. Create sample programs that manipulate those data structures in a loop, and time those programs running with single- and multithreaded versions of the corresponding libraries. If there's a substantial difference, tell your vendor, especially if you can tell from the size of the difference whether it's less efficient than it needs to be.

Library implementers are generally reasonable people. Certainly, all those I've met are. It's their business to provide the highest-quality code to their customers. If there's a competitive advantage they can gain over other library vendors, they're usually happy to hear about it and provide it. Getting rid of COW implementations falls into the "good optimizations" category in most cases (and general-purpose libraries care most about "most cases").

So why have COW and similar "optimizations" been so prevalent historically? Probably the biggest reason is inertia and the weight of years. COW has traditionally been a common optimization for decades. Even at the end of the 1990s, despite the volume of trade press about multithreaded code, it was far from clear how much we as an industry were really writing multithreaded business applications. That is finally changing. Now that it is becoming clearer to library vendors that a significant portion of their customers are using multithreaded builds of their libraries, a few major vendors have already decided to abandon possible false optimizations like copy-on-write. To me, and to many, this is a Good Thing. It is to be hoped that the rest of the vendors will follow suit.

The performance penalty COW exacts in a multithreaded program can be startling. Remember, though, the problem isn't just with COW. Any shared-information optimization that joins two objects in some way "under the covers" will have the same problems.

Summary

There's nothing wrong with optimizing complex data structures. The bad news is that some very common optimization methods actually aren't always optimizations at all, and can exact performance penalties that will get more noticeable as more of us write multithreaded programs or share libraries with others who do—especially when the libraries are written needlessly inefficiently because of inexperience with thread safety issues.

The good news is that other optimizations can give the same effect, but don't have performance impacts in multithreaded mode. For example, in C++, providing optimized custom allocators via a custom `operator new()` is usually a good way to deal with memory allocation performance issues. For strings, in particular, the small-string optimization (storing small strings inside the `String` object itself rather than in a separate buffer), delivers solid performance results time after time, avoiding memory allocations entirely for strings below a threshold size.

The trick is to use a true optimization, not a false optimization that, often unintentionally, optimizes library code only for single-threaded use.

Appendix B: Test Results for Single-Threaded versus Multithread-Safe String Implementations

This appendix contains supplementary details for Item 16 and Appendix A. The test harness source code can be downloaded via a link on this book's Web page at *http://www.gotw.ca/publications/mxc++.htm*, if you'd like to try it on your system.

Approach

To assess COW, I performed measurements of three kinds of functions:

1. Copying (where COW shines, its *raison d'être*)
2. Mutating operations that could trigger reallocation (represented by Append(), which gradually lengthens; this is to make sure any conclusions drawn can take into account periodic reallocation overhead due to normal string use)
3. Possibly-mutating operations that do not change length enough to trigger reallocation, or that do not actually mutate the string at all (represented by operator[]())

It turns out that the last two both incur a constant (and similar within about 20%) cost per operation, and can roughly be considered together. Assuming for simplicity that mutating-and-extending operations, such as Append() (235ms overhead), and possibly-mutating operations like operator[]() (280ms overhead), will be about equally frequent, the COW_AtomicInt overhead for mutating and possibly-mutating operations is about 260ms per 1,000,000 operations in this implementation.

Finally, for each of 2(a) and 2(b), I first used the data shown under Raw Measurements below to hand-calculate a rough prediction of expected relative performance, then ran the test to check actual performance.

SUMMARY FOR CASE 2(a):

PREDICTION

COW_AtomicInt Cost		Plain Cost	
1M shallow copies and dtors	400	1M deep copies and dtors	1600
667K mutations	???		???
667K deep copies	1060		
extra overhead on 667K deep copies	???		
extra overhead on 667K mutations	175		
	1635+		1600+

TEST
(program that makes copies in a tight loop, and modifies 33% of them with a single Append and another 33% of them with a single op[])

Running 1000000 iterations with strings of length 50:

Plain_FastAlloc	642ms	copies:	1000000	allocs:	1000007
Plain	1726ms	copies:	1000000	allocs:	1000007
COW_Unsafe	1629ms	copies:	1000000	allocs:	666682
COW_AtomicInt	1949ms	copies:	1000000	allocs:	666682
COW_AtomicInt2	1925ms	copies:	1000000	allocs:	666683
COW_CritSec	10660ms	copies:	1000000	allocs:	666682
COW_Mutex	33298ms	copies:	1000000	allocs:	666682

SUMMARY FOR CASE 2(b):

PREDICTION

COW_AtomicInt Cost		Plain Cost	
1M shallow copies and dtors	400	1M deep copies and dtors	1600
1.5M mutations	???		???
500K deep copies	800		
extra overhead on 500K deep copies	???		
extra overhead on 1.5M mutations	390		
	1590+		1600+

```
TEST
    (program that makes copies in a tight loop, and
    modifies 25% of them with three Appends and
    another 25% of them with three operator[]s)

Running 1000000 iterations with strings of length 50:
    Plain_FastAlloc    683ms  copies: 1000000  allocs: 1000007
            Plain    1735ms  copies: 1000000  allocs: 1000007
       COW_Unsafe    1407ms  copies: 1000000  allocs:  500007
    COW_AtomicInt    1838ms  copies: 1000000  allocs:  500007
   COW_AtomicInt2    1700ms  copies: 1000000  allocs:  500008
      COW_CritSec    8507ms  copies: 1000000  allocs:  500007
        COW_Mutex   31911ms  copies: 1000000  allocs:  500007
```

Raw Measurements

Testing Const Copying and Destruction: The Target Case of Cow

Notes:

- COW_AtomicInt always took more than twice as long to create and destroy a const copy as did plain thread-unsafe COW.
- For every copy of a string that was later modified, COW_AtomicInt added constant unrecoverable overhead (400ms per 1,000,000), not counting the overhead on other operations.
- Most of COW's primary advantage for small strings could be gained without COW by using a more efficient allocator, or the small-string optimization (for more about the small-string optimization, turn to Appendix A). Of course, you could also implement multiple optimizations—use COW along with an efficient allocator and/or the small-string optimization.
- COW's primary advantage for large strings lay, not in avoiding the allocations, but in avoiding the char copying.

```
Running 1,000,000 iterations with strings of length 10:
    Plain_FastAlloc    495ms  copies: 1000000  allocs: 1000003
            Plain    1368ms  copies: 1000000  allocs: 1000003
       COW_Unsafe     160ms  copies: 1000000  allocs:       3
    COW_AtomicInt     393ms  copies: 1000000  allocs:       3
   COW_AtomicInt2     433ms  copies: 1000000  allocs:       4
      COW_CritSec     428ms  copies: 1000000  allocs:       3
        COW_Mutex   14369ms  copies: 1000000  allocs:       3

Running 1,000,000 iterations with strings of length 50:
    Plain_FastAlloc    558ms  copies: 1000000  allocs: 1000007
            Plain    1598ms  copies: 1000000  allocs: 1000007
       COW_Unsafe     165ms  copies: 1000000  allocs:       7
    COW_AtomicInt     394ms  copies: 1000000  allocs:       7
   COW_AtomicInt2     412ms  copies: 1000000  allocs:       8
      COW_CritSec     433ms  copies: 1000000  allocs:       7
        COW_Mutex   14130ms  copies: 1000000  allocs:       7
```

Running 1,000,000 iterations with strings of length 100:

```
Plain_FastAlloc     708ms   copies: 1000000   allocs: 1000008
        Plain     1884ms   copies: 1000000   allocs: 1000008
   COW_Unsafe      171ms   copies: 1000000   allocs:       8
 COW_AtomicInt      391ms   copies: 1000000   allocs:       8
COW_AtomicInt2      412ms   copies: 1000000   allocs:       9
   COW_CritSec      439ms   copies: 1000000   allocs:       8
     COW_Mutex    14129ms   copies: 1000000   allocs:       8
```

Running 1,000,000 iterations with strings of length 250:

```
Plain_FastAlloc    1164ms   copies: 1000000   allocs: 1000011
        Plain     5721ms   copies: 1000000   allocs: 1000011 [*]
   COW_Unsafe      176ms   copies: 1000000   allocs:      11
 COW_AtomicInt      393ms   copies: 1000000   allocs:      11
COW_AtomicInt2      419ms   copies: 1000000   allocs:      12
   COW_CritSec      443ms   copies: 1000000   allocs:      11
     COW_Mutex    14118ms   copies: 1000000   allocs:      11
```

Running 1,000,000 iterations with strings of length 1,000:

```
Plain_FastAlloc    2865ms   copies: 1000000   allocs: 1000014
        Plain     4945ms   copies: 1000000   allocs: 1000014
   COW_Unsafe      173ms   copies: 1000000   allocs:      14
 COW_AtomicInt      390ms   copies: 1000000   allocs:      14
COW_AtomicInt2      415ms   copies: 1000000   allocs:      15
   COW_CritSec      439ms   copies: 1000000   allocs:      14
     COW_Mutex    14059ms   copies: 1000000   allocs:      14
```

Running 1,000,000 iterations with strings of length 2,500:

```
Plain_FastAlloc    6244ms   copies: 1000000   allocs: 1000016
        Plain     8343ms   copies: 1000000   allocs: 1000016
   COW_Unsafe      174ms   copies: 1000000   allocs:      16
 COW_AtomicInt      397ms   copies: 1000000   allocs:      16
COW_AtomicInt2      413ms   copies: 1000000   allocs:      17
   COW_CritSec      446ms   copies: 1000000   allocs:      16
     COW_Mutex    14070ms   copies: 1000000   allocs:      16
```

Testing Append(): An Always-Mutating Periodically-Reallocating Operation

Notes:

- Plain always outperformed COW.
- The overhead of COW_AtomicInt compared to Plain did not vary greatly with string lengths. It was fairly constant at about 235ms per 1,000,000 operations.
- The overhead of COW_AtomicInt compared to COW_Unsafe did not vary greatly with string lengths. It was fairly constant at about 110ms per 1,000,000 operations.
- The overall ever-better performance for longer strings was due to the allocation strategy (see Item 13), not COW versus Plain issues.

Running 1,000,000 iterations with strings of length 10:

```
   Plain_FastAlloc    302ms  copies:    0  allocs:   272730
          Plain       565ms  copies:    0  allocs:   272730
     COW_Unsafe        683ms  copies:    0  allocs:   272730
  COW_AtomicInt        804ms  copies:    0  allocs:   272730
 COW_AtomicInt2        844ms  copies:    0  allocs:   363640
     COW_CritSec       825ms  copies:    0  allocs:   272730
      COW_Mutex       8419ms  copies:    0  allocs:   272730
```

Running 1,000,000 iterations with strings of length 50:

```
   Plain_FastAlloc    218ms  copies:    0  allocs:   137262
          Plain       354ms  copies:    0  allocs:   137262
     COW_Unsafe        474ms  copies:    0  allocs:   137262
  COW_AtomicInt        588ms  copies:    0  allocs:   137262
 COW_AtomicInt2        536ms  copies:    0  allocs:   156871
     COW_CritSec       607ms  copies:    0  allocs:   137262
      COW_Mutex       7614ms  copies:    0  allocs:   137262
```

Running 1,000,000 iterations with strings of length 100:

```
   Plain_FastAlloc    182ms  copies:    0  allocs:    79216
          Plain       257ms  copies:    0  allocs:    79216
     COW_Unsafe        382ms  copies:    0  allocs:    79216
  COW_AtomicInt        492ms  copies:    0  allocs:    79216
 COW_AtomicInt2        420ms  copies:    0  allocs:    89118
     COW_CritSec       535ms  copies:    0  allocs:    79216
      COW_Mutex       7810ms  copies:    0  allocs:    79216
```

Running 1,000,000 iterations with strings of length 250:

```
   Plain_FastAlloc    152ms  copies:    0  allocs:    43839
          Plain       210ms  copies:    0  allocs:    43839
     COW_Unsafe        331ms  copies:    0  allocs:    43839
  COW_AtomicInt        438ms  copies:    0  allocs:    43839
 COW_AtomicInt2        366ms  copies:    0  allocs:    47825
     COW_CritSec       485ms  copies:    0  allocs:    43839
      COW_Mutex       7358ms  copies:    0  allocs:    43839
```

Running 1,000,000 iterations with strings of length 1,000:

```
   Plain_FastAlloc    123ms  copies:    0  allocs:    14000
          Plain       149ms  copies:    0  allocs:    14000
     COW_Unsafe        275ms  copies:    0  allocs:    14000
  COW_AtomicInt        384ms  copies:    0  allocs:    14000
 COW_AtomicInt2        299ms  copies:    0  allocs:    15000
     COW_CritSec       421ms  copies:    0  allocs:    14000
      COW_Mutex       7265ms  copies:    0  allocs:    14000
```

Running 1,000,000 iterations with strings of length 2,500:

```
   Plain_FastAlloc    122ms  copies:    0  allocs:     6416
          Plain       148ms  copies:    0  allocs:     6416
     COW_Unsafe        279ms  copies:    0  allocs:     6416
  COW_AtomicInt        380ms  copies:    0  allocs:     6416
 COW_AtomicInt2        304ms  copies:    0  allocs:     6817
     COW_CritSec       405ms  copies:    0  allocs:     6416
      COW_Mutex       7281ms  copies:    0  allocs:     6416
```

Testing Operator[] (): A Possibly-Mutating Operation, Never Does Mutate

Notes:

- Plain always vastly outperformed COW.
- Results were independent of string lengths.
- The overhead of COW_AtomicInt compared to Plain was constant at about 280ms per 1,000,000 operations.
- COW_AtomicInt2 fared better in this test case, but COW_AtomicInt did better overall. I am therefore focusing on comparing that with Plain.

```
[10x iterations] Running 10000000 iterations with strings of length 10:
   Plain_FastAlloc    3ms  copies:      0  allocs:      3 [*]
          Plain       2ms  copies:      0  allocs:      3 [*]
      COW_Unsafe   1698ms  copies:      0  allocs:      3
   COW_AtomicInt   2833ms  copies:      0  allocs:      3
  COW_AtomicInt2   2112ms  copies:      0  allocs:      4
     COW_CritSec   3587ms  copies:      0  allocs:      3

       COW_Mutex  71787ms  copies:      0  allocs:      3
```

[*] Results were within the measurement error margin. Both varied from 0ms to 9ms.

Testing Various Integer Increment/Decrement Operations

Test Summary:

- "plain" performs the operations on normal non-volatile ints
- "volatile" is the only case to use volatile ints
- "atomic" uses the Win32 InterlockedXxx() operations
- "atomic_asm" uses inline x86 assembler locked integer operations

  Notes:

- ++atomic took only three times as long as either ++volatile and unoptimized ++plain
- ++atomic does not incur function-call overhead

```
[100x iterations] Running 100000000 iterations for integer operations:
       ++plain    2404ms, counter=100000000
       --plain    2399ms, counter=0

     ++volatile   2400ms, counter=100000000
     --volatile   2405ms, counter=0

      ++atomic    7480ms, counter=100000000
      --atomic    9340ms, counter=0
```

```
++atomic_asm    8881ms, counter=100000000
--atomic_asm    10964ms, counter=0
```

Here are a few extra notes on the relative timings of various flavors of x86 assembler implementations of `IntAtomicIncrement()`. The timings were taken under the same conditions as above and can be compared directly (this is the one actually used above):

Instructions	Timing

`__asm mov        eax, 1`
`__asm lock xadd i, eax`
`__asm mov        result, eax`
	~11000ms

`__asm mov        eax, 1` `__asm lock xadd i, eax`	~10400ms
`__asm lock inc i`	~8900ms

Note that the non-atomic versions are much better and map directly onto the "plain" timings.

`__asm inc i`	~2400ms

Conclusion: There is, indeed, overhead introduced by the x86 LOCK instruction, even on a single-CPU machine. This is natural and to be expected, but I point it out because some people have in the past claimed there was no difference.

Finally, note that the Win32 atomic integer functions clearly do not incur function-call overhead. Never assume—measure.

Test Harness

The test harness and sample `String` implementations I wrote are available electronically via the *More Exceptional C++* home page at *http://www.gotw.ca/publications/mxc++.htm*.

Bibliography

[Alexandrescu00a] A. Alexandrescu. "Traits on Steroids" (*C++ Report* 12(6), June 2000).

[Alexandrescu00b] A. Alexandrescu. "Mappings Between Types and Values" (*C/C++ Users Journal* C++ Experts Forum, 18(10), October 2000). Available online at *http://www.gotw.ca/publications/mxc++/aa_mappings.htm*.

[Alexandrescu01] A. Alexandrescu. *Modern C++ Design* (Addison-Wesley, 2001).

[C++98] ISO/IEC 14882:1998(E), *Programming Languages—C++* (ISO and ANSI C++ standard).

[Gamma95] E. Gamma, R. Helm, R. Johnson, and J. Vlissides. *Design Patterns: Elements of Reusable Object-Oriented Software* (Addison-Wesley, 1995).

[GotW] H. Sutter. *Guru of the Week* (*http://www.gotw.ca/gotw*).

[Henney00] K. Henney. "From Mechanism to Method: Substitutability" (*C++ Report*, 12(5), May 2000). Available online at *http://www.gotw.ca/publications/mxc++/kh_substitutability.htm*.

[Koenig99] A. Koenig. "Changing Containers Iteratively" (*C++ Report*, 11(2), February 1999).

[Knuth97] D. Knuth. *The Art of Computer Programming, Vol. 1, Fundamental Algorithms, 3ᵈ Edition* (Addison-Wesley, 1997).

[Lippman98] S. Lippman and J. Lajoie. *C++ Primer, 3ᵈ Edition* (Addison-Wesley, 1998).

[Liskov88] B. Liskov. "Data Abstraction and Hierarchy" (*SIGPLAN Notices*, 23(5), May 1988).

[Meyers96] S. Meyers. *More Effective C++* (Addison-Wesley, 1996).

[Meyers97] S. Meyers. *Effective C++, 2ᵈ Edition* (Addison-Wesley, 1997).

[Meyers99] S. Meyers. *Effective C++ CD: 85 Specific Ways to Improve Your Programs and Designs* (Addison-Wesley, 1999).

[Meyers01] S. Meyers. *Effective STL* (Addison-Wesley, 2001).

[Murray93] R. Murray. *C++ Strategies and Tactics* (Addison-Wesley, 1993), pages 70–72.

[Niec00] T. Niec. "Optimizing Substring Operations in String Classes" (*C/C++ Users Journal*, 18(10), October 2000).

[Stroustrup94] B. Stroustrup. *The Design and Evolution of C++*, section 15.4.2 (Addison-Wesley, 1994).

[Stroustrup00] B. Stroustrup. *The C++ Programming Language, Special Edition* (Addison-Wesley, 2000).

[StroustropFAQ] B. Stroustrup. "C++ Style and Technique FAQ." Available online at http://www.gotw.ca/publications/mxc++/bs_constraints.htm.

[Sutter00] H. Sutter. *Exceptional C++* (Addison-Wesley, 2000).

[Sutter01] H. Sutter. "Virtuality" (*C/C++ Users Journal*, 19(9), September 2001).

Index

The C++ In-Depth Series

Bjarne Stroustrup, Series Editor

Modern C++ Design
Generic Programming and Design Patterns Applied
By Andrei Alexandrescu
0201704315
Paperback
352 pages
© 2001

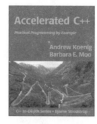

Accelerated C++
Practical Programming by Example
By Andrew Koenig and
Barbara E. Moo
020170353X
Paperback
352 pages
© 2000

Essential C++
By Stanley B. Lippman
0201485184
Paperback
304 pages
© 2000

C++ Network Programming, Volume 1
Mastering Complexity with ACE and Patterns
By Douglas C. Schmidt and
Stephen D. Huston
0201604647
Paperback
336 pages
© 2002

The Boost Graph Library
User Guide and Reference Manual
By Jeremy G. Siek, Lie-Quan Lee, and
Andrew Lumsdaine
0201729148
Paperback
352 pages
© 2002

Exceptional C++
47 Engineering Puzzles, Programming Problems, and Solutions
By Herb Sutter
0201615622
Paperback
240 pages
© 2000

More Exceptional C++
40 New Engineering Puzzles, Programming Problems, and Solutions
By Herb Sutter
020170434X
Paperback
304 pages
© 2002

C++ Network Programming, Volume 2
Systematic Reuse with ACE and Frameworks
By Douglas C. Schmidt and
Stephen D. Huston
0201795256
Paperback
384 pages
© 2003

Applied C++
Practical Techniques for Building Better Software
By Philip Romanik and Amy Muntz
0321108949
Paperback
352 pages
© 2003

Also Available

The C++
Programming
Language
SPECIAL EDITION

Bjarne Stroustrup
The Creator of C++

The C++ Programming Language,
Special Edition
By Bjarne Stroustrup
0201700735
Hardcover
1,040 pages
© 2000

Written by the creator of C++, this is the most widely read and most trusted book on C++.

Register
Your Book

at www.awprofessional.com/register

You may be eligible to receive:

- Advance notice of forthcoming editions of the book
- Related book recommendations
- Chapter excerpts and supplements of forthcoming titles
- Information about special contests and promotions throughout the year
- Notices and reminders about author appearances, tradeshows, and online chats with special guests

Contact us

If you are interested in writing a book or reviewing manuscripts prior to publication, please write to us at:

Editorial Department
Addison-Wesley Professional
75 Arlington Street, Suite 300
Boston, MA 02116 USA
Email: AWPro@aw.com

Addison-Wesley

Visit us on the Web: http://www.awprofessional.com